Stuttgart to Saipan
The Players' Stories

Miguel Delaney

MENTOR
BOOKS

First published in 2010 by
Mentor Books Ltd.,
43 Furze Road
Sandyford Industrial Estate
Dublin 18
Republic of Ireland

Tel: +353 1 295 2112/2   Fax: +353 1 295 2114
e-mail: admin@mentorbooks.ie
www.mentorbooks.ie

A catalogue record for this book is available from the British Library

ISBN: 978-1-906623-59-3

Cover: Mary Byrne

Typesetting and layout: Kathryn O'Sullivan
Editor: Una Whelan

Printed in Ireland by ColourBooks Ltd

Contents

Foreword

Jack Charlton was surprisingly flippant about it all as he stood in the centre of the Genoa pitch. 'If anyone misses, sod it, we've had a good tournament.' Surprising since this was a man who always wanted to win so much that, a few days beforehand, he had berated the Irish squad's priest for incorrectly reading out a history question in what was meant to be a friendly game of *Trivial Pursuit*. But, now that he had the opportunity to actually make his own history in a World Cup penalty shoot-out against Romania, there was no such abrasiveness.

In truth, of course, it was no more than a typical piece of psychology from a man-manager who was far more subtle than the bullish stereotype suggested. At this moment though, he could have said anything. As the Irish team – and, more specifically, David O'Leary – stood on the precipice of an unprecedented World Cup quarter-final place, it wasn't going to do too much to relax the players – current, past or future. Irish soccer had waited 60 mostly painful years to get to this point. Liam Brady had played in 16 of them. His voice dripped with that desire as, in the press box of the Stadio Luigi Ferraris for ITV, he implored O'Leary to 'just knock it in'. A few yards away from him, commentator George Hamilton memorably infused the moment with the words 'the nation holds its breath'. The Brazilian referee, José Roberto Wright, didn't care about wasting his own though. That much Packie Bonner remembers. The official had already told the goalkeeper, literally, to pull up his socks. And, with that in mind, Bonner had only just recovered from the relief of the overly fussy referee allowing his save from Daniel Timofte's penalty to stand after Andy Townsend and Tony Cascarino had broken FIFA rules by running into the 18-yard box to embrace him. Now, the official was being just as pedantic with O'Leary, ordering him to place the ball exactly on the spot. O'Leary padded the white paint down with the ball, only increasing the anxiety.

Back in the centre circle, Chris Morris was just pleased it wasn't him being put under that kind of pressure. Charlton's apparent ease at letting the players get on with the shoot-out themselves evaporated when no-one came forward to take the crucial fifth penalty. He had gone around all of the senior members of the squad only to be met with refusal. 'Well fucking hell, someone's going to have to take it.'

When O'Leary eventually stepped up, the uncapped Terry Phelan was at home wishing he was there but wishing even more that Ireland would prevail. In Bury, a 16-year-old Matt Holland was only watching because of his Monaghan grandmother, never imagining that he would be in the same position as O'Leary for the same country the next time Ireland were involved in a World Cup shoot-out 12 years later. Back in Dublin meanwhile, a generation of children such as Richie Sadlier, Robbie Keane, Richard Dunne and Damien Duff were watching alongside their families but really just waiting to get back out onto the grass to emulate the players. That was the real effect of Italia 90.

But it only had such an impact over time because of O'Leary's on the day. He hit the net. A nation went from holding its breath to the ultimate release. Rapture. Ireland were in the quarter-finals of the World Cup. It remains the greatest moment in the country's football – and possibly sporting – history. But it was also the peak of that history's most successful period. At eight barren years' remove, the era that began with Charlton's appointment in 1986 and ended with the World

Cup elimination to Spain in 2002 can justifiably be described as an Irish golden age.

Over those 16 years, a nation of around 3.5 million people qualified for the only four international soccer tournaments in its history. Alongside those three World Cups and one European Championship, a sport that had previously been the most popular pastime in only pockets of the country became a national obsession. It would take as stunning a result as that which was recorded in the German city of Stuttgart on 12 June 1988 to trigger that transformation. And that's proved by the numbers.

Before Charlton's Irish squad set off for Euro 88, only a few hundred fans turned up to see them off from Lucan's Finnstown House. And this was after the manager had publicly invited the Irish people to come down. By the end of a campaign in which Ireland beat England 1–0 and came to the brink of the semi-finals, thousands would fill the streets of Dublin to greet them home.

The innocent happiness that characterised that tournament was unthinkable by the time of the 2002 World Cup 16 years later. Certainly to that Irish squad's captain Roy Keane. The higher standards he demanded were among a number of factors that led to the infamous row with Mick McCarthy on the island of Saipan. Although the squad held together to reach the second round of that World Cup, the incident did more than threaten Ireland's chances at it. The split 'Saipan' caused within both the Irish football fraternity and the country at large effectively ended the era. In the stands, wonder at the team's progress would turn to weariness. On the pitch, the long-term effects of Keane's departure would see the Irish side enter a prolonged decline.

Nevertheless, the journey from Stuttgart to Saipan had gone over more peaks than valleys. Through more destinations that draw out good memories rather than bad ones. It really started back in Hampden Park where Mark Lawrenson's goal beat Scotland before taking in a detour to Sofia to see Gary Mackay's winner for that same Scottish side unexpectedly defeat Bulgaria. By then, virtually all of the players had jumped on for the ride. It would take Houghton's goal in Stuttgart for the rest of the country to follow. But, from there, celebration followed celebration in swift succession. There was Hanover and Ronnie Whelan's volley; Valletta and the victory over Malta that brought the first World Cup qualification; Cagliari and Kevin Sheedy's equaliser against England; Palermo where Niall Quinn poked home against Holland; the jubilation of Genoa; Alan McLoughlin's wonder-strike in Windsor Park and a gigantic performance against Italy in the Giants Stadium, New Jersey. The Charlton era would end and the wonders cease for a few years. But, either side of Saipan, there was still Jason McAteer's decisive half-volley against the Dutch and Robbie Keane's jump of joy against Germany. And all this from a small country that had previously only endured the agony of close calls or embarrassment of heavy defeats.

As the first book to cover Ireland's 'qualification era' in its entirety, these pages will detail what happened. But, also, how it happened. Because just as illustrative as the detail is the devil in it. The drama. What happened in the dressing room and on the training pitch. The banter behind the scenes, the arguments around them. The secrets behind the success. As much as a record of Ireland's most illustrious period then, it is hopefully a rollercoaster ride alongside those closest to it: the players.

In order to tell the story of the Irish team, it was decided to talk to the different types of men who made it up: the big names, those responsible for the best moments and those with the most interesting stories to tell. Because it wasn't just the team that transformed over this period, football itself did.

As an illustration of just how much, consider the contrasting situations of the Irish players setting off for the country's first international tournament and those who travelled first-class to the last. At Finnstown House in 1988, the Irish players weren't on radically more money than the few people who came to greet them. And they spent it in the same sort of pubs and shops as the supporters. It wasn't as if the squad were put out by their presence either. Indeed, the personal appearances the era eventually provided were opportunities for the players to significantly boost their income. Ahead of Italia 90, the likes of Packie Bonner and Kevin Moran were coming back every second week and quadrupling their earnings.

By 2002 the average salary of the squad was several multiples that of the average man. Roy Keane was one of the best-paid players in the world, let alone Britain. The money ensured footballers moved in drastically different circles. When celebrating, the Irish players now went to the pomp of the Piano Bar in Lillie's Bordello rather than the raucousness of Rumours nightclub. And, while the majority made so much they never had to work again, some of their predecessors subsequently sold Cornish pasties or entered the civil service.

This book is the story of both transformations. The individual experiences of all of Mark Lawrenson, Liam Brady, Tony Galvin, Packie Bonner, Chris Morris, Alan McLoughlin, Alan Kernaghan, Terry Phelan, Matt Holland and Richie Sadlier help make up the larger story of the team they played for and the sport they served. The final chapter attempts to bring together all their views, both on the football and the players' lives away from it. Because, while all were interesting, insightful and informative in their own ways, their versions of all those victories are merely the vehicles to again go down the most joyous journey Irish soccer has known. After all, the nation is still holding its breath for a reprise.

Acknowledgements

Thanks, first of all, to all those at Mentor Books. Special mention, however, must go to Danny McCarthy for initially approaching me about a potential project, ignoring the fact I look more like an under-21 player than a senior international and constantly hammering into shape both the writing and idea. Una Whelan also ensured no stone went unturned.

Thanks too to all the ex-players who agreed to be interviewed. Without their contributions the book could not have been completed. All of Mark Lawrenson, Liam Brady, Tony Galvin, Packie Bonner, Chris Morris, Alan McLoughlin, Alan Kernaghan, Terry Phelan, Matt Holland and Richie Sadlier were very generous with their time and thoughts. Their words are their own and have only been tightened for clarity.

I couldn't have heard them, though, without the help of an array of people literally far too numerous to mention. From journalists who write for local English papers to charity workers and underage football coaches, they all helped put me in contact with the interviewees and I hope they know who they are if they ever read this book.

Acknowledgement must also go to the writers of a number of other books, some of whom I personally know, others I've merely enjoyed reading. These pages were greatly bolstered by the work of Paul Rowan who wrote *The Team That Jack Built* (Mainstream Publishing); Sean Ryan's *The Boys in Green* (Mainstream Publishing); Paul Howard's *The Gaffers* (O'Brien Press); Paul Kimmage and Andy Townsend who co-wrote *Andy's Game* (Stanley Paul); Kimmage, again, and Tony Cascarino who co-wrote *Full Time* (TownHouse); Eamon Dunphy and Roy Keane who co-wrote *Keane* (Penguin); Tom Humphries and Niall Quinn who co-wrote *Niall Quinn* (Headline); Vincent Hogan and Paul McGrath who co-wrote *Back from the Brink* (Arrow Books); Andy Mitten who wrote *Glory Glory! Man Utd in the '90s* (VSP) and Martin Cloake and Adam Powley who co-wrote *The Boys from White Hart Lane – Spurs in the '80s* (VSP). This book was also informed by websites as varied as soccer-ireland.com and liverpoolfc.tv as well as publications like *Four Four Two*.

Thanks also to everyone in the *Sunday Tribune*. Shane Coleman first recommended me for this book while all of Pat Nugent, John Foley and Eoghan Morrissey allowed the (often extended) time and encouragement to get it done. My sports editor PJ Cunningham gave both that and much background to the text. Malachy Clerkin and Joe Coyle offered invaluable advice on either content or structure as they have done since I first walked into the building.

Both Conor McMorrow and Ewan MacKenna – who were enduring the writing processes of their own books – provided necessary sounding boards as well as merciful opportunities to merely vent.

Thanks to my college friends such as Ciaran, Donal and Declan for lending an eye and my home friends such as Karl, Richard, Joe, Iain, Ciaran and Brian for always being ready to lend an ear. Special thanks to Zoe for putting up with me while also propping me up through it all.

And, most of all, thanks to mum, da and Aisling for everything. Not just during this book but before and after it.

1

Mark Lawrenson

Breakthrough

The players looked on blankly. Because, at first, there was only confusion. Paul McGrath was named right-back, Ronnie Whelan left-back and Mark Lawrenson in central midfield. Three of the greatest players in Europe in their positions at that time, none of them actually occupying them. That cold February night in the Hampden Park dressing room, however, wasn't the first time that Irish squad had wondered, 'What the fuck is all this about?'

For a start, there was the new manager Jack Charlton's gruff delivery, odd idiosyncrasies and even stranger instructions. Only compounding the confusion, many of those instructions came from crumpled scraps of hastily scribbled-on paper, the writing on which even Charlton himself struggled to read. Moreover, they brought strangely alternating performances in his first two competitive games. Yes, there had been a spirited and disciplined draw away to Belgium in which Ireland had twice come from behind to draw 2–2. But also a dire 0–0 at home against Scotland with few chances, less excitement but an awful lot of apparently aimless punts up-field.

Even more odd, those first two games had seemingly reversed Ireland's usual style of result where hopeful performances would come at home, horrendous displays away. But they hadn't reversed any sense of momentum. Throughout the 1980s and even further back, a core group of quality players would prove capable of beating World Cup semi-finalists one year, losing 2–0 to Algeria the next; lose out on a place in a major tournament on goal difference in one campaign and miss out after just two matches in the following one. Ireland, it seemed, would eternally get so far only to then fall away. Someone was going to have to push the boulder over the edge, or just break it altogether.

The FAI attempted to end those trends in 1986 by breaking an older one and appointing a first ever 'foreign' manager. Yet, almost a year into this new era, there was still no real sense it was going to be anything other than the same old story. Irish football in general, it seemed, was in a state of confusion about where it was going next.

Until, that was, a supposedly ill-fitting team stepped out onto the Hampden Park pitch to meet Scotland. One of Charlton's positional switches paid off almost immediately. Ireland were awarded a free-kick near the Scottish goal and Lawrenson, in an unusually advanced position in midfield to take advantage, knew exactly where he was going. John Aldridge touched the ball a few yards and, finishing his forward run with a flourish, Lawrenson swept the ball towards goal. Not with any great technical expertise, it must be added, having used his much weaker left foot and kept his eyes closed. But maybe the strike should have been seen as a symbol of how Ireland's luck was about to change. Despite its deficiencies, the shot caught Scottish goalkeeper, Jim Leighton, unawares to nestle in the corner of the net.

Thereafter, the Scots never came close to doing the same. Part of that was down to the influence of the two improvised full-backs as the immense physical force of both McGrath and Whelan helped stifle the skilled but much smaller Scottish attack. Part of it was also down to an admirably drilled plan and performance by the Irish team. The actual execution may have been unspectacular but the outcome was anything but.

To put Ireland's 1–0 win over Scotland into context, it was only the second time the country had beaten, in a competitive away game, a nation that was prominent enough to have previously qualified for a World Cup. And it was the first time it actually mattered. The 1967 2–1 win over Czechoslovakia in Prague was meaningless for Ireland but allowed Spain a place in the 1968 Nations Cup.

This then was a very brave new world. Yet despite the unfamiliar surroundings, there was no longer any shred of doubt about what direction the team was headed. From then, and for the next seven years at least, Ireland were only going one way: Charlton's. Even allowing for a great deal of turbulence en route, it would take the side to unprecedented heights. As Lawrenson emphasises, 'If anyone hadn't bought into what Jack was doing by that game against Scotland, they bought the ticket, T-shirt, you-name-it, afterwards'.

It's one of the many ironies of the Charlton era that the man most responsible for that consciousness-shifting moment and most suited to the elevated stage it paved the way for never got to play on it. Injury ended Lawrenson's playing career mere months after the goal against Scotland. It's a greater irony that he has since been ever-present at such high-stakes international matches as a pundit.

Lawrenson is speaking on the opening day of the 2010 World Cup in South Africa and, although his exceptionally mellow manner only betrays hints of it, he is revelling in the excitement around France's match against Uruguay. It's the second game in the host nation's group and the first Lawrenson is covering. 'There's a real buzz about Cape Town. It's beautiful, 20 degrees and a perfect setting. If South Africa get even a point [in the opening game against Mexico] beforehand the place will go mad.'

They do, it does . . . but he doesn't. Much better used as a perceptive co-commentator rather than a studio pundit for the BBC, Lawrenson's laid-back – almost to the point of lounging – style can split viewers. Much earlier in his career though, it helped him become one of the most composed and unhurried centre-halves on the continent, forming a smooth but smothering partnership with Alan Hansen at Liverpool. Yet a partnership that was not without a bit of steel. The man who brought him to Anfield, Bob Paisley, considered Lawrenson one of the finest tacklers the club had ever seen and said that, if there was a desperate last-ditch challenge to be made in the area, he would 'trust the centre-half with his life'.

Indeed, so well-regarded was Lawrenson that he often got a tap on the shoulder from a prominent player or coach to say, 'You should be playing for England, son'. The likes of Ron Greenwood and Bobby Robson told him that, having won so many trophies with Liverpool, he could also have won over 70 caps for the country of his birth. Throughout the 1980s he was constantly referred to as the 'Irishman who should have played for England'.

Lawrenson, however, had made his decision at a mere 18 years of age. And, within a few months of it, he made what appeared to be an even longer-term one: to get married. At that age, the commitment only lasted nine months. But what seemed the more calculated choice, to declare for his maternal grandfather's country, would go much deeper. Once Lawrenson did so, he insisted he 'never thought about it again'. In any case, it was actually to the benefit of his career to play for the lower-profile nation. Although he didn't get to play in Euro 88 or any European Championships, he argues it helped him play in two European Cup finals.

'I think playing for Ireland so early in my career was one of the main reasons Liverpool signed me because it was a high level. So that experience of international football so early, I think, was absolutely priceless in terms of the development of my career.'

Lawrenson freely admits he knew 'diddly-squat' about Irish football. Or his Irish identity.

'I grew up in Preston and I considered myself English. I had been to Ireland a couple of times but I had no great conception of the country.'

The underlying influences were there though. His mother was Theresa Crotty whose large family moved from Waterford so her father could take a job as a foreman with a Preston construction company. Strongly Catholic, she had wanted the young Mark to train for the priesthood in Dumfries. But the school didn't have any cricket or football teams which were all he was interested in. So he was free to follow a route in sport that would eventually delight his grandfather. The links that actually got him to Ireland, however, were much more tenuous.

'I was playing for Preston in the old Third Division where Alan Kelly was reserves coach but also Johnny Giles's assistant for Ireland. Basically, because of my grandfather, he knew it was a possibility. When asked, I suppose the first thing I thought was, "What's the alternative?" Which was to play for England. And I said to myself, "I don't think that realistically is an alternative." I mean, when you're an 18-year-old, spotty-faced kid playing in the Third Division and someone asks you if you would like to play international football, the answer is going to be "Yeah".'

There was another factor though. Giles himself. Preston's manager at the time was Nobby Stiles, who had been Giles's teammate at Manchester United and was now his brother-in-law. 'Nobby told me that if anybody was going to turn the whole thing around and Ireland into a really professional outfit, it would be Johnny Giles. So I thought, "Yeah, let's give it a go".'

Lawrenson entered right in the middle of Giles's admirable attempt to modernise Irish international football and, after so much misadministration, actually make something of the side. By raising the levels of training, basic organisation and – most importantly – attitude and expectation, Giles got a team with a typically decent nucleus of talent to the point where they seemed only one bounce of the ball away from the big time. Indeed, he came close to making the breakthrough a good 15 years before Charlton.

'The set-up was very much Gilesy,' Lawrenson enthuses. 'It wasn't too different to what I later found at Liverpool. In terms of training it was all short, five-a-side, move the ball quickly. Very, very similar. Alan Kelly probably did more of the organisation off the pitch but it was a great education because I had never played with anyone as good as Johnny Giles at that stage of my career.'

The one bounce, however, never came. Indeed, as an effective outsider at that point, Lawrenson was arguably ideally placed to see the many factors that ensured Giles was always fighting a losing battle, to see the contradictions and uncertainties inherent to the side that would always seem to block the way. But these same factors were actually perfectly propped up for Charlton's bullishness to bulldoze.

For a start, beyond a core of quality players, the squad was startlingly shallow. That became apparent to Lawrenson on his first appearance in April 1977. Typically, it was a 0–0 friendly draw against Poland as the FAI returned the usual favours between the two associations with a fixture in Dalymount Park. Giles had thrown Lawrenson in on Kelly's advice without having seen him play – even if his club team, Preston, mightn't have been too happy at letting the teenager turn out.

'I remember I played for Preston on a Saturday, made my debut for Ireland on the Sunday and then came back and played again on the Tuesday. So three games in four days and one of them my international debut. The federations wouldn't let you now for health and safety reasons. That Poland were a really good team though. They'd got to the semi-finals of the World Cup in 1974 and still had players like Lato and Szarmach. In fact, I probably knew more about the Polish players than the Irish I played with that day.'

Certainly, League of Ireland stalwarts like Miah Dennehy and Ray O'Brien never got to play against such stars so regularly. So thin was the squad then that, as manager, Giles brought himself out of retirement on more than one occasion. Not that it was appreciated. Giles was wrongly seen as being in the job for the money during a period when his PR skills were at an all-time low. Yet, despite perceptions, his bank account was possibly even lower than that after the failure of a business venture. Giles was booed when he included himself for the first ever cross-border match with Northern Ireland during the Euro 80 qualifiers in September 1978. Even though the game was seen as an opportunity to foster peace, the boos only rang louder when, without a few of the more technical players such as Dave O'Leary, the passing game Giles always promoted only led to people almost passing out with boredom as the match ended 0–0.

That campaign also saw Lawrenson face the country of his birth for the first time in his seventh cap, a 1–1 draw: 'A strange experience.' Only on the bench that day, Giles was evidently thinking about whether he should manage, let alone play, for Ireland again. Once England ensured passage to Euro 80 by finishing way ahead of Ireland, the manager gave the 1982 World Cup qualifiers one game before finally giving up. Fed up.

That game, however, set up two thrilling years that brought the high points of Eoin Hand's regime and an illustration of how close the team could go when all key players were fit and on form. Drawn against the 1978 World Cup finalists Holland, Euro 80 finalists Belgium and the eventual 1982 semi-finalists and Euro 84 winners, France, Ireland's chances of reaching the World Cup in Spain looked terminal before even being tested. But they brought the group right to the death.

'At that stage we were a good team with some outstanding individuals. But we were always, I think, two players away from being a very good side. Ultimately we probably tried to play all our good players in one team when a lot of our lads played in the same position.'

Having opened the group with a 3–2 victory on an (eternally) tricky trip to Cyprus that saw Lawrenson score his first international goal, that imbalance of quality across the pitch was underlined in the second game, against the Dutch. Not for the last time in his international career, Lawrenson was picked to play central midfield. Not for the last time, it would reap rewards. Standard Liege's Simon Tahamata gave Holland the lead just before the hour only for Gerry Daly to equalise with 11 minutes left. A home draw against a team with Holland's pedigree wouldn't have been a disaster but wouldn't exactly have ignited enthusiasm again. Until, seven minutes from time, Ireland were awarded a free-kick.

'I think Liam took it. Basically, there was nobody marking me so I continued on my merry way into the box. The ball came in and I met it with a diving header. I knew I was going to score, don't ask me why. I could lie to you and say the timing of my run was brilliant but I wouldn't have any idea about that.'

After a creditable 2–2 draw with the Dutch in Rotterdam then, the crescendo came in a game Ireland simply had to win and any Irish supporter simply had to have seen. It remains one of the country's finest ever results and performances. Against the French side that would flourish in that World Cup in 1982 and prove themselves one of international football's all-time great attacking teams, Eoin Hand's Ireland went toe-to-toe and came out on top.

'It was just one of those old-fashioned, end-to-end games,' recalls Lawrenson. 'Our crowd at Lansdowne Road that day was almost gladiatorial. Fantastic. We just kept battering away at them. Some of our football at times mightn't have been the most scientific but it made for a great game, to say the least.'

That battering paid off after only five minutes when Philippe Mahut put into his own net. Bruno Bellone pulled one back three minutes later but, by half-time, some of the most lively football Lansdowne Road would ever see brought a 3–1 lead thanks to finishes from Frank Stapleton and Michael Robinson – set up by the finesse of Brady.

More drama awaited though. Still only Brady's understudy in the cast-list of great European creators, Michel Platini continued a habit of upstaging his predecessor at Juventus by shredding the lead with his third goal in four games against Ireland. It also shredded a lot of nerves since it came in the 82nd minute. Almost fitting that such a thriller ended with a fright.

Despite Platini's efforts, however, Ireland held on to win 3–2. Platini would ultimately ensure that Ireland wouldn't hold on to a qualification spot in the group itself though. The oddities of UEFA's qualification system at the time saw to it that, although the French match was Ireland's last of the campaign, their opponents still had two games to play. France knew it was imperative to win both to equal the Irish points tally having already equalled their goal difference. With Cyprus visiting Paris in the group's final match, all Irish hopes hung on Holland's same trip beforehand. Although Hans van Bruekelen and Ruud Krol kept it tight for a tense opening half, Platini eventually plundered the goal that would set up a memorable decade for French football. They went through behind Belgium and Ireland went out on goal difference. It was that close.

Indeed, it was that close in more ways than one. Dubious refereeing decisions in both Paris (a 2–0 defeat) and Brussels (a 1–0 defeat) had denied Ireland the point that would have been enough to bring a breakthrough six years before Charlton. And such seeming misfortunes were becoming as frequent a factor in Irish failures as missing personnel.

Lawrenson's competitive debut actually came in the 1978 World Cup qualifiers in a return match against Bulgaria immediately after a tempestuous trip to Sofia that saw four players sent off and Giles ludicrously have a seemingly legitimate goal ruled offside in a 2–1 defeat. A point might well have been enough to push Ireland into the finals in Argentina. Instead, it was another bad-luck story, another bad decision. Another coincidence?

Later in this book, Liam Brady claims otherwise, that there was most certainly some sort of conspiracy to keep big teams at events and small teams like Ireland out. Lawrenson doesn't quite put it so starkly but concedes some ground despite occupying, as he does, a place on both sides of the argument. He heard many claims over the years that his Liverpool side benefited from dodgy decisions. Were Ireland's troubles just a case of referees subconsciously favouring the more famous team, or evidence of something more sinister?

'Well, having played at Anfield for all those years, people said we'd always get a penalty there if we needed one. But we used to say the reason we do is because the ball generally is in the opposition penalty area 80 per cent more than it's in ours. With Ireland it was different though. Little-country syndrome does happen. We never really had the rub of the green. I just think it was very, very strange how there'd be one major refereeing decision in most of the games that cost us. That's not an excuse at all because these things happen but if the referee's decision had gone the other way . . . it really was a case of "what if".'

What if, too, the team's association had prepared like one with serious designs on reaching an international tournament? Roy Keane may have raged about Saipan but, back in Lawrenson's early international days, FAI farce was much more than a cliché. It was a calamity. He feels the effects on the team of such disorganisation, on top of weakness in depth and dreadful decisions, can't be underplayed. The nadir was a friendly away to – naturally – Poland in May

1981. Despite Hand's initial attempts at higher standards and despite the team being tantalisingly close to the five-star surroundings of the World Cup, the FAI made a fairly definitive statement about standards.

'A group of officials jumped off the coach at a big hotel in Warsaw, all with big bright eyes, saying "See you later, boys!" That was imprinted on our brains.'

It would stay there all the way to Bydgoszcz, which took in a bumpy five-hour trip in what amounted to a labourer's van. Incredibly, it got worse.

'The hotel, or what was classed as a hotel, was dirty. There were no towels, no toilet paper. It wasn't the manager's fault, wasn't the hotel's fault. It was the fault of somebody in a five-star hotel 200 miles away, lording it up. That was the first time I saw the players in danger of revolting. The secretary, Peadar O'Driscoll, waltzed into the hotel on the day of the game and we just went nuts. We told him that if our clubs knew exactly what we'd gone through they wouldn't release us again.'

Unsurprisingly, Ireland lost 3–0. Even more unsurprisingly, the players demanded to be returned to Warsaw straight after the match. However, as Paul Rowan wrote in *The Team That Jack Built*, the scene involving FAI officials they then witnessed in the lobby was like something out of a *Carry On* film. In the end, the players could only do what they always did: laugh. Even if it was beyond a joke.

"To top it off, more often than not we used to receive the details of travel and hotels when we got back from international matches rather than before we went,' explains Lawrenson. 'But you couldn't have gone in and said this was an absolute shambles and needs a change. They were an amateur organisation in a professional world and that doesn't work – does it?'

Noel Dunne wrote in the *Irish Independent* after the Polish debacle that 'this sudden slump by the Irish side back into the dark ages of football is quite baffling'. He didn't know the half of it.

The French game came five months after Bydgoszcz but, from then on, Hand would never again experience such a high. All elements seemingly conspired against Ireland at once – as opposed to isolated instances they could occasionally overcome. Not least a young, inexperienced manager's naivety.

Unlike the 1982 World Cup, Euro 84 was out of reach almost as soon as the qualification games began. Sure, there was false hope when Frank Stapleton's brace of goals brought a draw from a 3–1 deficit to eventual qualifiers Spain. Or when the all-time record win was wrought from an 8–0 rout of Malta. But the real downer came when an exciting new generation of Dutch players got revenge for their predecessors. With Ireland 2–0 up at Dalymount thanks to an early Gary Waddock strike and Brady penalty, the true turning point of Hand's tenure was signalled when Ruud Gullit and Marco van Basten ran riot and Holland ran out with a 3–2 win. The Dutch still didn't qualify that time. But it was becoming increasingly evident Ireland never would under Hand.

Despite an emergency FAI meeting, he survived that campaign. He wouldn't survive the next one though. An atrocious 1986 World Cup group saw Ireland finish fourth out of five, lose to bottom team Norway and end in a 4–1 thrashing in front of their own fans by a dynamic Denmark. The breakthrough never looked so far off.

'In many ways, we were only ever as good as our weakest player,' Lawrenson says, summing up the era. 'One of the problems was, not being disrespectful, more often than not we'd have a couple of players that played in the Second Division. Now it's very, very difficult for those players to sustain the level of those from the top echelons of the game. I don't mean that disrespectfully, that's just the way it was. Once you had a few more injuries, things became even more of a problem. We probably didn't have enough really good players so we could survive them [injuries].

'Eoin did come very close and should be remembered for that. The players liked him, they wanted to play for him. And there was a good spirit. All the lads went out together, drank together, there were no cliques. I just think, tactically at that level, Eoin was somewhat naive. We thought we could just go and play football against whoever and the best team would win. Away from home we were probably too open. Basically, the team was better going forward than it was defensively. We never really got that constant team ethic until Jack appeared on the scene.'

Notoriously of course, Jack almost didn't appear. Although the alternative will always remain another what-if story to wonder about. When the FAI executive met in February 1986, at least half of the 18 members initially wanted Lawrenson's old Liverpool manager, Paisley. Even among the names that had been touted in the build-up – Brian Clough, Billy McNeill – Paisley's was the most noted. And it certainly was compared to those left in the race: Charlton, Giles and another ex-manager, Liam Tuohy. Out of the Liverpool job for three years by then, Paisley had turned them from regular winners under Bill Shankly to relentless winners. His six League titles, three League Cups and one Uefa Cup made him Britain's most medal-laden manager until Alex Ferguson arrived. His three European Cups, however, ensure Paisley's record remains the most successful in the history of the Champions League. It would have been impossible not to be seduced by that kind of success. Lawrenson certainly was. Paisley brought him from Brighton to Liverpool in the summer of 1981, the circumstances being as slapdash as the FAI meeting which would eventually ensue in Merrion Square. It happened rather haphazardly at an airport and with almost as many clubs after Lawrenson as flights landing.

'Man United wanted me but hadn't agreed a fee. They wanted to send two or three players to Brighton in part-exchange but had also just signed Frank Stapleton which was one of the first transfers to go to tribunal. So Ron Atkinson was waiting for that but kept ringing to say, "Don't sign for anyone else. I'm building a team, I'll do a deal." Then I got a phone call saying Liverpool were interested and, within five minutes, another from Terry Neill at Arsenal. I went to Gatwick to see him but, to be fair to Terry, he didn't really sell the club to me. He said, "Come and play with David O'Leary", but the offer was less than I was on at Brighton.

'Then I got home and Ron was on again but I told him I was speaking to Liverpool the next day. He said he'd guarantee me more money than anywhere else. I just said, "It's not an issue of money – I mean, this is Liverpool!" The next day I went to Heathrow, met Bob Paisley, Peter Robinson and former chairman John Smith. I did hear Terry Neill was waiting in the hotel next door in case talks broke down. Within 20 seconds though I was saying, "Give me a contract and I'll sign it". It was a no-brainer. Liverpool had just won the European Cup so that was the chief appeal for me – that and the Bob Paisley factor.'

Despite the perception of Paisley as a paternalistic figure, Lawrenson immediately saw the competitiveness that made Liverpool so cutting edge.

'I remember two things about my debut: it was in a friendly against Atletico Madrid and I played in midfield in front of 50,000. Their midfielder told Bruce Grobbelaar not to do anything to wind them up because the crowd were going mad in the stands. The noise began to settle down, but then we heard a massive roar and I turned around and saw Bruce throwing oranges back into the crowd! I looked across at Bob and he was just shaking his head. Also the day of the game, in my first training session, Graeme Souness and Alan Kennedy had a fight. It was surreal.'

But successful. Many individuals might have frozen having suddenly been put into a European Cup-winning side. But, as seemed to happen with so many at a club that very rarely made a dud signing at the time, Lawrenson insisted it merely raised the level of his own game.

'The classic thing is that when you go and play with that quality of player, you generally improve yourself. I was lucky because, in those days, new signings generally spent 18 months in the reserves but I was straight in. Sink or swim. Fortunately, I swam. And, after a while, you'd know what to expect. The crowd at times were turning up at Anfield and virtually saying, "Go and win 5–0", because, in fairness, most of the time we were. But if there was a time where maybe we weren't playing as well as we could, a massive roar would go up and I'd just think, "Oh God, if it's like that for me, what's it like for our opponents?"

'There was an example when Ian Rush scored five goals against Luton on a Saturday then in training on the Monday missed the first chance he got. Ronnie Moran said, "Same player?" They were all about that, mind games. But you didn't realise how clever they were. The Boot Room was so far advanced in terms of the things they came out with.'

So far advanced that Liverpool won a fourth European Cup in 1984, ensuring Lawrenson entered an elite group of only 10 Irish players to lift the trophy. The others are Tony Dunne, Shay Brennan, Steve Heighway, Whelan, Robinson, Keane, Denis Irwin, Steve Finnan and John O'Shea. Given that the majority of those did so in the competition's first three decades as opposed to its last three, is there a sense the European Cup was easier to win then?

'I think it was easier to get through to the quarter-finals. To win? I'm not sure. Probably on a par overall. Other than the fact air travel wasn't great, there were no sports scientists, nothing about diet, recovery and we played over 60 games, we had some very tough away games. We beat Athletic Bilbao then battered Benfica before playing Dinamo Bucharest in the semis. When we went away, their manager reckoned Graeme Souness had punched one of their players and broken his jaw. I didn't see it but, like a lot of us, I heard it! So their whole focus for the second leg was about revenge. Immediately as our coach turned up it was ringed by soldiers. There were a few of us on the bus with long hair and moustaches and I remember this tap on the window. I looked around and the soldier was just staring at me, giving me the old slit-throat thinking I was Souey! So I'm shouting, "No, no, he's over there!" Then at the game, their players properly tried to break his leg. They caught him a few times and ripped his shin-pad open. But he just shrugged it off and said, "Bring it on". He loved that kind of stuff.

'We won that night. Rushie got a couple of goals and Bobby Robson, who was England manager, came in shouting, "That's the best European away performance I've ever seen, unbelievable!" Joe Fagan was just looking at him as if to say, "Oh no, Bobby, don't do that, they'll get arrogant."'

If not arrogant then certainly at ease, despite the final taking place in opposition Roma's own Stadio Olimpico.

'We'd been out to the pitch and came back in singing a Chris Rea song called "I Don't Know What It Is But I Love It". The story goes that when Nils Liedholm was giving Roma his team-talk, he heard this singing getting louder and louder and then saw the colour on his players' faces actually drain away.

They couldn't believe we were singing before the European Cup final. It wasn't a conscious thing to intimidate them. We wouldn't have sung Chris Rea.'

Liverpool did ultimately hold their nerve better in the penalty shoot-out, in part thanks to Grobbelaar's theatrics ('he never actually made a save', as Lawrenson makes a point of emphasising). The 1985 final would also involve Liverpool and an Italian club and would be settled by another penalty. But there would certainly be no singing. It was the night 39 people – the majority of them Juventus fans – died in the Heysel stadium disaster. To this day Lawrenson is one of the few Liverpool players involved who has talked publicly about it. Although, as he later admitted, his circumstances on the night were different to everyone else's.

'I had dislocated my shoulder a few weeks beforehand and, within about 80 seconds, the thing came out. Ahead of the game we waited hours and hours and nobody wanted to play. So then with the whole emotion of what happened, I just started crying. But I ended up in the same hotel as the dead and the dying. When I woke up, still in my kit, I was in an empty ward except for a soldier with a machine gun. He was there in case any Italians heard I was. I knew some people had died but had no idea quite how many until the morning. Some Italian journalists discovered I was there and were asking questions but I was only finding out information as they were telling me. The next thing Roy Evans came in with my wife at the time. He said it wasn't good and told me to put my tracksuit on inside out in case the badge was spotted.

'To this day it's the one game I've never watched. No footage. Joe cracked and quite rightly. In all the times the former players have met and shared a few drinks, we've never talked about Heysel. Ever.'

The authorities had to though. Liverpool fans were held responsible and, after over a decade of hooliganism and pressure from Margaret Thatcher's government, English clubs were banned from European competition for five years. Football goes on though. It always does. Despite a tragedy so far from the mundane, the nature of the sport and passing of each match attempts to render it so. Indeed, Liverpool would go – relatively speaking, as football jargon dictates

– from the low of that to one of the club's all-time highs. Within a season, they were celebrating a first ever domestic double of League and FA Cup and, in terms of excitement, arguably the finest football Anfield had seen.

Those were the last medals Lawrenson won other than that received for the 1988 title after his retirement, and ensured he finished with a haul of one European Cup, five Leagues, three League Cups and one FA Cup. They also made him the fifth most decorated Irish player of all time after Roy Keane, Irwin, Heighway and Whelan. Oddly, although clearly standing out in Irish football history, Lawrenson didn't seem to do so as much at that time. Despite the disappointment of the Hand era, the Irish squad still had a healthy concentration of players at premier clubs.

Perhaps all that was needed was a manager with the right mindset. By the end of that Merrion Square meeting in February 1986 though, it wasn't to be Lawrenson's old boss Paisley. Some members of the FAI executive – including those who voted for the former Liverpool manager in the first round – were irritated by the long process and also the manner in which Paisley's name had been promoted again so flagrantly and so late. Suddenly Charlton's original total of three votes transformed to a majority in the final round. He had the job – even if the FAI were struggling to get a hold of Charlton to tell him having not spoken to him in three weeks. It was high farce, but also the organisation's undoubted high point.

But what of those highs that may have been missed without Paisley? Not least in the style of play?

'I think even Bob would have admitted that he wouldn't have been able to do the job Jack did,' believes Lawrenson. 'He brought a completely different outlook. And, also for Bob, it would have been interesting to see how he would have done with a team that wasn't as good as his Liverpool.'

Certainly, Ireland could have done with the single-mindedness that was so striking at Anfield. Lawrenson hadn't a clue whether Charlton was going to be the man to provide it however. All he knew about him came from a 'no-nonsense' image and his brother Bobby – which, if there were any similarities, didn't bode well.

'I'd played for Bobby at Preston and he was very, very nervous. I remember seeing him in the dressing room with the opposition teamsheet before one of his first games in charge. It was an hour before kick-off and his hand was shaking. I remember thinking it didn't look good for him. He just wasn't cut out for it, didn't really want to be there. Another time he sent out four centre-backs in the same game.'

His brother Jack, of course, would eventually do the same in that match against Scotland. But the contrasting outcomes only emphasised how different the two brothers were on that level too. Lawrenson didn't actually play for Jack or meet him until six months and five games into his tenure – the first Euro 88 qualifier against Belgium. But there were already signs that *something* was afoot.

'Jack and Bobby are absolutely chalk and cheese. I didn't know Jack and hadn't been involved in the first few games but when you first meet him what strikes you is that it's all about the team. Not individuals. I think quite a few of us still thought, "Christ, I'm not sure about this". But it's like anything, you give it time. We had a really strong, very tight dressing room and I think the feeling among everyone was, "Let's give this fella a chance".

'And Jack was clever too. I think he suddenly spotted he had some good players here, people who could look after themselves and were quite bright. Realised, "I've got a bit of a team here". And that transferred to the players. He knew that we knew that he believed this was a team. The thing with Jack was his man-management was really, really good. There were no grey areas. He told you how he thought you should be playing, point out something he didn't particularly like. He never worried about upsetting anybody. But he was cute too. He'd put training back an hour for you on Monday if the players wanted to come over Sunday and have a few beers in Malahide. That helped a camaraderie that was already there.

'Belief in football ultimately comes from results. You can think you're in a really good team with really strong, committed individuals . . . and then lose games. So belief will always, always come from results.'

When the draw for the Euro 88 qualifiers was made, you could have forgiven the players for not having too much belief. There was only one qualification spot and the three other teams competing for it had all qualified for Mexico 86. Belgium, who Ireland were to face in that first game, had got as far as the last four. It was to become another irony of the era, however, that – other than Italia 90 – the tougher the group, the likelier Ireland were to get through. Those qualification groups for 1988, 1994 and 2002 are unmatched in difficulty in all of Irish soccer history except for 1982. As an illustration of how low expectations were when Charlton took over though, the FAI balked at his plan to play the most difficult away games first since poor results could harm attendances – and revenue – later on. But just as he did with the media, the backroom staff and the players, Charlton forced his way. It wasn't the only change. At 2–1 down going into stoppage time in Brussels, Ireland got the benefit of a referee's decision and Brady equalised. It was the sort of thing that usually didn't happen. In fact it was the reverse of what happened in the same city in 1981. Belief was breaking through.

'Yeah, we got a draw and the luck sort of changed. They say one of the best characteristics of a manager is to be lucky. And that was the early days, trying to buy into the way the team played. That's what I'm saying about results and confidence. We'd have probably gone to Belgium before and lost. All of a sudden we nick a goal and it's 2–2 and you think, "You know what, this is alright. That's something a proper side does, isn't it?"'

Next up were the back-to-back games against Scotland. The first temporarily knocked back any such notions. But the second set them in stone. And, fittingly, what stands out for Lawrenson other than his goal was the robustness of the performance.

'The Scottish team was full of quality but it had a few midgets if I remember. A few small players and, physically, we dominated them.'

Sheer strength was to become a standard.

'We weren't dirty or anything like that but teams knew we'd give you a real physical battle and, probably in the past, we didn't have that kind of asset. After we scored against Scotland we were really, really professional. There was a sense of realisation. I remember they didn't have too many opportunities and got booed off. Which, for an opposition team who weren't considered very good away from home, was a real fillip.'

The alliance of physicality and function pounded home that this was the start of something new. As Lawrenson argues, Charlton's crass dismissal of the norms and niceties of international football were in stark contrast to Hand's reverence and innocence.

'Very much so. I think it was almost an unwritten rule in international football that you have the ball, you play with it then we'll have the ball, we'll play with it. So Jack was like, we're not having any of that. We're going to force our particular style on the opposition and, with our very physical threat, let's see if they can cope. The majority couldn't, could they?'

Ultimately, Lawrenson's own physique betrayed him. The end of his story with Ireland came after captaining the side to an ultimately crucial – if surprisingly easy – win over Bulgaria at home. But the last chapter had begun to be written when he ruptured his Achilles just a month after his Hampden goal. The damage was such that there was no anguish about Euro 88. Only whether he would play even one more game for Liverpool.

'That would have been my first thought. I did my Achilles in March and you know sometimes when you're struggling. I was definitely, definitely struggling. So it wasn't as if it was a shock when I was told it was over. I knew early on it was always going to be a struggle to either play football again or, if I did, to the level people used to think I could play at. I tried all sorts of things to improve it but I knew. I remember one game against Arsenal, John Motson telling me it was strange that in the second half the ball came to me and I just hoofed it into the stand. It was because I knew. I just thought in the end that I was very lucky to have played for Liverpool, won championships, a European Cup, qualified for Euro 88. Imagine telling me all that the day I signed for Preston. That was my philosophy.

'I did watch a few Euro 88 games on television which, at first, was difficult because that realisation sinks in. But once they got close to picking up that first result I became a fan.'

Watching such games *for* television has, of course, been much easier for Lawrenson. Yes, there are occasions when he refers to both Ireland and England as 'we' but insists there's only one 'we' and the latter (England) are only referred to like that because everyone at the BBC does. There were a few other difficulties along the way to getting to such a comfortable position though. Like managing Oxford for Robert Maxwell's son Kevin.

'I quit because Bob nicked Dean Saunders from us for Derby. He pinched him after promising we could have him for a season. I went to see Bob to tell him where to stick his job. But he just paused, looked at me and went, "That's all very well but you know what? At the end of the day, all this has got fuck all to do with you." I walked out and we never spoke again.'

There was another short spell at Peterborough United as well as a season of gentle summer football in the Florida sun for Tampa Bay Rowdies before nominally filling the role of defensive-coach for Kevin Keegan's almost defence-less Newcastle United. He also went through another divorce which reared up a surprising amount of kiss-and-tell stories from the tabloids. At the time, Lawrenson merely shrugged, 'Whenever we played Everton the fans there said I was gay so I suppose leaving this so-called trail of women across Britain put up my street cred.'

Remarried and with a young son, Lawrenson is perfectly happy in the present as he goes off to watch the first game of the World Cup. It was one of the few stages he never got near himself. But he played a large part in ensuring his country ultimately did.

2

Liam Brady

Controversy, conflict . . . and a whole lot of class

Jack Charlton marches across the lobby. He's got something to say. 'Could've done with you tonight.' It's a few hours after Ireland's dismal 0–0 draw with Egypt in Palermo and Liam Brady is sharing a drink with the squad members who are by now ex-teammates of his. The same ex-teammates who simply couldn't find the moment of inspiration or innovation to produce a meaningful attack, let alone a goal, against the underrated north African side.

Brady would have.

'Only when you were at your best, mind,' Charlton adds, returning to Brady's table a few minutes later just in case an unqualified compliment became concrete in people's minds. The extra detail was unnecessary. And unfair.

But then, if you're looking for injustices from Brady's career, take your pick. There's the travesty that arguably Ireland's greatest ever footballer just missed out on Ireland's greatest ever football moments. There's also the fact that he never got to play on such a platform in international football at all. Then there were all those scandalous refereeing decisions that ensured that fact. Moreover, there was Juventus's dreadfully handled decision to replace him with Michel

Platini. This despite Brady bringing home the Serie A title with the penalty he knew could be his last kick for the club. Most of all though, there was the manner in which Charlton ended his career at the very highest level. He hauled Brady off in the first half of a friendly with West Germany to prove a point to the public that, surprisingly, he didn't have the courage to make in private.

Of all the distraught Irish faces when so many refereeing decisions had gone against the side in Sofia and Brussels, Brady's was the most internationally recognised. And the sight of him trudging off that day against the Germans was set to become the enduring image of another controversy: the debate over whether Charlton was sacrificing purism for progress. Was the country too willing to sell its soccer soul? That issue became the single great caveat to all of Charlton's conquests.

To an awful lot of people though – and to some extent Brady himself – much of that is empty talk. There was, after all, another great injustice to his time in the game: the fact he had so much ability compared to almost everyone else. It gave him a career that was, if not necessarily Ireland's most glorious in terms of medals, certainly the most glamorous. As he says himself, 'I was good and I knew I was good. You just know you are. I was confident, had the whole thing mapped out in my head. I'd be in the first team at Arsenal when I was 18 and then I'd play for Ireland.'

That he never got to play for Ireland in a tournament befitting his talent doesn't necessarily bother him. But some of the reasons do. Brady has been involved in five very questionable refereeing controversies during his time with Ireland, four as a player, three in Paris. Sitting now in the Merrion Hotel about to analyse the 2010 World Cup for RTÉ and with that Thierry Henry handball still fresh in the memory, Brady is convinced they're all part of the same continuum. Some incidents overt, some covert. All effectively conditioned to ensure the little guy loses out.

Does he actually believe there were outright conspiracies when he was a player though?

'Oh yeah. Without any doubt. We didn't have anything going for us as far as FIFA were concerned. We were really just also-rans as far as they were concerned and in referees' eyes as well – that referees could do things to us and there'd be no repercussions. Whereas, if it was England or a bigger nation there'd be such an outcry or maybe investigations they wouldn't take that chance. But with us it happened. No doubt about that . . . Certainly now, looking back, I feel very strong that there was a lot of skulduggery going on.'

The first example Brady cites came in his second campaign as an international and John Giles's second as an international manager. Despite missing out on Euro 76 by a mere point, the team had picked up momentum.

'Under John, performances had been better – got a few results. We went into that qualifying campaign with confidence. He was that kind of manager, said, "Look, we'll play this kind of game, believe in ourselves and be confident and we'll get good results." And he was right up to a point.'

To the point of the referee's whistle. For Argentina 78, Ireland were drawn in a tough three-team group alongside France and Bulgaria but weren't exactly put off by an opening trip to Paris. Nor by Michel Platini's opening goal. Even then, Ireland should have had the goal that gave at least a point.

'We lost under circumstances that were strange to say the least. We again got another good goal. I put a cross in, Gerry Daly pulled the ball back and Frank Stapleton knocked it in. For some reason, the linesman flagged for offside. We saw on television afterwards that it was ridiculous.'

St Etienne's Dominique Bathenay then added injury to insult with a scarcely deserved clincher which, as Brady says, 'kind of deflated the team'. But it didn't completely blow them away. Giles's side recovered admirably in the return game to claim an excellent 1–0 win – Brady illustrating his increasing ability by chipping between two French defenders to race clear and finish calmly. In Bulgaria then, Don Givens equalised Pavel Panov's opener and Ireland looked assured of claiming the away win there that would have put the side top of the group with only a game left. The pressure was beginning to tell. But not just on the Bulgarians. Also the officials. Givens was denied a penalty and Giles himself had a goal disallowed for another inconceivable offside ruling. Then, on the break, Andrej Zhelaskov scored 14 minutes from the end before getting sent off along with Krasmir Borisov, Mick Martin and Noel Campbell. They were the four players picked out of a 22-man brawl. As Paddy Mulligan bitterly remarked, it was 'possibly because they had red hair . . . it left a terrible feeling in the stomach'.

France went on to Argentina, Ireland to agitate over what might have been. But what was to come was going to be even harder to stomach. The 1982 World Cup qualifiers under Eoin Hand brought another trip to Paris, another undeserved 2–0 defeat and another controversy. Yet, incredibly, it was only a hint of what was to follow.

'That was another episode,' Brady laments. 'We had beaten Cyprus, beaten Holland and drawn at home 1–1 with Belgium, didn't do any damage there. That France away game would have been a big result for us though, would have tipped the group in our favour. We would have – had the referee been anyway fair. But, 1–0 down, Kevin Moran scores a legitimate goal. Robbed there again. Absolutely robbed.'

Still though, Ireland were in an exceptionally strong position. Cyprus were seen off 6–0 and qualification really was in clear sight. It might finally, actually happen. Ireland in a major championship. A point in the next game in Belgium could have done it. In fact, a point in Belgium absolutely would have done it. The way Ireland played that night they deserved much more. What they certainly didn't deserve was a sensational series of incidents that made the entire Thierry Henry scandal look like no more than a simple sleight of hand.

Lightning and relentless rain almost caused the match to be abandoned. But the real storm started just before half-time. Ireland had been awarded a free-kick on the right. Brady flicked it on, Stapleton finished. It was a move that had come off many times for the duo at Highbury.

'Frank and I had a relationship having grown up at Arsenal and knew each other very well,' Brady now explains, an element of irritation rising in his voice. 'With a free-kick I would wait for Frank to walk a yard like he wasn't interested, then he was going to come back and I just put it in where he was going to arrive.

I knew he was onside because we knew each other so well he would never be offside.'

The linesman apparently didn't think so either. As Brady says 'there was a lull'. Then a whistle. Referee Raul Nazare had disallowed the goal before, a full three seconds later, the linesman guiltily put his flag up.

'In hindsight, they must have all agreed, the officials, that if it was anything like that you flag for offside.'

If that was the case then they never agreed on an official version of events. When interviewed by the *Sunday Tribune* in 2002, 21 years after the game, referee Nazare first confidently asserted to Paul Howard that 'Frank Stapleton was offside. I remember this very clearly. It was not really my decision, you see. It was the linesman who gave me the indication . . . In fact, I remember now that I had blown the whistle before Stapleton touched the ball. So technically, you see, I did not disallow the goal because there was no goal to disallow.'

Yet, when presented with irrefutable evidence of the opposite – Howard asking him to watch Eoin Hand's personal videotape of the game – Nazare desperately backtracked and scrambled for other explanations. First: 'I made a mistake when I told you it was offside. I awarded an indirect free-kick. Nobody touches the ball before it goes in.' Then, when even his daughter disputes this version: 'The ball hits me and not Stapleton. That is why I disallowed it.' This despite the fact he is four feet from the ball when Stapleton volleys it into the net.

And still, it gets worse. Three minutes from the end of the game but only inches from the spot where Brady hit that initial indirect free-kick, Belgian captain Eric Gerets goes down a good foot away from the nearest Irishman. Again, Nazare gives an inventive interpretation. 'Yes he is clowning, there is no doubt, but there is some physical contact with this player, Steve Heighway.'

There isn't.

There is contact between the ball and the net though when Rene Vandereycken's subsequent free-kick bounces off the bar and high into the air for Jan Ceulemans to react first and decisively. Belgium got the win that ultimately took them to the World Cup. Nazare got a lot of abuse. First Mickey Walsh, familiar with the Portuguese referee from his time at FC Porto, called him a 'cheat'. Hand went further. 'You're a disgrace. You've been paid off. You've robbed us.' Brady, meanwhile, asked Walsh the Portuguese word for thief and put it to Nazare's face along with an accusatory jabbing finger. Was that real rage, or actual restraint?

'Well you can very nearly get banned totally from football when the likes of that happen. You'd have to stop yourself attacking the referee coming off the pitch. The sense of anger is, well . . . but it was really, really diabolical. I have a theory FIFA would prefer some teams to get to World Cups because of major sponsorships or money. And well it all came out that Belgium was corrupt. They were exposed as a totally corrupt federation and also at club level. Anderlecht had a title taken off them, there was the UEFA Cup game against Notts Forest. I reckon we were done in France and Belgium – we were hijacked. And then to lose out on goal difference shows we were good enough to qualify and that was probably the best group of players until the one Jack got.'

Missing out on Spain 82 remains – much, much more than Euro 88 or Italia 90 – his biggest regret.

'Well I never got to play in any major championships but the big one I would have liked to have played in was '82. We had the team.'

Did Northern Ireland's achievements in that World Cup, reaching the second group stage and last 12, only deepen the sense of regret?

'No, not at all. We were pleased for them. I played with Pat Jennings, Sammy Nelson, Pat Rice. And I was friends with Sammy McIlroy, Gerry Armstrong. It was great.'

That very tournament, however, raises another classic 'what-if' for Irish football. Soccer is the only mainstream sport on the island to be split across two bodies, owing to upheavals shortly after partition. The all-Ireland squad that could have taken on the world that summer is almost teasing to think about. What if players like Jennings, Martin O'Neill, Armstrong, McIlroy, Billy Hamilton and Norman Whiteside had gone to a tournament with Brady, Lawrenson and company?

But the 'what-ifs' for the Republic of Ireland began to evaporate soon after Brussels, as Brady freely admits. Instead, there were a lot of 'what-nexts?' All the dubious refereeing decisions couldn't explain some of Hand's judgements. A very decent man whom the players all had time for, it soon became clear he wasn't really ready for the job. Hand's inexperience, having only ever managed Limerick United, started to engulf him and he struggled to deal with both the deficiencies of his squad and the association that employed him.

'He suffered more than John [Giles] the pantomime that the FAI was at the time. Whereas before we would maybe take the piss, now we were getting a bit fed up with it. Now the gap between what we were doing with our own clubs and what the FAI were doing had widened. The lads were getting to be disgruntled and Eoin couldn't handle it. He didn't have the power or the bottle or the self-assurance to take on the FAI.'

Was it becoming a chore to appear for internationals at that stage then?

'No, no. But I think some of the friendly fixtures that were arranged might have become a bit of a chore, arranged to suit the FAI rather than what you were supposed to be preparing for. I don't think there was much co-operation between players, management and where we were going. The FAI wouldn't dare do it nowadays. We wouldn't be going to South America and playing Chile, Brazil and Trinidad and Tobago. The Liverpools and Man Uniteds said no to that. But Eoin didn't have the strength to say, "Sorry I'm not accepting this".'

That 1982 tour of South America was a particular FAI fiasco to trump anything that went on even in Poland. Initially scheduled for May and to first take in Buenos Aires and a friendly with Argentina, it was going to be difficult to get British clubs to release players at the business end of their season when they simply didn't have to. It was going to be impossible when the Falklands War broke out. The British government called for the cancellation of all sporting fixtures against Argentina and all the clubs naturally followed suit. Since this – in theory – had nothing to do with Ireland and meant, to some people's horror, British teams would de facto dictate Irish sports policy, the FAI was put under political pressure to fulfil the friendly even to the point of sending a League of

Ireland side. In the end, despite an initial announcement that the Argentina game would definitely go ahead, it was called off just a few days before departure. Hand still had to actually gather a squad to fulfil the other fixtures of the tour though. Both Manchester United and Arsenal refused while the Liverpool contingent were advised not to travel. The club 'had visions of the players not coming back'.

Although Brady was among the first to make himself available as an act of faith – what he concedes now was a foolish one – that meant at least eight senior internationals wouldn't be travelling. Of the 16 that did, seven played in the English second division or below, five earned the only Irish caps of their career on the trip. So a third of the squad were clearly completely unsuited to international football. And it wasn't just who played but how they played. Ireland lost 1–0 to Chile before being slaughtered 7–0 by a Brazilian team featuring Falcao, Socrates, Eder and Zico who would go on to set the World Cup alight.

'Funnily enough that would be one of the abiding memories of the trip,' Brady explains. 'At least I did play in Brazil and against as good a team as they ever had. OK, we were annihilated 7–0 but it's still a good memory. I can talk about playing one of the best Brazil teams. We all came back and decided to put our money on them to win the World Cup. They should have been certainties but just blew it against Italy because they were overconfident.'

The squad would make up the money lost on those bets though because, so humiliated were most of them by the Brazil match, they threatened to go straight home until the FAI paid out the thousand-dollar fee due for the tour. So instead of returning to Dublin, they partied in Rio. But having just endured the worst Irish defeat on record they then suffered the most humiliating: 2–1 to Trinidad and Tobago.

'Poor old Eoin had to put up with that kind of thing. But if he had been more assured of himself he probably wouldn't have done, particularly early on when he did well in that group. It was that kind of trip. I don't think there was any press on it, which shows there was no interest.'

Hand, however, was beginning to take an unhealthy interest in what the press said about him – to the detriment of his management, Brady believes.

'Eoin was never the most assured sort of man and I think he always put himself under enormous pressure. John [Giles] always had the self-confidence to be able to take on the FAI but with Eoin I thought it was different. Eoin didn't have that self-assurance. Maybe because he had only been manager at Limerick before he got the job, maybe – I don't know – they didn't pay him very well. Probably not. Did Eoin desperately need a job? Yes he did. And all that pressure he put on himself only increased when we had a poor campaign for Euro 84.'

The next qualification group, for the 1986 World Cup, would see it boil over altogether. After an atrocious 0–0 draw at Lansdowne against a weak Norway side, the few fans there began chanting, 'What a load of rubbish!' Back in the dressing room, Hand sat with his head in his hands complaining about the crowd and how the press would tear him apart. It was left to Brady, who had been substituted, to tell him to pull himself together and stop going on about them. Hand's response was to announce his intention to resign but the players managed to talk him around.

Worse though was when Hand let the press see just how much they were affecting him. Mick McCarthy, who had only declared for Ireland in 1984 and missed his brother's wedding for one cap, had come under constant criticism in that short time for his lack of pace. Hand's defence of his new player, however, only led to John O'Shea of the *Evening Press* betting that he could beat the then Manchester City centre-half in a 50-metre sprint. Incredibly, Hand accepted and then managed to coerce McCarthy into competing. 'Nah, nah, that's going to cost me 50 quid if you don't race,' was the argument. Contrary to the popular myth, it was O'Shea – and not McCarthy – who pulled up after the Yorkshireman won a first race. But a subsequent injury that forced him to miss the next qualifier was blamed on Hand's bet.

'You see when you work with a top manager – a top, top manager – he doesn't listen to that. But in those days it was "Look at what he's written now". Instead of Eoin completely ignoring John O'Shea and not giving him any kind of kudos, he got involved in it and all the players got involved in it and he asked

McCarthy. I mean Trapattoni and Giles . . . I don't even see Trapattoni reading newspapers. He'd know the guys to see but he doesn't know what they write or who they write for. Doesn't give a monkey's. That kind of confidence transmits to the players. But with Eoin it was transmitting bad vibes because he was getting upset about what they were writing. He was bringing more pressure on the players by showing this. He wasn't a confident man and that was transmitted to the team.'

Brady wasn't exactly spared criticism himself though. At that stage there was a body of opinion that argued he wasn't influencing the team as a player of his ability should. Dave Langan said 'everything depended on Liam and I think it was getting to him a bit'. One of his most strident critics though was one of the men who now talks up Brady's status as an Irish great the most: Eamon Dunphy. The then *Sunday Tribune* columnist described Brady, in just one example from a number of pieces, as 'rich promise turned to sulky self-indulgence' and a 'parody of a player of substance, the triumph of reputation over reality'. During all their years working together for RTÉ, did Brady ever bring it up with Dunphy?

'We laugh about it now – but at the time it wasn't funny. Your family live in Ireland and it's always coming back, "Oh, he's written this about you, written that about you". I confronted him once in an angry fashion but it was John who told me I'm better off just ignoring him and getting on with it. Eamon's opinions can fluctuate from black to white and back to black with no reference to when they were white. I mean Eamon went from "Jack must get rid of Brady" to, when he had the needle with Jack, "why isn't he playing? What's he done to Liam Brady?"'

'Jack did what he [Eamon] wanted him to do in the first place but then when he didn't like Jack any more he was using me as an example of what Jack was doing wrong. So John was right to say ignore him and I did. But it's difficult for your family, your mother and father.'

Dunphy was by far the most over-the-top critic of Brady. But he wasn't the only one. If some supporters were beginning to ask questions of Ireland's captain at that time though, it was only because he had provided them with answers so many times in the past – right from the start of his career.

On the day of his debut – that defining Euro 76 qualifier at Dalymount against the USSR – Ray Treacy would recall looking at the then 18-year-old Brady and wondering whether he had lost his bottle. 'I was nervous alright, but I think they were good nerves.' In any case, if the man who mattered most – the manager, Giles – thought along Treacy's lines, he had the technique to settle the teenager.

'John had a very reassuring fashion. "Seen you play – know what you can do – won't be a problem for you. Just concentrate on doing your job for the team and then when you get the ball do your own thing." Sure enough, they kicked off, the ball came back to John and he passed it straight to me as if to say, "Go on then, don't be frightened".'

Brady clearly wasn't. He produced what must have been one of the most promising – or perhaps promise-fulfilling – Irish debuts. He hit the bar from 25 yards and more than played his part for Givens to score a hat-trick in a thrilling 3–0 win. Seamus Devlin wrote in *The Irish Times* that he 'showed a footballing maturity that was positively amazing . . . the ability to spray his passes with an accuracy that belies description.'

'I couldn't have got off to a better start,' Brady recalls. 'We played really well on the day. I think that was a turning of a page in Irish football.'

Dalymount, as *The Irish Times* wrote, had never seen or heard anything like it. And, for a young man who had been inspired to follow a life in football by the electric atmosphere at the old ground he had experienced as a younger boy, it seemed appropriate that his career was mimicking the one he had mapped out for himself. That sense of destiny only deepened given the dynasty he was following. His great-uncle Frank had played for Ireland in the 1920s while his brothers Pat, Ray and Frank were with Millwall, QPR and Shamrock Rovers respectively. The day before Ray was to be capped against Austria in a crucial European Nations Cup qualifier in 1963, he brought Charlie Hurley up to the family home in Whitehall.

'It caused a major buzz around the place. All the kids were there knocking on the door. I was about seven or eight and awestruck. I was at the game then with my parents, beat them 3–2 and I was just . . . it was something that was special for me. Really wanted to be a footballer after that. That's when I really remember becoming obsessed with the whole thing.'

Obsessed to the point that he got expelled from school. Having been picked as captain for the Irish under-15s against Wales, Brady was warned by a head brother not to return to St Aidan's CBS if he played in the soccer game instead of lining out for the school's Gaelic football side. It may have been the height of the GAA's ban on foreign games and he may have won two Leinster medals with the school, but Brady played in Wales anyway. That trip across the Irish Sea would soon become a permanent move as, after sitting his Inter Cert at the technical school down the road in Whitehall, Arsenal turned his occasional training sessions from the age of 13 into a proper apprenticeship.

Even there though, that desire to just get out and play would almost delay his career before it had even started properly. Brady was expected to sit through English literature classes in a local polytechnic as part of Arsenal's apprenticeship package, while he himself had expected only to play football. So, he skipped school to go training. The head coach, however, didn't skip the chance to teach Brady a different type of lesson and hit him with a heap of demeaning duties. Every day, he would get back to his digs well after dark while his teammates took it easy. Disillusioned, Brady came home for Christmas full sure he wouldn't be returning to Arsenal. That idea only lasted two weeks. There was that ball to be kicked after all.

His independent spirit, both on and off the pitch, was always going to be an ingredient that would eventually prove unpalatable to a manager as controlling as Charlton. And, despite the ebb and flow of their relationship over the years, Brady recognised that fact immediately.

'My first impressions were, "this is not going to last between myself and himself". We [the squad] weren't that enamoured. John [Giles] had been in the running for the job as well and I wanted him and we got Jack in unusual circumstances,' Brady chuckles now. That would become a theme.

'It was amateurish in many ways. He was a person who could be laughed at because he was so disorganised. He would give totally ridiculous team talks, get the names of half the guys wrong . . . One time he showed a match but it wasn't the opposition we were supposed to be playing – it was their under-21 team. This sort of thing. We'd just laugh at it. But I still had that kind of feeling, "Why is he here and John's not?"'

Another future workmate was very much in the picture though. 'Eamon Dunphy was behind the campaign, "Brady has too much power in the Irish team, Jack has to sort him out". I think Jack and Eamon at the time used to socialise and mix together and I think Jack had that in mind. So there was that kind of tension to begin with.

'But Jack didn't really have any respect for anything, you know what I mean. To Jack the Irish job was a salary. Then he began to understand the Irish, what a great people we are. They looked after him in a manner he couldn't believe. Initially though, I don't think he had any idea about what might happen and what might snowball.'

First though, Charlton had to get the players to believe in his way of playing. Or, if they didn't want to believe, just go along with it. Brady forced himself but, with one of the most analytical minds in the game, he was never happy about such a compromise.

'John had a belief over how he wanted the team to play from the back through midfield, passing the ball around. And that's a way of playing that appeals to every player. Jack was taught in the FA at that time, brought up by a guy called Charles Hughes. And his theory was that the more times you get the ball in the box, the more goals you score. Get possession of the ball in their half, get possession of the ball by pressurising, getting throw-ins, getting corner-kicks . . . that leads to goals.'

And Hughes's goal at the time was clearly to influence all of English football. Having written coaching manuals such as *Soccer Tactics and Skills* in 1980, the lessons from which the FA eagerly implemented, he was then part of an unofficial think-tank that included Graham Taylor. Hughes never quite managed to make it soak into all of English football but the imprint could be seen on Taylor's Watford, Egil Olsen's Norway and, of course, Charlton's Ireland. Brady, however, is as sceptical of the so-called science Hughes attempted to use to prove his theories as he is of the style itself.

'It's a way of looking at it. Nobody has to play the same way in football all the time. But Hughes had a licence that he took upon himself to describe what was a pass and what wasn't. For example, did you see Denmark's second goal against Cameroon [in the Danes' 2–1 World Cup win in South Africa 2010]? That's a creative goal as far as I'm concerned. Keeper throws it out, Bendtner turns well, hits it, Rommedahl makes a good run, hits him, turns inside, goal. Jack's play wasn't about that. And Hughes would use that goal as an example of what it's not.

'With Jack, the ball would never have gone to Bendtner in the first place. Bendtner would have had to chase it. In fact, Bendtner wouldn't have got into Jack's team because he wouldn't put himself around. But the forward for Jack had to put himself around, chase the ball into the corner, fella made a mistake, we won the ball to get a cross in, scored or got a corner-kick. Then, if the defender got a header away we would then look to win possession.'

It's not too much of a stretch then to describe possession as almost an afterthought in that kind of approach. Which was always going to be a problem for a player who prized it.

'He couldn't leave me out because I was playing well but I probably didn't do myself any favours. I couldn't change the way I played. I always played naturally on the field. The ball would come to me and I'd do what came naturally – dribble, maybe, in midfield. If I did it successfully nothing was said. If I didn't I'd have people roaring at me from the sideline but I just ignored it. I accepted that I had to go along with what he wanted for the most part, yet I didn't toe the line completely. It was that bit of rebellion that wouldn't allow me do it totally his way.'

But, little by little, a balance was struck between the two philosophies for the betterment of the team. 'I think he figured out in the end that the good outweighed the bad and I had a bit of a licence to play the way I wanted to play but I did adapt my game a bit then. I went far less back to receive the ball because I knew, one, he would be unhappy with me, two, he'd give a bollocking to the centre-half who gave it to me. That was where the modifying of the way I played came into it.'

Brady is also keen to stress the point that there were aspects of both Charlton's philosophy and delivery that were universally beneficial.

'First of all, Jack had plenty of self-confidence. That assurance Eoin didn't. He also had a group of good players who were desperate to get to a major finals and he led them well. Second, the foundation was correct with Jack. Having been a defender, he would single out their best player and make sure we stifled him which was always good in a coach. He was also good at free-kicks, corner-kicks, for and against us. We weren't giving away any stupid goals. Things that Trapattoni has introduced in many ways now. And, like Trapattoni and Giles and all good managers, Charlton had a knack of building team spirit.'

With all the talk of the famous camaraderie of the squad being one of Ireland's great strengths, Gordon Strachan's infamous line is put to Brady, that 'team spirit is an illusion created in victory'.

'Strachan's talking rubbish there. Team spirit is what leads to victory. OK, team spirit might be fortified by victory. But team spirit is the manager getting through to every one of his players that one hundred per cent workrate is required no matter what position you're in, no matter who you are. All the best managers can get that out of their players. Giles had it. Trapattoni has it. Charlton certainly had it at the time.

'Charlton wouldn't be frightened to confront someone if they made a mistake but he was fair. It wasn't like he was picking on one guy or he had his favourites. Everyone got encouragement, a bollocking when they deserved a bollocking. And those are common denominators among those three managers.'

The result was what Brady believes was his very best football for Ireland.

'All through that campaign I'd played really well. I played all the games, every single one of them. Scored the goal against Brazil, got man-of-the-match awards. Jack realised I was a very good player for his team, maybe gave the creativity it needed at certain moments. That spirit he introduced, that discipline he introduced, still needed that creativity.'

Brady mentions the 1987 1–0 friendly win over Brazil but, although important in the evolution of the Charlton era, the fact that he himself illustrated his ability against such international opposition by wrong-footing keeper Carlos so elegantly – and gaining personal revenge for 1982 in the process – has seen it afforded a mythical status that it perhaps doesn't entirely merit. For a start, only five of Brazil's 1986 World Cup squad played. More importantly, none of Socrates, Zico, Falcao or Julio Cesar did. Secondly, only 17,000 turned up at Lansdowne Road on a May afternoon to watch – less than would watch Luxembourg in a Euro 88 qualifier four months later. Nevertheless, despite what a large section of the country's soccer supporters seemingly thought, it was still Brazil. And it was still only a third win in 11 games as well as, incredibly, a first at home. As such, the players went out that night and the following in celebration before flying to Luxembourg. Just like the Scottish match at Hampden Park a few months beforehand, it was all helping to build belief and momentum for tougher tests ahead.

One of those tests would prove much more crucial in retrospect than at the time. Despite the completely different approach Charlton had brought, it seemed the end product would ultimately be the same as ever: a narrow miss. Ireland knew they had to beat Bulgaria in their last game to stand any chance of making Euro 88. But it was still going to be a very slim chance as, regardless of the result at Lansdowne Road, an anticipated Scottish defeat in Sofia would send the Bulgarians through. It was that sense of futility that perhaps saw an otherwise exceptional Brady (his performance was described in the *Irish Independent* as a 'tour de force') lose his cool and get sent off for elbowing Ayan Sadkov with five minutes left of a surprisingly easy 2–0 win secured by goals from Paul McGrath and Kevin Moran.

'I was being man-marked the whole game. Kept getting fouled, kept getting fouled, And the referee I don't think even booked him. They were lenient towards those kind of man-markers at that time. Sure remember Gentile with Maradona in 1982. You'd be off the pitch in 15 minutes now. So there was no real protection for that kind of man-to-man marking and I just said to myself . . ."

UEFA said to Brady 'four-game suspension' and he thought 'that was it'. 'I seem to remember thinking, "Well that's my international career finished". I might have been thinking "OK, I'm going to stand down. There's no point hanging on."'

Completely unexpectedly though, Scotland would hang on after Gary Mackay scored the only goal late on in Sofia. Not that Brady or any of the Irish squad actually saw too much of that game given that it was barely aired anywhere in Britain.

'I was playing golf with Pat Jennings and, when we got back to the clubhouse, the barman had this strange look on his face. "You won't believe it, Scotland won 1–0. You're going to the European Championships."'

Before that though, Brady had to go cap in hand to UEFA about his suspension. He was told to relax, an appeal was being sorted. But Brady still contacted Juventus chairman Giampiero Boniperti to see if he could help pull strings within UEFA. Eventually, Brady travelled to Zurich for the hearing with the then FAI president Pat O'Brien and Des Casey.

'Pat was a lovely man but he had a really strong Cork accent and even I had trouble understanding him. Anyway, we go into this room with several UEFA officials from different countries and booths at the back of the room for translators. Pat opens our appeal and I wasn't sure what he was saying so I could see the translators shaking their heads and shrugging their shoulders. I'm worried obviously but Des tells me everything's going to be fine. So then, Des is on his feet and he's really doing his best. "Liam Brady has been a great player for Ireland, he's waited so long to get to this stage. What you have to appreciate is that Liam Brady is to Ireland what Michel Platini is to France and what Diego Maradona is to *Brazil*." I'm laughing to myself at this stage thinking "I've got no chance".

UEFA actually reduced the suspension from four games to two but, in the end, it made no difference as a cruciate ligament injury cost Brady the chance of playing in a major tournament. He was 'gutted' but, having been asked by Charlton to travel with the squad, he remembers Euro 88 as one of his most enjoyable experiences with Ireland.

'I still felt part of the team that got them there. Look, if I had have been suspended and lost my place and couldn't get back in the team, that would have been hard to take. But I was on crutches, trying to get myself fit and didn't actually play until October. So it was different. But I felt part of the team.'

On one particularly thankless occasion he was actually put in control of the team. Charlton charged him with sending them to bed after the victory over England.

'That was the hardest job I've ever had to do. I think I got the last of them to bed at 7 in the morning.'

Charlton's good-natured invitation to Brady to travel to Germany also illustrates the easy nature of their relationship at the time.

'I always got on with Jack on a personal level, played cards together, laughed together, shared jokes together. But there was this difference of philosophy over how the game should be played. I would argue that if we had Giles at the same time he would have done it in a more attractive and pleasing fashion. He would have, in a creative sense, availed of the players who were available to him at the time. That never left me so there was always that suspicion of one another.'

That potential problem finally played out very publicly in a September 1989 friendly. Up against World Cup favourites – and eventual winners – West Germany at Lansdowne Road, it wasn't to such blue-chip opposition that Charlton wanted to make his point. Throughout qualification for Italia 90, players who 'stuck the boot in' – as the manager put it – like Andy Townsend had occupied the midfield places. Yet, when the calls inevitably came for Brady to be returned to a creative role at the end of a campaign he had barely featured in, Charlton responded disparagingly. 'What Brady can't do at 33 is give me 90 minutes at a pace and work-rate our style demands.'

To emphasise it, he chose to 'put 'em on display'. As Charlton later said, 'With Ireland, they don't give up their fuckin' heroes easily, so you've really got to show 'em.' But, with 33 minutes gone, Charlton's old guard were showing Germany. Frank Stapleton had scored after 10 minutes and Ireland were dominating. Despite that, Charlton was roaring at Brady to 'pick players up' before turning and declaring, 'Right, that's it!' It was – in almost every sense.

Brady, arguably Ireland's greatest ever player, was humiliatingly hauled off long before half-time. He didn't show much emotion as he trudged off to gasps around Lansdowne Road but he certainly did in the dressing room. Stapleton even had to interrupt a face-off between manager and captain to remind everyone, 'Hold on, hold on, there's a game to be played here.'

That sight of Brady shuffling disconsolately off the international stage has been held up as the defining image of Charlton's approach to football and the whole debate around it – the blunt manager derisively substituting the country's most nuanced player ever. On reflection now though, even Brady admits that interpretation is a little too simplistic. While still perturbed about the manner in which Charlton removed him, he no longer faults the rationale.

'I was 33, had a serious cruciate tear. I wasn't the same player, maybe wasn't able to do what I'd done prior to qualifying for Euro 88. The injury had really killed my career at international level but, rather than Jack saying to me, "Liam, I really need somebody in the team that maybe has more legs, I don't think you can do it anymore so I'm not going to pick you", he went out of his way to create this thing against Germany.

'The more success Jack got, the more bolshie he got. People are different . . . if Jack hadn't qualified for '88 he might have been coming around to the players, "What do you think we should do?" – you know what I mean? But '88 went well, we all came home in an open-top bus and he got bolshie. What happened in '89 – he was probably feeling he could do whatever he wanted. But I knew my time was up.

'And, really, I didn't want to be a sub, sat on the bench at the World Cup wondering whether I was going to get a game. My time had gone, good luck, cheerio, goodbye.'

Despite the perception since, Brady was selected for one more game – a send-off friendly against Finland just before the 1990 World Cup. That and the meeting in a Palermo hotel lobby after the game against Egypt show how he and Charlton had, to some degree, repaired their personal relationship. In any case, he found Italia 90 almost as rewarding as Euro 88 as a co-commentator for ITV. When David O'Leary readied himself for that fifth penalty against Romania, Brady can be heard desperately imploring, 'Come on David, just knock it in'. He was later seen outside the stadium embracing loved ones in tears of joy. One of the greatest moments of his life in football?

'Yeah, it was. It was great to see our arrival on such a stage with a team that was actually a good side. The team gave a great account of themselves and so did the support. It showed people we deserved to be there. I hadn't been there because of what FIFA allowed to go on, or encouraged to go on. It was very enjoyable to be part of it because we were hanging around. Jack never had a problem with us being around the hotel. We were all good friends. In the media job I was doing I was promoting games and defending them.'

An added bonus was the reception Brady got when he went back to Italy, particularly in Genoa where he had played for Sampdoria. When he initially moved to the country in 1980 though, it was only because Arsenal were so reluctant to move on themselves.

'Arsenal helped me become a footballer and I owe them a great deal. The 1979 FA Cup final [in which Brady inspired the side to a last-minute 3–2 win over Manchester United who had been 2–0 up with five minutes left] is among my best football memories. But we should have kicked on from there. Never built on all the good young players we had. But Terry Neill, a good manager, was happy with the success we were getting. On our day we could beat anybody but we weren't good enough to be at the top of the league. We couldn't challenge the likes of Liverpool week in week out and I felt it was never going to happen. Allied to the fact I didn't feel I had been rewarded properly, I left.'

So, Brady went from a club where fourth or fifth in the league and a decent cup run were considered 'somewhere', to one where anything below first was nowhere: Juventus. Manchester United were an option and he even met then manager Dave Sexton in the Burlington Hotel. But the call from Italy couldn't be refused.

'Kevin Keegan had gone to Germany and, from all the documentaries and programmes about him, he seemed to take to it really well. I thought I'd like some of that. Luckily for me, Italian clubs decided to let foreigners into the league again in 1980 after a ban and Arsenal had knocked Juventus out of the Cup Winners' Cup a few months prior. I played OK and they made their minds up.'

He also made up his own mind to make the most of the move.

'I'm the kind of person that's interested in culture, history, no matter where I go. So when I went to Italy I decided to learn what it was all about, learn the language as quickly as possible and I think the locals appreciated that. You become friends. I was never going to be someone, like some footballers, who go over and lock themselves in their apartment because they're just over there for the money that's going into their bank account. I overcame the language barrier and then got on well with my teammates. They knew I was serious and professional and wanted to get results with them and win with them and was there to integrate.'

Whatever his new teammates thought of him though, Brady insists they couldn't have been as impressed as he was with his new manager, Giovanni Trapattoni.

'Even with the language barrier and not yet fully understanding what was being said, I could see straight away he had the total respect of the players. Didn't have favourites. Wasn't sneaky with the media. There are a lot of managers who ruin their relationships with the players by thinking that they have to keep in more with the media than they do with their team and a lot of them fail like that.'

While Brady enjoyed the full faith of his formidable new manager from the start, he couldn't say the same about the club directors.

'My first league game was in Cagliari and it was boiling hot and I couldn't raise a gallop. But, by this time, I'd picked up some of the language and one of the directors was on the bus and asking how Inter, who were the champions, had done. They'd won 4–0 and their new signing, the Austrian Herbert Prohaska, had scored. So I heard the guy say, "We made a mistake with our foreigner". I remembered that when he was putting his arm around me after we'd won the championship.'

That was the first of two consecutive titles. So integral had Brady been that when his form dipped in the second season, the club's famous owner, Fiat's Gianni Agnelli, approached Brady to say, 'Come on, you're better than this'. It didn't click with Brady then but, such were the standards expected at Juventus, Agnelli was starting to look elsewhere. It did click, however, when he got a call from an agent completely out of the blue informing he could be 'fixed up'.

'Fix me up with what?'

'Don't you know, Platini's in and you're out.'

'It was Agnelli's call and what Agnelli wants, Agnelli gets,' Brady later revealed. 'To be fair, he wasn't a bad judge, but it was a crushing blow at the time and I did feel somewhat betrayed after playing so well. I realise I was replaced by someone who went on to become arguably the best player in the world but I'd played against Platini for Ireland and he'd come out on top largely because of refereeing decisions. So, at the time I didn't feel inferior to him.'

He attempted to prove it. Despite the situation and despite Fiorentina putting Juventus under severe pressure for the Serie A title with a mere three games left, Brady stepped up in every sense. With 10 minutes of the season to go and with the knowledge he was about to leave now widespread, he scored the penalty against Catanzaro to give Juventus the two points that sealed the *scudetto*. 'Since then I have this reputation in Italy as the ultimate pro. I didn't deserve it, but I got it.'

From there it was on to the genial surroundings of Genoa with Sampdoria before the amphitheatre that was the San Siro with Inter Milan. The only regret from a 'brilliant time' in Italy was a brief spell at lowly Ascoli which he describes as a mistake.

It was, ironically, the link to Italy which brought Brady back to Ireland and

Trapattoni to the FAI. When the association first sounded out the Italian, he contacted his one-time playmaker for advice. Brady told him it would be a 'beautiful experience' and Trapattoni agreed – on the condition Brady assist him and Marco Tardelli in making the transition.

'It was great. I was only too happy to help Giovanni and Marco because I think initially they may have needed a guiding hand as regards certain things and think they needed me to get them over that – portray exactly what they wanted to the players. What also pleased me was that I got on very well with the players and enjoyed working with them, never felt there was any animosity because I had maybe been critical of them as a pundit.'

The job was also Brady's first experience of working with senior professionals since his own attempt at management in the early 1990s with Celtic and then Brighton. Looking back now he feels he had neither the experience nor the finances to do either to the standard expected.

'Myself and management weren't successful. But neither job was disastrous either. I didn't really understand the Celtic job until I got there. That was huge pressure and I couldn't cope with it.'

It hit him straight away when news of his appointment as Celtic manager was among the main news headlines rather than the sports headlines. His wife Sarah turned to him and asked, 'Sure you know what you're doing here?'

Many Celtic fans asked the same question in a different way when his side lost 5–1 to Neuchatel Xamax in the UEFA Cup or when he dropped Packie Bonner and bought a confidence-shot Tony Cascarino, Stuart Slater and Andy Payton for a club already in debt. But there was also a long unbeaten run and an awful lot of financial and political problems to put up with behind the scenes. One director, Fintan Cassidy, even handed Brady a slip of paper at one stage with his requested first XI on it. Brady got up and walked out.

'Glasgow is a demanding city and although I didn't achieve what I'd hoped to, I've no regrets. To have managed a winning team in an Old Firm is something you don't forget. We tried to change the way things were run too and play attractive football. Nearly got there but Rangers had so much financial power at the time.'

Brady eventually found another calling, however. Where once he created chances on the pitch for Arsenal, he now created quality players off it as head of the club's youth development. Although it was an opportunity to directly return the favour for the nurturing they had given him as a young man, his gratitude was itself rewarded when a manager with Arsene Wenger's philosophy arrived to manage the first team a few months later in 1996.

'I'll put it this way,' Brady smiles. 'I'd hate to be working as head of youth development at a team where the first team above you were playing Jack Charlton football. I probably wouldn't want to stick around doing it.'

It was his sense of duty towards Arsenal that ultimately stopped Brady staying on with Ireland. He felt it was unfair to be taking so much time out of his day-job, particularly now that both Trapattoni and Tardelli knew their way around theirs. But, just as he eventually worked with both Italians again and just as he ended up right back where he started at Arsenal, Brady was given one more reminder of football's cyclical nature: another qualifying controversy.

'The Henry thing was one of the worst incidents in my footballing life. We didn't say it to the players before the game but I always had a feeling . . . people wanted France there. I think FIFA were paving the way for this to happen. The changing of the draw exposed them totally to what they're all about. If it had been Serbia finishing second in their group they would never have seeded that draw and that exposed them totally to what Blatter and FIFA are about. It conditions the officials.'

In the end, Brady doubts whether anything will ever change. He need only look back through his own career though. As Charlton showed a generation of Irish players desperate for qualification and Brady himself in that hotel lobby in Palermo, cycles are there to be broken.

3

Tony Galvin

Outsider on the left

T ony Galvin is keen to debunk a myth. Well, not just debunk it but shatter it once and for all. The myth goes that, when he was making his name at Tottenham Hotspur in the early 1980s, a diligent FAI official noticed how Irish it sounded, made a few background checks and then delightedly informed Galvin he qualified to play for Ireland. The winger, so that FAI official would have liked everyone to believe, apparently didn't have a notion about his ancestry.

'Rubbish. Absolute rubbish,' Galvin scoffs now. 'And, anyway, it was on my mum's side not my side. My side are four or five times removed from Ireland. They all came over in the 1800s. But my mum's dad was a Tucker. He was from Limerick. And my mum's mum was Scottish with an Irish grandfather, grandmother. I knew my grandfather was from Ireland, obviously. So nonsense that. Rubbish.'

It's a story that may well have been started to serve the career of one ambitious official but that it was so widely spread and believed only illustrates the image many had of the 'Republic of England' or 'England B' at the time.

More justification for jokes about players declaring because they had once drank a pint of Guinness or worn green. Spitting Image even devoted a sketch to it.

For many other aspects of his professional life, Galvin has got used to being cast as something of an outsider. His broad Yorkshire accent caused a few puzzled looks in an awfully Cockney Spurs dressing room that almost set the stereotype for flamboyant Londoners. It also, however, hid an intelligent mind only sharpened by the college education his late start in professional football allowed. That Galvin had actually attended university was enough to perplex his teammates; he didn't even need to get to the fact it was in Russian Studies. And, since then, he is one of very few footballers from that time to have made a complete break with the senior game. No media work, no coaching. Instead of giving his opinion to Richard Keys or Gary Lineker as a pundit, he's letting colleges know whether they qualify for funding as a civil servant.

When it comes to his international career though, Galvin isn't so content to be portrayed as such a brazen interloper. Indeed his story was becoming common enough among that era of Irish players.

'Chris Hughton had already declared and obviously I played with Chris at Tottenham and we had a conversation about my Irish ancestry. He mentioned it to Eoin Hand and then it snowballed from there. Then it was just a question of finding out where my grandfather was born and that. That was the only background check. They found the proof and I said I was more than happy to play for Ireland. No problem and off we went.'

Galvin, then, did qualify through the infamous 'Granny Rule'. That was always something of an unfair misnomer though. Throughout the last few decades, Article 18 of FIFA's rules on nationality and eligibility merely read 'any person who is a naturalised citizen of a country in virtue of that country's laws shall be eligible to play for a national or representative team of that country'. Unlike most countries, however, Ireland's citizenship laws entitled a passport to anyone whose grandparent was an Irish citizen. Hence the 'granny rule'.

The FIFA law had actually been introduced at the end of the 1950s to stop scenarios where the likes of Alfredo Di Stefano, Omar Sivori and Lazlo Kubala turned out for multiple nations, while Ireland's citizenship laws had been passed in 1956. Only sheer ignorance saw it go unexploited for years. Manchester United full-back Shay Brennan was the first English-born player to be capped but there were potentially thousands of others including half of Celtic's 1967 European Cup-winning team. It was only when John Giles took over in 1973 – and thanks to his numerous contacts in the English game – that the possibilities offered by the rule started to be properly pursued, a fact reflected in the numbers thereafter. During the 1982 World Cup qualifying campaign, eight of the 24 players used were born outside Ireland. By 1990 it was the majority, their contingent boosted by the advertisements for players Jack Charlton circulated in clubs.

Those figures, however, naturally raised a few questions. First of all, how Irish did the players actually feel? The issue of dual nationality is a difficult one to explain to anyone who simply hasn't got it and requires something of a double-think. It's almost an extreme version of having two counties in Gaelic games. Galvin's experience of it certainly wasn't as intense as Mick McCarthy's – whose father would rather he played hurling for Waterford – or Tony Grealish's, who actually did play minor hurling for London. But, like almost everyone bar perhaps Michael Robinson or John Aldridge, there still was an experience of it.

'The family used to always talk about it and where they were from in Ireland, when it was they moved over. When I declared, I just had to find the exact details. But then that was it. I was Irish. That was my team. Full stop.'

Second was how Irish the fans felt the players really were. Galvin insists this was 'never, ever' an issue and almost everyone else echoes that. When Hand's Ireland, including Galvin, drew 0–0 with Norway at Lansdowne Road in the Mexico 86 qualifiers, many supporters were heard to chant 'fuck off back to England'. Rather than a rejection of the so-called 'Anglos' though, it is likely that this was as much an insult to the Irish-born players who earned their money there. Certainly, Giles always felt there was an inferiority complex in Irish football that ensured English accents would be afforded more credence than those from home.

Finally, of course, there was the question over the quality of the players. Certainly, they were hugely important in filling in gaps in the squad. As an example of its imbalances during Hand's time, he had to choose between two of the best left-wingers in the English game – Galvin and Kevin Sheedy – but was forced to reach much lower on the right side. Charlton, however, solved that issue by using the rule as an effective transfer market and picking out players for his two problem positions – right-wing and up front – with Ray Houghton and John Aldridge filling those gaps.

By the same token, there was the issue whether many were only here because they weren't good enough for England. At least in many English minds. The opportunity to prove otherwise would come though . . .

Long before that, however, Galvin had to prove that he was good enough to even play professional football. His was a route to the top that's almost inconceivable in today's game. But, as long ago as it was, it seemed to take someone – anyone – even longer to realise just how promising the bustling young Galvin was. Twenty-two years to be exact. As a teenager he'd had a trial at Huddersfield and played a youth-team game for Leeds United but 'hated it, didn't like the lads and just buggered off home. I was never really obsessed with football.'

He did like it enough to keep playing for Northern Premier League side Goole Town while training to be a teacher. From there, word of his performances in an FA Cup run eventually got back to the likes of Scunthorpe, Hull and a one-time double-winning manager.

'I was playing one really wild, horrible night for Goole and been told someone was coming to watch. I didn't have a clue who and thought, on a night like this, they probably won't turn up. But Bill Nicholson did. He just decided on the one game to sign me, then buggered off, made the recommendation to Keith Burkinshaw at Spurs.

'Keith then gave me a take-it-or-leave-it offer but said the best thing I could do was finish my teacher training course because it might not work out. So I'd be at college all week doing my qualification. Then on a Saturday I'd be on a train at nine o'clock to London to play. If I had a bit of time off I'd come down to train but it was all a bit weird. I was mixed in with the reserves, youth-team players. Didn't really feel part of it. Bit of a stranger.'

Galvin's education marked him apart even more. He began the teacher training course after graduating from Hull University, where his form for the college team initially attracted the attention of Goole. Indeed it was stock *Shoot* trivia in the 1980s that Tony Galvin, in fact, had a degree in Russian Studies. Why Russian Studies though?

'Well it was politics, language, all that stuff. I went to grammar school and we did it there and it was something I quite enjoyed. It became quite popular at that time in the 1970s in universities. Obviously it was the height of the Cold War and Russian became quite popular. Now that of course changed down the line but it was very interesting. I even went to Russia a couple of times. It's a fascinating country. I was very interested in the politics and the history and still am. I never got to use my Russian qualification though.'

Talking in his home a few weeks before the 2010 British general election, would it be safe to make a few assumptions about his vote given his choice of degree?

'I'd never vote Conservative, put it that way. When you get older you get mellow but I used to be quite keen. I was a member of the Labour Party. I'm not now and not allowed to talk about that because I'm a civil servant but, yeah, I tend to be left-leaning. I would be on that side of things!'

His politics were something else that placed him apart from a generation of English players who, if they did actually vote, often went Tory. Not that it was voting habits which were picked on in the Spurs dressing room.

'They used to take the mickey out of me at Tottenham because I was a student, because I was a Northerner, a Yorkshireman too. Then my dress sense too. That more than anything. I'd be coming down to London and I'd be in a scarf and student gear, whatever that was in the late 1970s. Long coats, jackets out of fashion. It was old-fashioned stuff because I didn't have the money. Tottenham first offered something like £50 a week. But I was a student so it was useful. So I used to get the mickey taken out of me for both those things. Paul Miller and Gary Brooke used to be right piss-takers.'

With his academic mind, surely Galvin was able to keep up with them barb for barb though? Indeed, having come from outside, what does he make of the general perceptions of footballers' intelligence?

'I think a lot of footballers are quite sharp, witty. Lively minds. Maybe hadn't been directed down the academic route. So the banter is quite hard at first but you get used to it. It toughens you up. It's actually quite good.'

It wasn't the only element Galvin had to tough out to get up to speed with. There was also the training and the shuddering shift, not just from amateur to professional, but from one of England's bottom rungs to its very top.

'It is a big jump to go from part-time to full-time football. It took me a while to adjust. The training's a big thing to get used to, five days a week. And, maybe because I was a bit older, it took me longer to get used to. The touch would be the first thing you notice. Making that step up. If you mis-control, someone takes the ball off you or, equally, a better first touch means you've got more time on the ball. It's crucial, especially for forward players, being able to control the ball under pressure and then do the next thing. There's the pace of the game, especially in the final third. Everybody's fitter, everybody's quicker. Eventually it came good, got my opportunity and it was a good team to play for.'

Galvin eventually made his debut in February 1979, a full year after signing, in a 3–0 home defeat to Manchester City. Not exactly a portent of things to come. It would take another two years to actually get a regular run in the team but, just like on the ball, he would then prove almost impossible to dislodge. Galvin's strength and crossing provided a different, more direct outlet to a flowering team that also had the flair of Ricky Villa, Ossie Ardiles, Steve Archibald and Glenn Hoddle and was about to enter another dimension itself. Galvin forced his way into the first XI at an incredibly fortuitous time.

'Yeah, we had some great players. Very different types of players and it was a good team to play in. We played some wonderful football. Won two FA Cup finals in 1981 and 1982, lost in extra-time in the semi-finals of the Cup Winners'

Cup in quite a contentious game against Barcelona and then won the UEFA Cup in 1984. Obviously that 1981 cup run was my first experience of anything. Tottenham hadn't won anything for a while so it meant so much to the supporters. It was massive.'

Galvin also had a cameo in one of the most mythical moments in both the club and the competition's history, feeding Ricky Villa for the otherwise individual goal that beat Manchester City 3-2 in that 1981 final replay.

'Yeah, taking the ball up the field, gave it to Ricky and the rest is history. It is nice to be part of that goal even though it is very much Ricky's!'

The fuss made about Spurs' other Argentine World Cup winner, Ardiles, became almost as memorable. 'Ossie's Dream' was the title of the cup final song written by Chas and Dave and featured the ludicrous line 'in the cup for Tottingham'. Galvin remembers the rest of the experience being just as much of a laugh.

'It was great craic. We were on *Top of the Pops* two years running. They used to give you plenty of drink so you could lose your inhibitions. It used to be a bit of a joke really. When you heard the record, it was heavily produced. Even in those days. It sounded a lot worse than that. But it caught the imagination. Fun Boy Three and Bananarama were there and we all got pissed. Fun Boy Three were down-to-earth and the girls were too. Some of the lads were friendly to them!'

Drink, of course, was as big a part of both Ireland and England's football cultures at the time as crowd violence and tight shorts. As Galvin admits, 'We'd play, we'd train properly but afterwards we'd be going wild'. It was the summer tours though where things got really out of hand. As the story goes in the book on Tottenham, *The Boys From White Hart Lane*, the club went to Swaziland two years running to play exhibition games. The first saw them get on famously with a Manchester United side containing Bryan Robson and Kevin Moran who were of a similar mind to say the least. But the second tour showed Spurs just how distant they were from the perennial champions Liverpool. In every sense.

'There was never a good feeling between us [Spurs and Liverpool], maybe because they were successful, maybe because we were Londoners, but we didn't mix. On this trip some of their lads were just legless, never sobered up. I've never seen people drink like it. They weren't bothered because they'd just won the European Cup. The first game we drew then played again a week later. It was fucking boiling and on the Saturday before the Sunday game we had a few drinks in the casino and started to mix a bit. One by one our players went to bed but at four o'clock they're still up and there was just me and Gary O'Reilly. They were taking the piss out of us, calling us lightweights. It was six o'clock before they went to bed and we thought we were going to fucking stuff them when we play.

'But they absolutely hammered us, hammered us. We lost 4– or 5–1 and they didn't run, were just pinging the ball around. It was one of the most embarrassing things I've ever seen because they literally couldn't run. And that shows what a good team they were.'

It obviously wasn't just a resilience to alcohol that made Liverpool ensure a thrilling Tottenham side would never get near a League title, as often as Spurs did threaten to.

'We had two or three seasons when it looked like we were going to be pushing but didn't quite have it in the end. Remember in those days the squads were nowhere near as good as they are now. We had a few injuries. Liverpool didn't have a big squad but it was always near 15, 16 players and always stronger than our 15, 16. That's why they'd usually win the title. They were very good buyers, very careful about who they bought. Look at Mark Lawrenson's case. They were a bloody hard team to play against. I know that. I think we possibly could have done more but maybe we needed one or two other players to make the difference, make us harder to beat or give us something else. We probably just about achieved as much as we could. We could have been more consistent and, at the end of it, the team that wins the League are the best. Away from home we would sometimes not play as well as we should have done. We had some outstanding players but, occasionally, they would go missing.'

That was a criticism directed most commonly at Hoddle. Galvin doesn't think he was the most culpable though.

'Glenn was magnificent. A magnificent passer of the ball, great free-kicks and set-pieces. Unfortunate with the England scenario, could have played more times for England. Ossie always said that had he played in any other country he would have been the kingpin. He felt the team could be built around him. But England managers didn't seem to have faith in him.'

Hoddles's personality was also cited as a problem. Before his idiosyncratic religious beliefs saw him lose the England manager's job in 1999, there was an immense ego that the likes of Cascarino criticised.

'He had strong opinions about football. Very strong opinions. He was serious but not that serious either. I was never really aware of some of his beliefs. I think that might have happened towards the end of his career. But he's always polite. I don't see him that much and wasn't that close to him but to me he always seems the same bloke I used to play football with.'

Ardiles may have been loudly defending Hoddle but soon had to do the same for his country. The Falklands War broke out in April 1982 between Britain and Argentina – a problem for an English club with two Argentinian players.

'It was quite difficult for Ossie and Ricky. Ossie used to get quite a bit of abuse when it first kicked off, then he went and played abroad for a while to Paris. Yeah, they got abuse. Simple as that. It was quite tough. Ossie would argue his case though, call it the Malvinas [the Argentinian name for the Falkland Islands]. He saw it from Argentina's point of view. Said they belonged to Argentina, that was it. There may have been tension in the dressing room but just arguments really. Ossie was a very intelligent bloke and he was educated to believe they belonged to Argentina. That was it. Some in the dressing room saw it different.'

Around that time Galvin himself was delving deep into the effects of Britain's age-old foreign policy. Or, rather, what moved his family to England in the first place. And from where exactly? Once the fine details were determined, Galvin finally made his debut for Ireland in the opening game of the Euro 84 qualifiers against the Dutch. Ireland started the series as they limply finished, making no discernable impact in a 2–1 defeat. Gerry Daly's late consolation would have an effect on the group though as it ensured, in the final game, Spain would have to beat Malta by only 11 goals rather than 12 to trump the Dutch for top spot. As ludicrous as it seemed, the Spanish won 12-1.

It wasn't until the 1986 qualifiers that Galvin got a regular place in the Irish team. Unlike with Tottenham though, it was possibly the wrong time to get a taste for international football as the collapse of Hand's regime was looming. Mickey Walsh's strike gave Ireland a 1–0 win over the USSR and a surprisingly good start to the group but thereafter the team was scuttled in Scandinavia, beaten in Norway and thrashed twice by Denmark. As Galvin puts it, there wasn't so much a sense of pessimism but the feeling it was always those few players or few moments away from ever happening. 'It was a lack of confidence.'

Someone was going to have to instil it. Although that someone's initial lack of organisational skills didn't exactly inspire confidence in him.

'One of Jack's very first training sessions was in a gym that was like the size of a school's. Twenty of us running around it. What were we doing? It was a joke, rubbish! Training left a lot to desire in terms of equipment too. And when it wasn't in a gym we didn't half train on some crap pitches. Sometimes in the airport hotel. It was awful. Imagine international players training on pitches like that?'

More glamour awaited. For Charlton's first summer, the FAI agreed to play in the Iceland Triangular Tournament involving the hosts and Czechoslovakia to celebrate the 200th anniversary of the founding of Reykjavik. But, while the tournament was hardly going to make any news, the squad named for it made plenty. Because, for the first time in 10 years, David O'Leary wasn't in it. Worse, Charlton told the press this before he told O'Leary.

The story goes that Charlton had made his decision long before, as early as his first game – that 1–0 home defeat in a friendly to Wales in March 1986. Despite the common feeling that O'Leary was one of Ireland's few genuinely world-class players – in any era – his style of standing off a forward and using his speed to win the ball was definitely not what Charlton considered world-class in a 'stopper'. Jack himself certainly didn't do it that way for Don Revie at Leeds

United. So, when Ian Rush's 17th minute free header proved enough to win against a team which physio Mick Byrne had picked, Charlton blamed O'Leary. He walked off swearing the Arsenal man would never play for his Ireland again.

Charlton would soon be denied the choice though. When it emerged that Ireland's Merseyside contingent of Jim Beglin, Ronnie Whelan, Mark Lawrenson and Kevin Sheedy were off on an end-of-season holiday, the manager shamelessly rang O'Leary to coax him into coming to Iceland. But O'Leary had made his own plans and wasn't inclined to change them. Charlton's response: 'OK then, forget it!' He certainly made himself forget about O'Leary. For three years.

'When he didn't go to Iceland that was it for Jack,' Galvin recalls. 'He wasn't the most forgiving if you crossed him and he felt Davey crossed him.'

The Iceland tournament ended up a bit of a holiday itself. The players arrived with crates of duty-free alcohol because they had heard there were no pubs in the country. But, other than the boozing helping to strengthen spirit – O'Leary's absence notwithstanding – Charlton also felt the retreat was the perfect way to re-educate the players into his way of thinking. They proved fast learners. Ireland beat Iceland 2–1 and then Czechoslovakia 1–0, both with late goals from Gerry Daly and Frank Stapleton respectively. It was the first tournament Ireland had ever won and remains the only senior trophy in the FAI's cabinet. Kevin Moran has always emphasised the victory's importance while Charlton himself later said, 'The Czechoslovakians couldn't get out of their own half. They didn't understand what was going on. And it caused so much chaos. Just one simple ball played in behind and everybody chasing it.'

From Reykjavik, Charlton went to Mexico for the 1986 World Cup. Diego Maradona may have confirmed himself as one of the all-time greats but, for the most part, Charlton was 'bored stupid'. 'After two weeks, I hardly made a note,' he would say. 'I saw nothing new.' So, Charlton would provide world football with something new. Whatever about the manager's sense of organisation, Galvin was immediately convinced by his tactical acumen and impact.

'He used to get quite focused coming up to games. How he wanted to play, the shape of the team. He would be good at coming up with a different trick for each game. "Stand at the near post against them, their player doesn't like it if you close him down on this side, get onto him quickly." He was also obsessed with the playmaker type, stopping them playing. But he wouldn't give you a lot of unnecessary detail. He was very tactically astute. He's never been given enough credit for that.'

The one flaw to Charlton's framework was that it worked much, much better against teams nominally stronger than Ireland than those weaker than them. It became a recurring theme of the Charlton era that Ireland would struggle to break down minnows. Indeed, Galvin's only goal for his country came in such a game and proved far more important than the opposition would have indicated. With Ireland toiling away to Luxembourg in one of the last games of the Euro 88 qualifiers, Galvin struck in the 44th minute to set the side on the way to a 2–0 win. Ireland eventually made it to Germany by a solitary point.

Waiting there, of course, were England – for the first match of Ireland's first major tournament.

At over 20 years' remove, whatever words are used now can't quite do justice to the elusive, conflicting feelings behind the fixture back then. There was excitement versus anxiety, fever versus fear. This was a brand new stage but up first were Ireland's oldest rivals, England. And, as arcane as it may all seem now, there was an awful lot of history swirling around the game before the Irish team could make their own history – the fact that it was England's sport, 700 years of conquest, the Northern Ireland situation. On a much more personal level then, England was also the birthplace – and, for most of their lives, the first country – of 12 of Charlton's 20-man squad. So, to go with everything else, the players had to endure some odd emotions of their own.

'Obviously when we found we were playing England it was very uncomfortable. Nervous really. I'd never played against England in any game. Some had, but this was a bit special.'

Surely there must be some sense of conflicting loyalties?

'It didn't bother me at all. I'd played for Ireland quite a few times by then.

My team. I was playing for the supporters. Some other people might have had a problem with that but I didn't. None at all. I was wearing the green shirt and that was it. No problem whatsoever.

'We all knew each other though – didn't we? We all played in the same league, same clubs. It was a weird feeling. I knew these players.'

To illustrate Galvin's point, Ronnie Whelan rang his Liverpool – and Irish-descended – teammate Steve McMahon a few days before the game filling him with stories that 'my head's falling off. We were out on the piss again last night.' On the other end of the line, an incredulous McMahon couldn't quite believe what he was hearing.

There was a dark side to that humour though. McMahon mightn't have been able to believe it but many others would have had no problem. Ex-teammates of those Irish squad-members such as Tony Grealish had spoken of how they always had to ignore all the stereotypes about Ireland when growing up in England. All the old Irishman jokes, all the asides about alcoholism. Apart from a general dismissal of the team as well as odds as high as 50–1, many Irish players are still irritated now by how arrogant the English media were before the game. Jimmy Hill had said Ireland were only there to make up the numbers and made typical noises about 'English' players. Over on ITV, when Brian Moore suggested the same thing, his co-commentator Liam Brady turned to him and asked 'well where was John Barnes born?' As Brady said for this book, 'we were the butt of a lot of jokes in England so it was a bit of a funny story for them in the newspapers. So I thought it was pertinent to point out Barnes was born in the Caribbean. Brian was embarrassed by it. Hit the nail on the head.'

Moore wasn't the only Englishman to be proven wrong that day. One would be proven emphatically right though. 'They've written us off already,' Charlton said just before the tournament. 'I think that's a mistake.'

Early in the day it became clear that Irish fans – who had travelled by cross-continental trains, very few planes but an awful lot of banged-up automobiles – were greatly outnumbering the English. The players walked out into the Neckarstadion in Stuttgart at 2.25 p.m. Irish time on 12 June 1988 to, as one put it, 'a curtain of heat, a sea of green and a wall of noise'.

'When you went out there before the game the atmosphere was unbelievable,' Galvin remembers. 'Highly charged, incredible. The day was hot, tense and edgy.'

Well, it was tense and edgy for all but about one minute of the 90. And Galvin played his part in that minute.

'What we did early on in that game was put them under pressure when they weren't settled. I think that rattled England – didn't let them relax. The idea was to get the ball in areas they'd have trouble dealing with. All I remember is the ball coming into the box and the next thing I'm playing it across, bounces up . . .'

Then, fiesta.

'Ray's headed it in the perfect place. As soon as he had I knew Shilton hadn't a chance.'

Nor did anyone else have a chance of reacting with anything like a regular response. It was rapturous. Aldridge and Whelan famously piled on top of Houghton in jubilation. Charlton infamously smashed his head off the roof of the dugout as he leapt up. Chris Morris ran to the opposite corner, pumping his arms at the fans. Galvin can't quite remember what he did.

He does remember the rest of the match, however, slightly differently to the accepted narrative of English onslaught.

'In the first half they had chances but we dominated. Worked really hard and it could have been a totally different game had we got the second goal. Obviously, at 1–0, they came out in the second half and had a real go. But we were hard to break down, bottom line.'

And the bottom line on the Stuttgart scoreboard ultimately read 'England 0: 1 Rep. Irland'.

'My favourite moment in football is probably when the whistle was blown for that game. It was as happy as I've ever been for a game of football. I was substituted late on with total exhaustion and still remember the joy at that moment. I've obviously been to a UEFA Cup final, FA Cup finals but to play in that game . . . you knew it was a historical moment.'

Shortly after it, Galvin went up to his former Tottenham teammate Hoddle to swap shirts. Hoddle had promised it to someone else beforehand but was so stunned he just blankly handed it to Galvin. At that point all manner of dignitaries and celebrities were crying and dancing into the Irish dressing room. Galvin saw none of that though. His story of the Neckarstadion ended in a cold officials' room.

'Unfortunately I got dragged off for a random drugs test. I missed all the celebrations. And then you're waiting to go to the toilet. It took the edge off because you really don't want to be there at a moment like that. I had to go straight from there to get changed and to the bus. But we had a good night that night. Jack let us have a few drinks and I've never seen a room with so many excited people. Jack was good like that. "Enjoy the moment but there's a game around the corner."'

That next game against the USSR saw, as Galvin and many others believe, Ireland produce one of their greatest ever performances. He also finally got to use his degree, stunning a Soviet player beforehand by speaking Russian as they went through the pre-match handshakes. The rest of the USSR squad would soon be equally stunned by the high-energy manner in which Ireland played around them, through them and pressed them in. Whelan also scored the opener with one of Ireland's finest ever goals. The fact his flying volley partly came off his shin perhaps encapsulates the display though: great to watch but, in the end, not quite perfect.

'The few years I played for Ireland, that was the best team performance I played in. We should have gone 2–0, 3–0 up. I was taken down by that famous goalkeeper Rinat Dessaev. You know sometimes it felt when you played for Ireland that referees always gave the benefit of the doubt to the bigger teams. It was a blatant penalty. Ridiculous. And 2–0, the game's over. Then John had a really good chance, was really frustrated he didn't score. But these teams, they'll punish you. One chance and it's in the back of the net and so it proved.

'But we murdered them. Not so much with our usual high tempo but we actually played a lot of good football. That was definitely the best we'd ever played. Jack was frustrated, disappointed we didn't win. But proud. We showed, yeah, we could compete but we could also play good football.'

That 1–1 draw with the USSR prevented immediate progress to the semi-finals but the late 1–0 defeat to the eventual winners, the Netherlands, killed it altogether. Galvin, however, is by no means regretful in summing up Euro 88.

'We were disappointed with that final game against Holland but we were run ragged by some of the best football I've ever seen. We couldn't get near the ball. I think over the three games we achieved the maximum. We could have nicked it and gone into the semi-finals and then you never know do you? But it wasn't for want of trying. We gave everything we got.'

Giving everything was also how many summed up Galvin's own career. By that stage though, injury was beginning to force its end. The break-up of that Spurs team brought in David Pleat as manager who, to Galvin's enduring irritation, simply didn't fancy him and sold him on to Sheffield Wednesday. Another back injury interrupted that until he enjoyed something of a swansong with old teammate Ardiles at Swindon, helping them to the 1990 Second Division play-offs.

That form saw Galvin play his last game for Ireland – and only his second game since Euro 88 – in the notorious 1989 friendly with West Germany. He was afterwards named by Charlton as one of the three players – along with Brady and Stapleton – he wanted to prove couldn't play at the top any more. Despite being shocked by Brady's half-time blow-out with Charlton, he remembers his own end more benignly. Perhaps because, unlike with Brady, Charlton actually filled him in.

'I was at Swindon and had injury problems but Jack said to me that if you can show me in this game you can still do a job you can still go to the World Cup. Jack was loyal like that. I hadn't been playing but was in squads and did well. It [the Brady-Charlton row] all went off at half-time obviously, but at the end of the game Jack said to me, "you stay fit, you go to the World Cup". But then I had further problems with my back and an operation. I did go and do some training with them in the end. I stayed for the first game, the England game, which was a great atmosphere. But I came home and missed the main moments. Even though I wasn't in it, you felt you contributed to the team moving forward.'

While Ireland were doing that, Galvin himself was moving on.

'After finishing playing in 1990 I was coach at Swindon and then Newcastle with Ossie [Ardiles]. Ossie got sacked and then, I don't know what happened, I just thought it was time for something else.'

That something else, though, was a long way from Wembley or the European Championships. Instead of spending his days on sidelines like virtually all of his former teammates, he spends them in an ordinary London office. From big crowds to the quiet life. Surely it's a huge change to get used to?

With his educational background and experience of a life outside football into his twenties, it was always going to be easier for Galvin to make a clean break with the game though. Indeed, it's probably because of that that he is one of the few from that generation to actually do so.

'I had my eyes on an alternative career alright. Didn't know what that was going to be but I knew I could do something outside football. I do notice when you meet people on the fringes of football you wonder have they really made the break? What do you do on a Monday morning? What do you do Monday–Friday? Just play golf? I think you have to have a bit of purpose in your life, a bit of structure.

'So now I'm a civil servant. I work for the Skills Funding Agency in London. We fund colleges. I don't teach anymore, we provide the money for training colleges. It's fulfilling when you go out and talk to the colleges, see what they're doing. It can be a bit bureaucratic. Some good, some bad. Like most jobs. But, as I say, gives you structure in your life and it's reasonably productive. Such is life!'

What isn't so productive is trying to explain to ex-teammates and those still in football what exactly it is he does.

'In the end you just stop trying. I just say I work for government, educating and training. "What's that then?" You just say forget about it, don't ask me again. It's difficult to explain and footballers probably aren't that interested anyway!'

Despite admitting he can easily stay away from the game, he does retain interest in what they do though.

'Don't get me wrong, I do like football. I stayed involved at an amateur level and still coach at the weekends. My son's the manager of a local team in the United Counties League so I'm helping him and I can still get passionate now. I can have a row with anyone on the sideline, don't worry. I'm completely divorced from professional football though. Nothing to do with it. I watch it on telly and go to Tottenham a few times a year but I don't really have time and you don't want to be spending six or seven hours of your Saturday going to a game.

'I go to the occasional reunion, really enjoy that. Still play. We have an ex-Spurs team for charity. Meeting up with the old players is nice, we have a few drinks. Like the other day we had Mark Falco, Les Ferdinand. They're properly organised, recognised by the club but they're a laugh and a good laugh. We're trying to get some of the younger ones to play as they're a bit fitter! But the truth is that the recently retired players have either made too much money or they're just not interested. You'd be amazed. The supporters come along, bring the old books and say to you after the game it's nice to actually be able to come to a game and talk to someone about football.

'That's the sad thing about football. It's become a bit sanitised. The big stars, the great players are celebrities. They're distant. Like pop stars aren't they? You're never going to bump into them in a pub or a restaurant. That's the way of the world, what can you do?'

And, once again, Galvin is the outsider looking in. Although, this time, he's perfectly happy to be.

4

Packie Bonner

Keeping an eye

Packie Bonner is on the road. Again. Another day, another few hundred kilometres of tarmac to get through for the FAI's Technical Director. First up, he's got to attend an event for the Special Olympics in Limerick. Later, a club function. Next, a very quick stop-over in Brussels. Then . . . well, whatever the diary demands.

A lot of hours on the go then? 'It's non-stop,' he laughs. 'I suppose because of the work I do it's during the weekend and then during the day you've got other things so it's long.' So long that you've got to really believe in the job to work those hours. Obviously, Bonner does. He's completely bought into the big vision of restructuring the FAI from top to bottom for the future of Irish football. And, although Bonner's area is primarily the grassroots, it naturally branches out into all sorts of things.

All of a sudden there's another car whizzing by a little too close, an exasperated curse and Bonner cuts off conversation. An elderly lady in a tiny jalopy just went down the wrong side of the motorway. 'The police should know about that.' He puts in the call.

Now, there's an easy line for this of course. The goalkeeper attempting to keep things safe, as ever. That's a little too simple in more than one sense though. Because Bonner did much more than just keep things safe for Ireland. He became a symbol of the Charlton era, involved in all of its most cherished moments. That's hardly surprising for a goalkeeper in a team built most distinctly on a defensive foundation. But then at Italia 90 he was effectively Ireland's most creative player. With two assists from powerful punts, he was involved in both Irish goals. His long kicking was key to Charlton's whole gameplan. As such, although Mick McCarthy was always identified as the extension of Charlton's management on the pitch, that arguably applied more to Bonner. You only have to listen to him talk about it. Just as he has now bought into the FAI's vision, he clearly did Charlton's. It becomes apparent the second he starts explaining the mechanics of the manager's approach. More than any other player interviewed, he best sets out the team's tactics and why exactly they were so effective at that time. And all that without commentary or interpretation. Just the logic of it. Listening to Bonner makes it all sound so simple.

There is an old theory in football that goalkeepers make the best managers because they're always overseeing everything that happens on a pitch. Whatever the truth of that, it's little wonder Bonner took it to the next level and applied his mind to such an all-encompassing job. One of his main concerns now is to streamline the structure of Ireland football and create seamless pathways for pre-teen players to professional careers, ensuring no-one of any notable talent gets lost in the ether. After all, he himself almost did. Football then was a different world. There was a haphazard nature to the process of how he ended up first-choice keeper for both club and country.

'I was playing Donegal youth football and got picked by the Irish youth team for that. We were down at Mosney's and, from that then, Sean Fallon, the chief scout at Celtic, got wind and just turned up to watch a few games. So I was sent over for a trial. I had been over and back at Leicester City during that period too but they never signed me and Celtic came in and offered me terms. Jock Stein came over to Donegal to sign me and I ended up his last signing before he left the club.'

With 10 Scottish titles, a 1967 European Cup medal and a six-foot-plus frame, Stein must have made Bonner's hometown of Burtonport shake when he arrived?

'He was a big, intimidating man of course. I didn't have too much involvement with him when I was at Celtic. I was in the reserves, some good people in there. I was only with Jock for a month or so but he was very much an intimidating man. I met him a few times after that before he died. Even at that stage he had an aura about him. Powerful.'

Bonner himself soon outgrew the reserves.

'Within six months I'd made my debut. I was over in July 1978 as a 16-year-old and I made my debut on St Patrick's Day 1979. Played two games, actually, against Motherwell twice in 10 days, then went back out of the team again for another 10 months. Peter Latchford, Bob Latchford's brother, was the goalkeeper then. He was a very good player but then, in 1981, Peter broke a bone in his hand. You need a bit of luck and I got in during Danny McGrain's testimonial and basically kept the place.'

By that stage, Bonner had worked his way up Ireland's junior teams to the under-21s. His call-up to the seniors still carried an element of coincidence to it too, though. Eoin Hand's Limerick were playing a game in Holland at the same time as Celtic so the manager hung around to have a look and promptly included Bonner in the next squad.

After turning out against West Germany B in May 1981, Bonner then made his official debut in the 3–0 defeat to Poland, that game Mark Lawrenson so lamented earlier in this book. You'd think picking the ball out of your own net three times in such miserable surroundings would be an awful way to celebrate your 21st birthday. Especially since it was a trip many other players described as a nadir for the FAI. But it was all too new for the birthday boy to be anything other than exciting.

'I didn't have visions of international football because I hadn't played. I remember under-21 football, going out to Toulon with Johnny Giles as manager and Alan O'Neill in goals. Alan hit his head and I had to play against Yugoslavia. But no, I didn't know what the first team was going to be like. Maybe that was the best thing so I could learn what it was about.'

Bonner made just eight more appearances over the next five years and only two of them competitive. Still in his early twenties and particularly young for a goalkeeper, that was understandable. He would be coming into his prime at an opportune time though. The lack of a top-class, first-choice goalkeeper was cited off the record by some players as yet another factor in so many failures through Giles's and Hand's tenures. Charlton was going to have no truck with that. He made very plain the importance of a forceful goalkeeper to his system in Paul Rowan's *The Team That Jack Built*. Bonner's particular abilities fitted the wanted ad.

'You start with the goalkeeper. Now the first thing I said to the goalkeeper is, "You do not, under any circumstances, throw the ball out to one of your full-backs. You kick every ball." In other words, we're going to start playing from the other end, not from this end. Now, you make it very plain. What you say to the goalkeeper is, "I want you to kick every ball long, as high as you can into their half of the park."'

And how. Charlton evidently made it very plain for Bonner.

'Jack was a confident, powerful individual. Said this was how we were going to play. We had tried to play an international style under Eoin, had good players but maybe not enough to play that style. So Jack probably looked at it slightly differently. He adapted to put other teams under pressure rather than us trying to play their style. We were set up very defensively, with Jack being a defender of course. Attack-wise, people who were playing in those roles maybe had to adapt to a different type of game. Frank Stapleton I remember had a particularly hard job to do, dropping back to midfield and, to be fair to Frank, he did. He was a great player getting that little bit older but he put his shift in. Also, because we hadn't qualified for anything, he wanted to give it a go.

'The training wasn't anything too different to what had gone before. But there was a lot of talking about tactics off the field.

'The one thing that he did change which probably united the team was that lads weren't allowed to leave the hotel after training. We used to be driving all around the country. The Dublin lads would be all off around the city at home for an afternoon with their families, then me coming from Donegal. And the boys from England would be around the hotel on their own. That wouldn't be great. So Jack stopped that and it helped create spirit. We'd go to the horseracing, or Mick Byrne and Charlie O'Leary would create an atmosphere around the hotel for the players to enjoy.'

Despite most pinpointing the Hampden Park game on 18 February 1987 as the definitive date Charlton became the team's manager in mind and spirit and not just body, Bonner still feels it was more gradual. He does concede, however, the first XI that night was probably – overall – the strongest ever put out by Ireland. That was the conclusion of many former stars when a large group sat to reminisce the evening the FAI gathered every living Irish player who had been capped before the first game at Croke Park in March 2007. The line-up read: Bonner (Celtic), Paul McGrath (Manchester United), Ronnie Whelan (Liverpool), Mick McCarthy (Manchester City but soon to be Celtic), Kevin Moran (Manchester United), Liam Brady (Ascoli), Lawrenson (Liverpool), Ray Houghton (Oxford United but soon to be Liverpool), Frank Stapleton (Manchester United), John Aldridge (Oxford United but soon to be Liverpool), Tony Galvin (Tottenham).

'When you look at that team, a lot of stalwarts were there, all playing for big clubs at the time, and physically it was very strong. And the results helped players believe. We weren't leaking goals, we were very strong defensively.'

The stats alone tell that story. In the three campaigns before Charlton took over, Ireland conceded an average of over one goal a game (1.29). Under him, that dropped to 0.5 goals a game. A particular high – or, perhaps, low – came in the Italia 90 qualifiers when Bonner let in only two goals in eight games, both in the same match away to Spain. In addition to Charlton's discipline, Bonner puts such parsimony down to the fact that three of the backline – himself, McCarthy and Chris Morris – played together for Celtic. Indeed, with his club winning the double in their centenary year, his country qualifying for their first international tournament and the keeper himself in form that would see him earn continental recognition, 1987–88 must be regarded as the finest season of Bonner's career?

'Yeah, the three of us all had that. From a Celtic point of view I did have a few injury problems with my back so I worked very hard that year but it corresponded with us only conceding 24 goals in the league. But we were playing really well and I was playing really well. I missed the Scottish Cup final but going into the European Championship then I was at the top of my game confidence-wise, fitness-wise. I was in good shape.'

Bonner still needed some help from his friends in Scotland though. Even if he didn't expect any. For their final Euro 88 qualifier, Bulgaria required only a draw against a Scottish team that lay fourth of five in the group, had been hammered 4–1 by Belgium and would go on to draw 0–0 with lowly Luxembourg. For 86 minutes in Sofia it looked like that game was heading for 0–0 too and Bulgaria for Germany. Deliverance seemed so unlikely. But then the saviour was equally so. Hearts' 23-year-old midfielder Gary Mackay was only 41 minutes into his international debut when the ball landed at his feet in the Bulgarian box. Despite two defenders running across his line, he swept it into the bottom corner and Ireland into the 1988 European Championships.

At that moment, Charlton got a phone call saying 'Congratulations'. 'What for?' he replied. Without realising it he had been watching a delayed transmission of the game with only half an hour gone. In Glasgow, Bonner had the benefit of the live show.

'I was in the house watching it and was shocked. Didn't expect it. But Scotland played well on the night and I remember Roy Aitken and people like that at Celtic did a fantastic job. If it wasn't for Gary Mackay doing what he did you never know what would have happened. We mightn't have had the impact we did over 10 years. I was asked by the FAI to go down to the airport with a bottle of champagne. And I did. Met them coming off the plane that evening. Glass of champagne and a few pictures.'

Fast-forward seven months and Bonner is in the Neckarstadion dressing room with a few gifts of his own for a tense Irish team. In the 48 hours before the match with England it had been all the squad could talk about. Attempts to divert their minds inevitably deviated back. Any sort of psychological trick was going to help.

'I had been sent clay from a relic in Donegal. I went home for a couple of days when Jack gave us a few off. Went to get my mind right in my mum's and I was given this soil so I felt obliged. There was a note on it 'for the players' – so it ended up in everybody's boots. Those are the things you do when you're under pressure. If they work, fantastic!'

Something certainly worked for Bonner that day. He was inspired. Although he claims that, once the pageantry of the occasion began, it was hard not to be.

'I think we all look back on the anthem playing and seeing the flag waving on that stage. A great moment. Makes it.'

On the line, Charlie O'Leary was in tears as he sang. More would follow. Ireland made England work in the first half, although Bonner remained the most admirably focused even after the goal. Since so much emotion could have unsettled the team's gameplan, Morris remembers his keeper immediately shouting and reorganising the backline for kick-off. Such defensive discipline does have one drawback though. 'In the last 20 minutes you almost inevitably psychologically concede the ground and try to hold on to what you've got,' Morris recalls. 'England piled on the pressure.'

Memorably, Bonner was equal to it in what was probably his very best display for Ireland. Time and again in the second half, England would create a chance. Time and again, Bonner would turn it away. Was it as tough to play in as it looked?

'It was, it was. But I was feeling really good. Glenn Hoddle didn't start which was a big shock to us. He was fresh when he came on and put through some fantastic passes for Gary Lineker.'

One of them, with only minutes left, sent Lineker one-on-one with Bonner. He had enough time to pick his spot. But Bonner pulled out a stop. It was at that moment, many English players later conceded, they knew it wasn't to be their day.

Unadulterated joy naturally overcame all reason and it undoubtedly energised the team for the next game against the USSR. But behind all the emotion was an exceptionally well-executed gameplan. Despite the scoreline at the end, that second game against the USSR was almost a distillation of everything that was right about the Charlton era (in which case the moral victory of a draw was arguably an apt result given how often his side achieved them). Ireland were playing a notionally more celebrated and technically superior team but were intimidated by neither fact and instead frightened them with force.

Bonner's explanation of how they did it, meanwhile, almost serves as a blueprint for Charlton's brilliance in this regard.

'Jack's tactics that night were spot on. Russia had players like Rats, Belanov and a mix from Dynamo Kiev. And they played with a sweeper which was a different style we wouldn't come up against too often at club level. But what Jack talked about was how they'd try to lure you over to one side of the pitch. Their goalkeeper would then transfer it across the other side so the sweeper eventually ends up with a lot of time on the ball and the opposition is all over the place. That was their way.

'Jack said, "Well, we're not going to allow that to happen" so the tactic he set up was that, instead of everyone shifting across, we keep the wingers wide on each side and fill the gap in the middle with people dropping off. So then, when the ball was played to their left-back and then back to the sweeper, when he went to change the play there was always somebody out on that wide guy. Then, when we put them under pressure, the sweeper could only knock it back to the goalkeeper who himself could only knock it down the middle to Kevin Moran.

'One of the other things was that he deployed Paul McGrath in the middle of the pitch because he wanted Paul to drop back in when the ball was played wide and our right- or left-back would go out. Paul being there meant that the other full-back or centre-half didn't have to shift across too far so we always kept a very strong back-line.

'Attack-wise, Jack kept things simple, wanted to create space in front of goal for midfielders arriving in and we did that by keeping the ball away from goal rather than the striker's feet. John Aldridge probably got unfairly criticised over that period for not scoring enough goals. His role was very clear though and Jack told him not to worry about it. He'd be in areas he wouldn't have been in at club level, getting on the ball and setting it up for Ray or whoever was on the other wing to get into the box. And then the other forward was normally a big guy – Tony, Frank or Niall – who would go to the back post to create space. So, with John going one way and the other centre-forward going the other way, that pulled centre-halves around the place and they didn't know how to cope with it. Then we had midfielders getting into the box into space.

'So those were the tactics and, from there, we played really well. Really, really well.'

Ireland, however, couldn't make the most of it. Their luck ran out at the wrong moment. And so did George Hamilton's.

When interviewing Bonner before the match, RTÉ's then soccer correspondent had mentioned the keeper's Irish record of going eight matches without conceding a goal. That added up to 729 minutes by that stage. For fear of tempting fate though, Bonner didn't want to talk about it. Hamilton infamously – and understandably – couldn't stop himself late in the game when Ireland were looking to close it out. 'And Bonner has gone 165 minutes of these championships without conceding a goal. Oh danger here . . . '

It was self-inflicted danger as Ireland fell asleep for an instant and Oleg Protasov slipped the ball past Bonner.

Ireland's luck would then take a – literally – ludicrous turn against Holland even if, once again, Charlton appeared to get his gameplan absolutely right.

'It was very difficult because it was three in the afternoon in the heat of Gelsenkirchen and that may have cost us in the end. But I think Holland were afraid of us because they knew we were physically strong. They were technically very good and Ronald Koeman at the back was a great passer of the ball. He would pick it up and play a 30- or 40-yard pass to the wide-men. He didn't like people putting him under pressure though because normally at club level that wasn't the norm. When we did it he just kept turning and giving it back to Hans van Breukelen. That was how we stopped them and it actually worked in the World Cup [Italia 90] so there was a similarity between both games.'

Except for the outcome. Just as they would have exactly two summers later, Ireland had in their hands the point they needed to make it through the group for yet another unprecedented feat. McGrath had even smashed the ball against the Dutch post. But, after two games in those temperatures and at that tempo, they were beginning to feel the heat in every sense. Holland were now looking to exploit every angle. Eventually, they found one. A wicked one. With seven minutes left, a scrambled Koeman snapshot found its way to substitute Wim Kieft. His stretched header was still going wide until, improbably, the ball flicked up off the pitch at 90 degrees and into Bonner's net.

'They were a fantastic team and for us to go out there and match them and be very unlucky to lose out to a bit of a fluke goal shows you. What stands out for me was Van Basten was offside. And the rules at the time were if you were in an offside position you were offside. That annoyed me, but the way the ball moved after it hit the ground, it's something that may happen again – it may not – but there's nothing you can do about it.

'I think it showed for us though when both Russia and Holland got to the final. We grew in confidence after that, playing against Russia very well and then taking on Holland. The thought was "we can actually do well if we get the chance to qualify again because we're not afraid of anybody now".'

If anything, as Belgium's cautious approach at Lansdowne Road first hinted in April 1987, Ireland were now one of the sides to fear in Europe. That would be emphasised in the Italia 90 qualifiers. When the draw was made it might have initially looked difficult. Spain had the core of an exciting young Real Madrid team led by Emilio Butragueno and Michel, while both Northern Ireland and Hungary had qualified for Mexico 86. The first two results wouldn't have suggested it was going to be much simpler than Euro 88 qualifying either. Ireland drew 0–0 in Belfast with military helicopters whirring above, and were then soundly beaten 2–0 in Seville. That sort of defeat though was something that was becoming increasingly rare. Ireland were in fact about to go on the longest unbeaten run in the country's history: 17 games. Five of the next six qualifiers were won with Bonner keeping a total of seven clean sheets. Seville was also avenged with Michel bullied into conceding an own goal at Lansdowne Road for a 1–0 win.

Northern Ireland and Hungary may have qualified for the previous World Cup in 1986 but neither offered any evidence they would get near this one. In the end, it was a surprisingly easy way to enter the promised land. It was also an Irish campaign drastically different to every one before or since. Or maybe the team was just at its peak. Either way, the manner in which qualification was eventually secured summed up the group. It was all so routine for such a long-awaited breakthrough.

Sure, the final night could have gone wrong. But that would have taken a turn of events far less likely than a Hearts midfielder scoring his first goal in his first cap. Having dismantled Northern Ireland 3–0 at Lansdowne Road, Ireland would have to lose to Malta with Hungary somehow beating Spain in Seville. Bonner is still a little reluctant to describe either the task or qualification as elementary though.

'No group is easy. I think, going out to Malta, you're never sure until you get that goal but we were confident we could overpower them. For a goalkeeper those games are difficult though because you're only one shot away from making a mistake. So concentration is key for all those types of games, keeping everyone in front of you organised, keeping them on their toes, don't let them lose it. There was so much at stake, that wasn't going to happen. But you still had to perform even though you're getting very little to do. You come off the pitch knackered. Mentally more so than physically. You're sitting at the back hoping we get this goal, get this goal. You know then when John Aldridge scored the first, and then the second, you think "we have it now".

'We always seemed to qualify on the road though. But it was good to be on an island where the fans could enjoy it . . . and we could enjoy it too you know! Just release. That was the unique thing too. We had a really good connection with the fans.'

Aldridge can certainly testify to that. When rushing for the toilet in a nightclub later that night, he was lifted above the shoulders of the crowd and carried around. The party was only just getting started. Typically though, Bonner had to concern himself with the more mundane details that ensured it ran smoothly. In the build-up to Ireland's first World Cup, everyone wanted a piece of the team. Someone had to organise who would be making what appearances and where.

'Yeah. Myself, Liam and a few others took on the role of making sure everybody had their job to do. So the team shared the responsibility. But the thing was that, at the time, you needed the money. It was different to today. So we were responsible to sponsors, the people who had paid, so there was all that to do.'

Given his working hours, Bonner can come across as a bit businesslike, always in a hurry. Once settled and speaking though, he's not like that at all. Granted, the gritted teeth probably never helped that perception. They formed an image as intrinsic to Ireland's Italia 90 experience as that of the squad piling on top of David O'Leary. They also helped Ireland get to the point where they could pile on him. Bonner's determined bite gave two long punts the extra push that put Ireland into the second round. It was clearly needed. In the first game against England in Cagliari, the fortuitous goal Lineker had bundled past Bonner clearly put the team on edge as the clock ticked towards the 70th minute.

'The gritted teeth were very much because of Mick and Kevin coming back and looking for the ball off me. The only time Jack wanted me to give the ball to people was when we were charging forward with it. But Jack still didn't want me feeding them to play it through midfield and put ourselves under pressure. So play it long and then get it back and play from there. But they were looking for the ball off me, looking for the ball off me, looking for the ball and it wasn't about that. Eventually I got tired and gave Mick a bit of an ear-bashing. That's when the camera caught me, after giving out to Mick. But it was to gee everybody up!'

It certainly did. The ball immediately fell kindly for Kevin Sheedy who drilled home Ireland's first ever World Cup goal and banked the first ever World Cup point. The first ever knock-out game would them come after another Bonner clearance-cum-assist forced Holland's Berry van Aerle and van Breukelen into a mix-up for Niall Quinn to plunder.

Ireland were into the last 16 and mainland Italy at last. It was only at that point, surprisingly, that Bonner felt they were actually part of the festival.

'Being out on the islands was unfortunate in many ways. You do feel detached. Unlike some of the other lads though, I never felt really bored. I had Gerry Peyton who was very good, we got on well together. And, being from Donegal anyway, I was used to going for long walks so I had a lot of little things to keep me occupied. Other people were different though and that was the job of the manager to suss that out and make sure everybody's comfortable and that.'

One time Charlton made everybody feel distinctly uncomfortable though was when the boardgame Trivial Pursuit came out.

'We had a very intelligent team now. But you always had to watch Jack because, according to him, the questions were inevitably wrong. The priest who was with us, Monsignor Liam, was the question-master and he got a few volleys from Jack. Questioning the cards, questioning the answers. The answers must be wrong if Jack's wrong. There was good craic that way.'

On one occasion when the senior players beat a team consisting of Charlton, Mick Byrne, Maurice Setters and a few other backroom members, the manager let rip in a manner normally reserved for a centre-half who passed the ball to a midfielder. 'What a crap team I've got here! Did you answer one question? Did you answer one single fucking question all night?'

'Otherwise I wouldn't say there was anyone you'd pick out who were off the wall and kept everybody entertained,' Bonner explains. 'If you did have any who were a bit mad it could wear you down. But Mick Byrne was probably the one who kept everybody going.'

Not least when he accidentally backed into – and smashed – a prize model ship in one of the family hotels the team were staying in. Cue apologies, a failure of communication and finally a huge argument with the owners.

Byrne and the rest of the Irish squad were about to be waited on hand and foot by hotel staff though.

'The hotels on the islands were OK, don't get me wrong. Jack's usual way of looking after us. But for the second round then we were up in Rapallo in Genoa and I think it was a five-star hotel. Scotland had stayed there for the whole term but were knocked out,' he chuckles. 'They were in luxury while we were down in the islands. It was only then we could compare.'

Once Ireland caught the plane to Genoa their World Cup also caught fire. The Stadio Luigi Ferraris was host to what were probably the most jubilant scenes ever witnessed in Irish football. Although purgatory had to be endured before reaching heaven: 120 minutes of anxious, tense football against Romania, then the distilled drama of a penalty shoot-out.

Ireland, however, had been preparing. Even if it was just to entertain themselves rather than actually practise.

'What had happened was that Niall and Dave had this little book for after each training session. A fiver if you scored all three penalties and a fiver for us if they missed one. Almost every day after training that was going on. I don't know if money was paid in the end! But what it did do was create a bit of competition. And Dave was practising penalties. Who was to know that would be important later on?'

It also helped sharpen Bonner.

'All I had to do was prepare myself. Of course we'd thought about it. I'd had a shoot-out against Aberdeen that season and I'd only gone right for one of them. So I had to think about it and myself and Gerry came up with a scenario. We had a kind of process.'

Isolated from the team down at the centre of the pitch, Bonner's experience of the shoot-out was obviously completely different to the rest of the squad.

'Everybody was up at the centre circle but I went off to set my mind right and do some stretches. The thing I remember is the referee from Brazil. He was very pernickety, made everybody pull up their socks, which was a bit mad after 90 minutes and extra-time in boiling heat.

'Gerry had been working out the scenarios with me though. That gave me confidence and I was getting closer and closer even though the first few penalties were good penalties, very good penalties. I was still going the right way. I knew from their run-up which way the ball was going and I had a little thing where I could go one way then the other way very quickly to gather momentum and dive as far to the corner as I could. That's what I did myself but I anticipated by the way they ran up they were going to hit the ball into a certain area of the goal and all you can do is dive into that area.'

For the record, all of Gheorghe Hagi, Danut Lupu, Iosif Rotariu and Ioan Lupescu had put the ball in areas just out of Bonner's reach. Kevin Sheedy, Houghton, Andy Townsend and Tony Cascarino – just – responded. Then up stepped Daniel Timofte. The Romanian was the regular taker for Dynamo Bucharest and came armed with information himself. Word of a Bonner injury at Celtic had got back to their camp. Lupu, the second penalty-taker, thought he noticed this in Bonner's dive and advised his teammate to change his style. The Irish keeper, his thinking went, wouldn't make any shot he had to move for. So, for the first time in his life, Timofte didn't blast a penalty down the middle. You could tell, as Bonner remembers.

'Not a great penalty, good height, no great pace on it and it was there to be saved because I went the right way.'

The diving save defined Bonner's career. His leap in that distinctive pale-blue jersey became one of Irish sport's most iconic images and was fossilised forever in a thousand ads that read 'Packie saves with Irish Permanent'. Timofte would even name a pub after him.

Despite his jump of joy, Bonner couldn't let himself get carried away – yet. And not because whoever Ireland's fifth penalty-taker was going to be still had to score.

'The only people allowed in the box were the two goalkeepers and whoever was taking the penalty. But when I saved that penalty Andy and Cas had already taken theirs and ran from the halfway line to hug me in the box. My fear at that moment was that this (the saved penalty) would have to be retaken because the two lads had broken the rule of staying in the centre circle . . . and I didn't know Dave was taking one!'

The referee Jose Roberto Wright didn't flinch though. And neither did O'Leary. Then, 'bedlam'.

Among the many players who were involved in both games a debate has arisen over which was the more joyous occasion, as if such things can be measured: Stuttgart or Genoa? Despite what defeating England meant, Bonner is in no doubt.

'Romania was the one because everyone was involved. Normally it was the one who scores the goal but this was different. It was fantastic when you can show your emotion. I always look back to it. Little Charlie O'Leary attempting to jump up and he couldn't . . . fantastic!'

These were giddy new heights. Little Ireland, with one of the lowest populations in the tournament and poorest economies, were left as one of the best eight teams in the world. And this just five years after a campaign when the World Cup never looked further away. How quickly football moves.

In every aspect though. Irish fans would always remember Bonner's save against Romania but hope to forget another in the 38th minute of the quarter-final.

'Italy's goal was unfortunate. But we gave the ball away, the one thing Jack didn't want. It allowed them a rare counter-attack. Donadoni picked it up in an OK position and had a shot. I had read it to go wide so that's where I moved. But it moved a metre in the air back into the centre of the goal and, as it turned, I lost balance. All I could do was put it into the area where it was going and had to pull it with me, which I did. But, just before that, Schillachi had made a little diagonal run across the box and the ball went straight to his feet, open goal. Looking at it now though I don't know if I could have done more because of the nature of the shot and how I moved.'

The fact Ireland pushed Italy so far and were only 90 minutes away from a World Cup final has brought a lot of fanciful talk about the full potential of that World Cup. Typically, Bonner attempts to look at it with a logical bent.

'I always had the feeling Italy were going to win that game because they were at home. It was the quarter-final and they needed to go through. The referee was from Uruguay and wouldn't have been used to our style. But they had Argentina in the next game and, the way they played – knocked it about, one-twos – that would have suited us. Press them high up the pitch. We could have done them.'

What many feel was the great missed opportunity though, was Euro 92. Particularly given Ireland's strength in depth at the time but especially given how a moderate Denmark went and won it. Uncharacteristically, defensive lapses against England and, above all, Poland, cost them. David Platt breached the Irish backline at Lansdowne Road for a 1–1 draw but that wouldn't have mattered had Ireland closed out their 3–1 lead in Poznan in the second-last match.

'We lost some bad goals against Poland. A diagonal ball into the box. Kevin probably should have headed it away. I shouted at him and the guy dives in and gets a header on it. That was a bad goal to give away. Three-all. The England game was a sickener too. At home, we should have beaten England.'

So should Poland. Ireland could still have gone through had the Poles preserved their early 1–0 lead over England on the final night. But, as Ireland were waiting anxiously for news while winning 3–1 in Turkey, Lineker scored 13 minutes from time.

Bonner would still enjoy one more great day for Ireland. A display that fit the Giants Stadium as the Italian defeat was avenged. Bonner pulled off a few good saves, most notably from Beppe Signori, but overall remembers it being remarkably run-of-the-mill in terms of actual goalkeeping because of the epic performances of those in front of him.

'Personally I didn't have a lot to do. The Italians obviously didn't like Paul McGrath breathing down their neck and we stopped them quite easily actually.'

It would prove a premature peak to an underwhelming tournament. Ireland's second World Cup ultimately wound its way down to Bonner spilling a Wim Jonk shot in a 2–0 second-round defeat to Holland.

'It probably summed up the tournament in one way for me. He picked the ball up, had a bit of space, struck it. I think I was thinking about what I would do with it next, more than anything else. It was just an error, one of those things you can't legislate for. But it wasn't as enjoyable as other tournaments. We were way too long in Florida, conditions were atrocious, that heat, preparation. The tournament itself was all over the place. There were no connections with other areas, TV was crap and then the water. Not being able to give the guys water when they should have been. All of that. Crap. The only positive out of it was that we got through the group stage. But we were getting older too for those conditions. I was 34.'

He was also getting too old to adapt to some of the changes in the game. There had already been the introduction of the backpass rule in 1991.

'It destroyed me! It came in almost overnight and I don't think the managers, outfield players and goalkeepers adapted to it quickly or well enough. At the time none of us were comfortable with it. If you go and ask Pat Jennings, Peter Shilton, Ray Clemence . . . we were not brought up in that system. Bruce Grobbelaar was used to playing outfield in five-a-side so he got away with it.

'The training had to be changed to make the goalkeeper almost an integral part. In the past goalkeepers went into the corner, dived around a bit, did reaction work and a bit of fitness. But now they have to deal with the outfield players. We didn't and it took us a while. I was coming to the end of my career so I don't think we had time to adapt and change. We didn't understand the concept of space as it relates to passing. If the left-back gives you the ball that means there should be space on the right-back's side. Even now I don't think the goalkeeper coaches get enough time at it.'

Such is the isolation of the position and detachment from the rest of the team in that regard, Bonner feels there is a 'definite uniqueness' about goalkeepers.

'That starts at underage level. The goalies always room together and work together, do everything together. Room, train. You have to respect each other and back each other up. There will be a time when you will expect the same from the other goalkeeper. Declan McIntyre is in charge of the goalkeeping side of the

FAI and has taken on that philosophy with the young players. I was very fortunate at Celtic. Peter Latchford helped me considerably. Then with Ireland, myself and Gerry became very close. We'd still chat on the phone today.'

The empathy with other keepers can even reach across borders as strong as the Old Firm.

'One stage at Rangers, Andy Goram was making mistakes and the crowd was on his back. I remember going up to him in the players' lounge at Ibrox after one game and chatting to him and trying to gee him up. From then on, he was brilliant and we ended up losing some championships because of him! I made a mistake . . . well, not a mistake, just something you do naturally. But you have a feeling for goalkeepers. Tomorrow it could be you.'

Part of the reason might also have been that, for a decent period during Bonner's time at Celtic, Rangers weren't even the main threat. Both of the so-called New Firm of Alex Ferguson's Aberdeen and Dundee United occupied a top-three place more often than Rangers between 1980 and 1986. And on the final day of the 1985–86 season Celtic had to break Hearts to steal the title.

'We went into that game against St Mirren having to score four or five goals with them [Hearts] having to get beat so we didn't have a lot of, I suppose, hope. When you play for Celtic you have to win every single game. But this game we just had to play and hope for the best. We scored early on, got a few – then news came through Hearts were losing 2–0. To be honest those teams were fantastic teams. It was before the real money. Scottish football was very strong then.'

On eventually retiring, Bonner took up a job as goalkeeping coach with Mick McCarthy's new Ireland, ensuring he was one of very few individuals to be involved in all of Ireland's qualifications to date, in some capacity.

'That was enjoyable, working with Alan Kelly and young Seamus [Shay Given]. I took all the knowledge I had to help them. I was fit and young and could do the job well. So it was great to be still involved.'

He wasn't just involved in the success though, but the drama. Saipan. Notoriously, Roy Keane's nuclear temper was first directed at Bonner when he argued against using his over-worked goalkeepers for a training match. Having never spoken publicly about it before though, Bonner simply doesn't want to start now. The question is cut off at source.

If Keane took a bit of interest in what the FAI do nowadays, he would realise many of the smaller changes he requested at that time have long been implemented. Indeed, Bonner has bigger ambitions for his own job.

'When I first came into it, the role was very much about education, youth development. Those were the two pillars and it still is. But very quickly that whole area of social responsibility came into it. We're charged with looking after football as a whole, not just the best players. To affect areas of social disadvantage, people on the margins, at risk and so on. We have the likes of Richard Dunne who's helped us with that as a social ambassador. So football is the carrot and the rest comes with it.'

Bonner cites a staff of over a hundred and how important they've been in getting the base of Irish football stable. Once that's done it's all about unifying all the disparate strands of the sport, from the regional leagues to the national league, and creating proper pyramid structures with correct coaching. It's the way countries as small as Bonner's eternal bane, Holland, have stayed so competitive.

'That's the future. We have to get the infrastructure right and we haven't quite got there yet but there's been huge improvement in some of the facilities also. We're actually quite different to England and Scotland. Up to 16 years old we have an influence on the best players. Unlike there where the professional clubs own them. We have that influence. We look at it very much from a development point of view, giving them a broader knowledge. We've just got to get the balance right.'

Anything to stop kids as talented as Bonner falling through the cracks as he almost did. Even if he did eventually follow his own road.

5

Chris Morris

Can't beat the feeling

few days before the 2006 World Cup, Chris Morris was taking time
out from the family Cornish pasty business to reminisce about his own
experiences of the tournament for Radio Five Live.

'I was on with Tony Cascarino and I probably gave all the stock answers.
Olympic Stadium, meeting the Pope, penalty shoot-out. Then the presenter goes,
"and turning to you Tony, what were your overriding memories?" "The Coca-
Cola girls."

'A class line, I just fell about laughing. I just thought, "you . . . I wish I
thought of that." Only Tony.'

Morris does himself a bit of a disservice though. Open and articulate, he's
all too able to tell a story well. What's more, when he does give the 'stock
answers' as he puts it, he describes them with almost a supporter's sense of
emotion. The scarcely believed glee at actually being involved in so many
revered moments can be heard in his voice. A sense of realisation that 'Yes, I
was there'. Perhaps that's because he thinks he was 'lucky enough to be in the
right place at the right time'. Perhaps that's because he had to come from fairly

83

far away to actually make it in the sport. Growing up in the rugby town of Newquay where there was scarcely a football club let alone a scout, Morris stayed in school and sat his A-Levels before eventually forcing a trial for Sheffield Wednesday. Or, perhaps it's because he felt a 'gatecrasher' from the very start of the good times.

'I had just made my debut against Israel in Tolka Park when I was part of a TV panel with Mick McCarthy for when Scotland beat Bulgaria. Most of the squad had departed so I just tagged along with Mick really. I was a little bit sort of embarrassed because I had only played in one low-key match and to be sort of commentating on qualification where everyone else had done the hard work was a bit . . . Nonetheless, I was happy to be involved. You take your chance when you get your chance but I did feel I had used somebody else's spot really.'

Specifically, that was the popular Dave Langan's spot. With Jack Charlton having publicly stated how important full-backs would be to the future development of the game after the 1986 World Cup – and Langan already beginning to feel the injuries his endearingly abrasive style brought – the manager wanted a more athletic mould of player.

'I fitted the bill,' says Morris. The experiment against Israel went well with Ireland winning 5–0, Morris performing adequately and fellow debutant David Kelly scoring a hat-trick. Morris, however, had already received something of an unusual endorsement before the match even began.

'I was out on the pitch doing some stretches and didn't see Jack come up behind me. He just booted me right on the shin then said, "I don't know if you'll play regularly but now you're here you'll be around the squad for quite a long time". I just went "OK". Oddly enough then I played something like 20-odd games on the bounce thereafter.'

If Morris still felt like a gatecrasher when he was included in the squad for Euro 88, most of the country didn't. Most of the country, in fact, didn't even care the team were preparing for the competition. Talk about the calm before the storm. The atmosphere before the tournament, not to mention the general attitude towards football in the country, was at odds with everything that was to immediately follow it. It was still only the hardcore that actually bothered too much, as the numbers who went to Finnstown House in Lucan to see the team off proved. And then the numbers who turned up at the last home friendly against Poland emphasised.

'That Poland game stands out alright. We won 3–1 in front of barely anybody. Some of the warm-up games were low-key and there was a little bit of a danger of people doing other things. It was all very relaxed though. Finnstown House was a fantastic location, idyllic really. It did help to calm everyone.

'We prepared for the most part in the normal way. We trained hard for it, had a bit of down-time. Jack didn't want to flog us to death because obviously we'd played in long domestic seasons. He did stress the sort of things he wanted done as part of his gameplan and methodology. Also got the balance right with down-time. He allowed us a bit of golf.

'But, Jack being Jack, we did some things that were perhaps a little unusual. We had a great day at the races, had a few beers. Jack picked something like seven out of eight winners on the day and still only won about a tenner because he put so little on. We were having a bit of a laugh on the way back then and trying to get Jack to stop for another beer. All the boys singing, "We love you Jackie, we do". That usually got him. He said, "OK, we'll stop for one more". We went to the Hill 16 and of course Jack paid by cheque, it went on the wall and of course he didn't pay.'

That atmosphere of relaxation had evaporated by the build-up to the England game. The team were staying in what amounted to an army barracks but that seemed to fit the feeling. It was taut, tense. Morris especially. With good reason.

'I do remember the English press really trying to get into me personally because perhaps they didn't know much about me and I was due to be playing against John Barnes who was then football writers' player of the year. And they really, really tried to get into me. It was a particularly difficult press. They tried to set me up a little bit. I didn't appreciate that very much and I think that made me all the more determined to give a good account of myself. It wound me up to fever pitch. I felt quietly like a coiled spring, waiting to get in there and compete.'

At least he was going to. Kit-man Charlie O'Leary wasn't but was more worried than anyone. The night before the English game he was sitting up praying and pondering when Charlton came into him and got him to shuffle across the tiny little camp bed. Jack sat down and asked, 'What's wrong with you?'

'Just thinking about tomorrow,' O'Leary answered.

'What about tomorrow?'

'If we get beaten, you know?'

'Why? Who's going to beat us? England? Don't be daft.'

O'Leary was composed enough to do his job correctly the following morning though. In those days, the squad got into their full kit before hopping on the bus to travel to the ground. Morris had only just got all his kit however.

'I was playing in Puma boots and they sent me over the wrong ones so I had to get another pair arranged. They didn't arrive until the day before the game so I didn't have time to break them in. Odd little things like that seemed to happen quite a lot but we used it as fuel to overcome adversity and give it our all and I think that's what we always did.'

Whether Charlton gave any sort of particularly motivational team-talk before the England game, Morris was far too preoccupied to even remember.

'He probably did. But by the time I got to that bit I probably hadn't blinked for two hours. For me, you go into your own little zone of focus and, half the time for really big matches like that, you don't hear what the manager's said. He's only gone over what he's said before and he's going over key moments. But I remember nothing about what Jack said before that.'

Much like the aftermath.

'I can't remember what I did at the end of the game. I probably just collapsed and I think everybody was going ballistic. Everyone in the squad was coming on and racing around to the players. I did change shirts with Tony Adams. Probably the overriding memory I've got is the amount of politicians, dignitaries, officials who came in and were so overcome with emotion. Everyone was crying.

Incredible. The impact that result had and, particularly, over England.'

Other memories that stand out for Morris are the Irish fans comfortably out-singing the English, the heat, O'Leary and the subs smothering the first XI with ice-cold towels at half-time and, of course, his own display.

'Yeah, I did have a good game. I always enjoyed working with Ray Houghton. He was very energetic just in front of me and I think we always worked pretty well together. He covered a lot of ground. But all around that team you had a lot of support. Mick McCarthy was constantly in my ear just inside me.

'And I always remember afterwards, John Barnes – very magnanimously – said what a great game I had against him and how difficult he'd found it. Which was nice of him.'

After the 1–0 over England and 1–1 with Russia, it was on to the German town of Narl. And more heat. At least now the players were finally in a proper hotel rather than barracks or university campuses they had become accustomed to in the first week of the tournament. That had its own surprises. As tends to happen in Germany when it's that hot, many of the residents took every single item of clothing off to go swimming. With the players in an effective nudist resort, this created the comical sight of Charlton running around trying to prevent tabloids getting photos of his boys sunbathing beside naked women. 'Only the FAI at the time!' Morris laughs.

There was still a degree of confidence the team would do the job against the Dutch and, as UEFA effectively dictated, plans had been made for a potential semi-final. Just like his team though, Morris's participation ended earlier than it might have.

'I banged my head against Holland and my eye swelled up so I could barely see. I had to be taken off. I was watching from the bench and it was torture.'

The pain had a pay-off. The players returned to a transformed country, one that – from the England game – had realised its love for football and the team. The squad got a glimpse of what awaited them immediately after the Dutch game. Thousands of fans stayed behind chanting, 'We want Jack'. He came out after half an hour to a rapturous reception.

The squad started drinking on the coach after the game. Some bottles were even brought down to a delighted few fans hanging around outside the ground. And, although Narl proved a bit too detached from the Irish supporters sending the tournament off that night, the party continued for the players onto the plane and after.

'There were hi-jinx to say the least. We did all have a few drinks, then had to get ourselves together.'

Throughout the flight, scissors were brought out to cut the smart ties of anyone who fell asleep. Once half the squad's had been tailored, Charlton suddenly turned around to roar, 'What the fuck are you lot doing?! You've got fans and dignitaries greeting you!'

The players had no idea and watched with drunken but delighted faces as their coach brought them up O'Connell Street and down to the Municipal Gallery for a reception. There the fans started singing, 'Who put the ball in the English net?' for Houghton to respond – at the urging of his brother – 'I did, I did!'

The appetite had been whetted. And the anticipation for Italia 90 was drastically different.

'I think with Euro 88 nobody knew what to expect. That was a particularly difficult tournament to get to because only eight teams qualified. Therefore the expectation was just to give a good account of ourselves, perform credibly. It was somewhat muted really.

'But for the World Cup, having seen how well we could perform against the big teams on the top stage, I think the expectation quite rightly was, "Hey, let's see what we can do here".'

The players had a lot to do before they left. There were the appearances, the suits to be measured for, and of course the songs.

'It was great. I loved being involved. It was always good fun when we made the songs and that sort of thing. "Give It a Lash Jack", I loved that.'

The song that really captured the spirit of the times, to the point it was sung on the terraces and at almost every joyous Irish event thereafter, be it football or not, was 'Put 'em under Pressure'. Produced by U2's Larry Mullen who was a long-time supporter and friend of the squad, it featured a number of different elements that created a raucous soundtrack for the tournament. Built around a riff from Horslips' 'Dearg Doom' – itself taken from the traditional song 'O'Neill's March' – Clannad's Moya Brennan sang the haunting intro while the chorus was adapted from the familiar chant of 'Olé Olé Olé' and a reworking of the optimistic words from Scotland's own 1978 song 'Ally's Tartan Army'. Above all though, there were the samples of 'MC Charlton' and an interview the manager had done: 'The game is about being effective, being aggressive, getting on with the play . . . we'll put 'em under pressure'.

'Yeah, Jack's voiceover. I can't remember too much of that recording to be honest though. I think I was one of the lads down at the pub while the rest were singing. There in spirit! Singing wouldn't have been my strength.'

For the pre-tournament training camp, instead of Lucan, the squad returned to the site of qualification: Malta. Or rather, the site of Charlton's usual family holiday.

'It was the hotel Jack and his wife Pat had stayed at some years before and they wanted to book it again. Nobody from the FAI had bothered to go and check the place out. When we got over they had just opened the hotel for us. People were taking dust-sheets off the furniture when we arrived. It was a disaster. The swimming pool was empty. Nothing worked. I remember getting stuck in the lift for 45 minutes, me, Pat Bonner, David O'Leary. It was just crazy.

'We would laugh about it, get on with it and what else could you do? The training pitches weren't very good, we didn't have very good kit. I remember Niall Quinn used to come down and there was never a shirt that fitted him. It would always be riding up his belly. The socks. It was all mix and match. Just funny. I remember going for the team photo at Old Trafford and it wasn't organised properly. People didn't know they had to bring this or that. Little Charlie O'Leary had to stand in the back row because he'd forgotten his boots and was there in his black leather shoes with his tracksuit on. You could see it underneath and that was the World Cup photo!

'Just little things like that would make you laugh. We were sharing a training pitch in Malta with Scotland and all their training kit was matching. Everything just seemed super-organised . . . but not always in a positive way. I remember watching them train and there were that many cones and grids it looked like roadworks on the M1. Whereas we just had a couple of things Jack wanted to do. Short, sharp five-a-sides. All the Scots were laughing at us and our minging kit but they were home before the postcards.'

Other than that, there was actually little interaction with other squads.

'We only came across the Scots in Malta. They were sharing their training base as well. Little bit of banter there. We did see the Argentines at one stage. Didn't know them or anything like that. Just envied their gear!

'We were isolated down there really. Down on the islands. But then so were England. They had a particularly bad time with the supporters. But we were up for that, ready for that.'

Ireland's first ever game in the World Cup brought a strange sense of déjà vu despite the novelty of the occasion and the long wait to finally be there. An exciting new stage but one again occupied by Ireland's oldest rivals.

'There was perhaps a little bit of a reverse of the game in Stuttgart. England scored first then we had to chase the game but I think we did that very creditably and were well worthy of our point – if not more.'

They might have got more had England's star-in-waiting not tricked Morris with something other than his ability on the ball.

'I remember closing down Paul Gascoigne chasing his own goal. He was really, really fiery and didn't like the fact that I'd clipped his heels a couple of times. I'd had a little bit of a bite of him trying to get the ball and then he snapped a little bit which he was well capable of. He threw a big punch at me. Just sort of swung over my shoulder a rabbit-punch which just missed my right ear. We ended up in a heap on the byline and he said to me, "Quick, get up, shake hands before we get into trouble". And, as I'm shaking his hand, I'm thinking, "Before you get into trouble you mean!" He conned me right out of it then. What a character he was, a beauty.'

The match, however, was anything but a beauty. After a relatively dismal

1–1 draw, one Italian newspaper ran the headline, 'No football please, we're British'. It got worse though as there was even less on show in the 0–0 draw with Egypt. The first two games were hardly what was expected from a tournament Ireland had waited 60 years to reach. Back home in the RTÉ studio, Eamon Dunphy couldn't stand any more. Having spoken about how qualification was 'glorious and golden' before the Egypt match, Dunphy angrily threw around far harsher words along with his pen afterwards.

'Anyone who sends a team out to play like that should be ashamed of themselves. We know about the upside of Jack. We know how hard these lads work. We know about their courage. But football is a two-sided game, when you haven't got the ball and when you have got the ball. When we got the ball we were cowardly, ducking out of taking responsibility.

'I feel embarrassed for soccer, embarrassed for the country, embarrassed for all the good players, for our great tradition in soccer. This is nothing to do with the players who played today. That's a good side. I feel embarrassed and ashamed of that performance, and we should be.'

Even harsher words were used when Dunphy travelled on an already-arranged trip to Italy for Charlton's press conference before the crucial third game against the Dutch. Once Dunphy tried to ask Charlton if he felt the way of playing in the qualifying matches should be different to the actual World Cup, the manager immediately interrupted.

'You're not allowed to ask a question . . . you're not a proper journalist.'

An argument broke out about Dunphy's entitlements between English and Irish reporters – most of the latter on Charlton's side – culminating in *The Guardian's* Ian Ridley being told to 'Fuck off back to England'. Dunphy himself said 'He's bullying lots of journalists . . . I've just decided I'm not going to be bullied any longer.'

Much like the debate over Liam Brady's departure from the squad, this latest controversy appeared to concern football philosophy: Dunphy's purism against Charlton's pragmatism. There was, however, a personal element to it. The two had drunk together until Charlton read some of the opinion pieces that had turned so many of his players against Dunphy. When they then came across each other at a Hanover hotel during Euro 88, Charlton couldn't help himself.

'You, you little cunt. I tell you something. I've gone along with you and I've tried to help you. But now you can fuck off. 'Cos I'm joining their fucking ranks. I want fuck all to do with you.'

He made that perfectly clear two years later as the press conference drew to a close.

'I am entitled as an individual to speak to who I want to speak to. I think that's pretty straightforward and I don't want to talk to him.'

Were his players talking about it though?

'We did get to hear about it,' says Morris. 'The press were looking for our reactions to it. Dunphy said this or that or whatever. We all knew. But with Dunphy that was par for the course, wasn't it? So we ignored it. Maybe it was one of those eminently forgetful games though. I haven't seen it. Obviously we were disappointed with the result.'

Whatever about the performance, the result should be placed in some sort of context. The European champions Holland couldn't defeat Egypt either having drawn 1–1 and it would take England over an hour to breach the expected minnows. Eventually, Mark Wright travelled up from the back of Bobby Robson's surprising new sweeper system to head home the goal that would open up a deadlocked group. As the four teams entered that final round of group matches, they were level on points and goal records. Wright's goal gave breathing space. It would also change the dynamic of Ireland's match against Holland. After just 10 minutes, Ruud Gullit completed a quick one-two with a drilled shot into the bottom corner for Holland's one moment of class in the tournament: 1–0. Bonner's long punt on 70 minutes, however, caused enough chaos in the Dutch box for surprise starter Niall Quinn to equalise. The party got started again.

And, having been Ireland's tormenter, Gullit suddenly turned to peacemaker. Word got to the players that England were winning and, with the competition's odd structure ensuring three teams went through from four of the six groups, the result would be enough to send both Ireland and Holland through.

'There was something that went on and Gullit was going around saying "ein-ein" to all of them. I don't remember Mick saying very much but there seemed to be a bit of a pact and the referee couldn't do much about it.

'We were happy just to keep it and they weren't putting us under pressure. We were almost taking turns. You make a bit of a token effort but we were happy with that. The only one who seemed not to be bothering with it was Van Basten who was still trying to score! You did feel that if the Dutch tried to go at it again, it would have been hard. They were that good. But I think at that stage we were both happy to go through.'

Holland perhaps should have tried a little harder though. With identical records, lots were drawn that sent Ireland into second place and the Dutch to a meeting with the tournament's stand-out team and their most bitter rivals, West Germany. That match would end in a 2–1 West German win and a literal spat as Rudi Voller left the pitch with Frank Rijkaard's phlegm in his perm. When asked on ITV what he would have done in Voller's position, Charlton didn't engage in the usual media-speak. 'I'd 'ave chinned him.'

Ireland didn't exactly get off easy though. They were up against a Romania side that had the core of Steaua Bucharest's 1986 European Cup-winning team, the belief that they could actually win the tournament and a player Morris feels was the best he ever came up against.

'Aw, my favourite was Gheorghe Hagi. I thought he was absolutely fantastic. The game we played against him, he'd shoot from absolutely anywhere. But also his acceleration and power. He was absolutely awesome and a real handful.'

Not enough of a handful to hit the net until it came to the very first penalty of the shoot-out. Hagi stepped up and smashed it into the top corner. Ireland's World Cup experience rested on an effective game of Russian Roulette.

'Everyone's got different memories and I remember thinking we were lucky. Cas's penalty hit the ground and bobbled underneath the keeper. As they were going 1–0, 1–1, 2–1, 2–2 and so on . . . getting to 4–4, Jack was in the centre-circle saying, "Right, who's next?" We'd had our nominated players and he's looking at the senior ones. Mick McCarthy's saying, "I'm not taking one, I'm knackered." And then Kevin Moran's there saying, "Not me, Jack". Then next minute Jack's looking at me. "Right, you can take the next one."

'I'm like, "Jack, I've got cramp, my calf has knotted up". That's what I remember, the pressure mounting from that point of view. And Jack's there, "Well fucking hell, someone's going to have to take it".'

The most surprising figure of all finally did. Making the long walk from the centre circle was the player who had only come on as an extra-time sub for Steve Staunton. A defender no less who had never taken a competitive penalty in his life, who had been missing from the squad for three years, who Charlton swore would never play for Ireland again, whose cultured football abilities appeared to represent everything the manager's style wasn't . . . and here was David O'Leary about to decide whether Charlton's star would implode or go supernova.

'The nation holds its breath,' George Hamilton would proclaim.

O'Leary held his nerve.

Ireland exploded.

In the Stadio Luigi Ferraris, almost every member of the travelling party descended on O'Leary in delight. In Dublin Castle, veteran journalist John Healy would cry tears of unrestrained joy at the EU summit. In the rest of the country, those who weren't dancing did pretty much the same. More Irish people had watched that event than any other in history.

'Phenomenal' is how Morris simply sums up the moment.

One question on it though. Considering he could have stepped up before O'Leary, does Morris have any regrets about not taking a chance at immortality?

'No, none whatsoever!' he laughs. 'It could be nice if you could guarantee you were going to score!'

He does struggle to find words for what awaited the squad next. The quarter-finals weren't the only heavenly stage Ireland would reach. With Rome on the horizon should Romania be beaten, Charlton had joked to physio Mick Byrne that he would take him to meet the Pope if Ireland qualified. The priest travelling with the team, Monsignor Liam Boyle, wasn't laughing when he made the call to the Vatican to arrange the visit though. The squad were granted an audience with Pope John Paul II in the auditorium.

'I think the occasion and actual presence of the Pope are such that it beggars belief. I'm Catholic and it meant a lot to me but meant a lot to everyone. Just incredible. You really have to be part of it to feel it. I think it had an overriding impression on everyone. Absolutely universal on that. Whatever denomination anyone was from, they couldn't fail to be moved by that occasion.'

Morris insists that 'nothing is sacred' when it comes to jokes in a football dressing room but, such was the awe, he can't remember anyone laughing or giggling. Not even when Charlton nodded off.

'I don't particularly remember anything being said! It was just a momentous, reverent occasion that moved everybody. I'm sure somewhere there were a few comments with a degree of cheek but I didn't hear any!'

The Pope had a few words for his fellow goalkeeper Bonner and 'the boss' as he called Charlton. The general feeling might have been though that, given the euphoria around the country, all Ireland was blessed. Such emotion led to Con Houlihan's famous lament of the tournament: 'I missed the World Cup. I went to Italy.' Even as a direct participant, it's something Morris doesn't necessarily disagree with and it was a thought that particularly struck him the night before the quarter-final. As the population were battling nerves on the eve of what was probably the biggest sporting event Ireland had been involved in, he was battling boredom.

'Con was different class and I know what he means. It did feel a little bit like that. The frustration was that, when we were doing well and progressing, you could hear so much about what was going on back home in Ireland. The country had almost come to a standstill but we weren't getting any of that. After games it was very low key.

'I remember before the quarter-final, I sat in my room, nothing to do. This fan on in the ceiling, just whizzing around watching it. You're that far removed from it. Up in the hills above Rome, a very isolated place. You're contemplating the biggest match in the country's history, so many people watching and it's so low key. The only thing you can think of are your own personal standards and "please don't let it be me that drops a clanger". It is really tough, really tough.

'Then, though, we got a phone call from Jack. "Get yourself downstairs to reception." He brought in a barrel of Guinness and we all had a few pints. It was just class Jack because he read the script and we were all bored. We were all thinking and knew the importance of the game. It was well capable of getting the better of you but he brought us all down, got us all a couple of pints, good night's sleep, off you go.'

They gave the Italians a difficult night in Rome but ultimately fell short. Like almost every other player involved though, Morris feels that wasn't entirely down to Ireland's failings.

'It was extremely difficult for us to get past the Italians. I'll never forget what a raw deal we had. Every single moment the game was broken up by officials. Italy got absolutely everything. It was so frustrating. We couldn't go anywhere near them. Kevin Moran got booked because he applauded the referee. It was tough.'

Is he suggesting the subconscious influence of the host nation on refereeing decisions – as Italy experienced themselves against Korea in 2002 – or something more treacherous?

'I don't know. I just think the odds were stacked against us and perhaps we were playing uphill most of that game. It was always going to be difficult. Could you see, in Italia 90, the Italians turfed out by the humble Irish in the quarter-final stage? That was not written in the script and it was a script they intended to stick with. It's hard to say.'

Alan McLoughlin concurs.

'Being honest I don't think we were ever going to beat the Italians on their home soil. Italy were good but we, equally, held our own against them. There was no way the referee was going to give us anything. There was only going to be one outcome, by hook or by crook, and that was Italy winning. In my own mind, no matter what we did that night, eventually something would have happened that led to Italy winning the game.'

In the end, Toto Schillachi's opportunism was enough. And it shouldn't be forgotten that he also smashed the crossbar with a free-kick that another linesman might have given as a goal when it bounced down off Bonner's line. With one of the six strikes that would help him become top scorer, Schillachi had got enough off the Irish though. As Morris would know all too well.

'Just as the match finished I ended up right next to Schillachi. I just shook his hand and he sort of gestured to me do I want to swap shirts. So I swapped shirts, that's great . . . then he gestured again. Did I want to swap shorts because we had matching numbers on the shorts? So I thought may as well get a complete set. But what he didn't realise was that we had the old Adidas shorts with the centres built in. So I've got no underwear on. I'm thinking "Do I want those shorts or am I going to maintain my modesty?" So I thought bollocks to it and took the shorts off. Of course then, because he'd scored the winning goal, there's a bank of photographers snapping away and I'm stood there, boots, long socks and nothing else. And Schillachi trying to protect my modesty!'

Shortly afterwards, Charlton would come back out onto the pitch to be serenaded by the supporters. It was only a flavour of what was to come. The players would finally get to see the full effect they had on the country. As their plane for home approached Ireland, the captain had an announcement. "I am changing the route slightly. We are going to fly in over O'Connell Street and I want everyone to look out." The squad was silent as, below them, over 300,000 filled the street just for them. That was 250,000 more than greeted the West Germany team that won the World Cup.

'It was incredible,' recalls Morris. 'We had some reception after Euro 88 but Italia 90 was just . . . amazing. In some ways we were glad to be back. A lot of us would have liked to have gone further but, nonetheless, it was brilliant to get that kind of reaction. I've never seen scenes like that. Just amazing. The amount of people who came out for us.'

So many that Charlton couldn't actually enjoy the open-top bus trip through the city. He was too busy roaring at kids to keep a bit of distance for fear they might be run over. When he finally got to address the crowd, Charlton raised an even bigger cheer. 'We've prepared properly, had a little bit of sun, ate well and we drank very little.'

Pause for effect . . .

'We're going to change that tonight.'

And they certainly did as Morris remembers.

'It was a chance for everybody to let their hair down a bit. Everyone liked a bit of craic and beers and everything. We'd worked hard during the tournament and achieved a measure of success. It was good to be back to share that and be part of what was going on in Ireland. Because, as you say, even the players felt they missed it a bit!'

Although it comes across like a cliché, the camaraderie derived out of such sessions was anything but. Drinking for the team was, much like the general population, a crucial part of their make-up. Training hours would be moved around to accommodate sessions, players would rush over from England a day early to get them in. For the squad, some of those memories are as cherished as the matches.

'Undoubtedly. The kind of camaraderie we had I'm sure they don't have that these days. It's much more of a regime. More strict in a lot of ways. But we had so much going for us in terms of that spirit. And the right mix of players who made the most of it.'

And make the most of it they did. The upshot of all the success was the players – who still weren't exactly on mega-bucks – never had to pay for a drink in Ireland again. Nightclubs would be begging them to make appearances and offering them free drink for the night. The first match after the World Cup 90 was against Morocco and it was a carnival where Charlton realised he could command the crowd with a wave of the hand. And the circus around the Irish squad now brought a few other perks, as Tony Cascarino freely admitted in his autobiography.

'When we weren't opening shops, modelling clothes or doing fashion shoots for magazines, we were fending off girls literally queuing to be screwed by one of the 'boys in green'. Some handled it better than others and resisted the temptations . . . but it was so ridiculously easy.'

There would be a difficult side though. Not least for Morris. The squad's main haunt at that stage was Rumours nightclub on O'Connell Street. It would more than live up to the name. One hostess took Morris to court in a paternity suit. He won. Although Morris appears a little uncomfortable talking about it now, he answers questions on it fairly.

'Yeah, there's blame at my door. Instead of being on the back pages I found myself on the middle pages. What you've got is people who are high-profile. Does that attract attention? I think undoubtedly it does, rightly or wrongly. I guess it's how you react to that kind of attention. I can only speak for myself and I found myself on the wrong end of a tabloid frenzy. It's not very nice. But I suppose it depends on how you do react. You look at the situation with John Terry and I think you've got to hold your hands and try and make it right. I can only speak for myself.'

It's put to Morris that many other people around the squad considered him its 'ladies man'. One even tells what he described as a fairly typical story: Morris, with highlights in his hair, holding court for a group of blondes in one of the team's hotel lobbies.

'I think it was a bit over-played really. It wasn't something I tried to live up to. I made a bad choice and got myself in a bit of trouble and the label stuck, rightly or wrongly. From there on in the boys used to just wind me up about it.'

The trappings of that kind of football fame were a long way from his early days in the game. So indifferent was his home town of Newquay to the game he found it difficult to initially forge a path in the sport.

'It's not a football hotbed, not a place where there are dozens of scouts at every game. Rugby union is the number-one sport. I had to go through a convoluted process to get where I wanted in the end. But maybe that was right because as a very young lad I probably wasn't ready for that. Obstacles are there to be overcome if you want it badly enough. I ended up staying at school and taking on my A-Levels. So I went through the representative sides and ended up playing under-18s for England before Ireland.'

A mother from Monaghan would see that change. Morris would also move from a town ambivalent towards football to one obsessed with it.

'I was offered a trial at Sheffield Wednesday. It was there I came across Jack first before Howard Wilkinson came in. He got a hold of me and really developed me from what I was – a midfielder/winger – to a full-back. Teaching me how to play the game really. Howard had a huge part in the development of my career. He was a fantastic coach. Dominant but with a very positive influence. We did have a very, very tough training regime. The fittest I think I've ever been. It was Howard who made me realise in football circles I could be a top athlete. I had capabilities that he brought out – under duress! – and I knew I was capable of competing athletically with almost any footballer.'

Morris saw the full effect of Wilkinson's expertise in the 1983–84 season when Wednesday won promotion to the First Division.

'It was so thoroughly, thoroughly prepared. Howard, from day one, chalked off all the fixtures and told us how many wins we needed to be promoted. He wrote them out on the board before we'd kicked a ball and after every game he'd chalk them off. Then the dossiers you'd have, the thoroughness. The attention to detail was incredible. In some ways I'd gone from the sublime to the ridiculous because, although on the training pitch everything was fine with Jack, with everything else it seemed you didn't know what was going to happen next.'

Which old-school sergeant major was worse for an ear-bashing though, Charlton or Wilkinson?

'Ooh . . . both strong characters. But Jack is a lot taller and has a louder voice. I wouldn't want to be on a bollocking from either to be honest though. There were a couple. I remember I once miscontrolled the ball right in front of the dug-out and Howard came storming out, kicked the bucket with the sponge and it completely soaked me. I was on the pitch! And I had a couple off Jack. One of the first times in the squad I dared to play a pass from the back into a midfielder's feet and Jack absolutely went for me. I shit myself!'

After Wednesday it was on to Celtic in the summer of 1987 and the connection with Bonner and McCarthy that would eventually see him declare for Ireland. Glasgow, of course, would make Sheffield seem like Newquay when it came to football.

'It's a fantastic city. You do have to be a little bit careful. And probably for me it was the first time having that kind of profile. You can get caught up with it. I remember once my wife at the time was pregnant. We lost to Rangers and I went down the town with a friend for a quick bite and we were being surrounded by a group of 19- to 20-year-old Ranger supporters. It was threatening to kick off with a heavily pregnant lady there. But generally it was pretty good-natured. I felt like I was a decent player for Celtic and I got a good bit of respect from the Rangers supporters as well. One of the highlights I have is scoring at Ibrox, 25 yards out, silenced the place. Fantastic. It was at the other end to the Celtic supporters. It took about 30 seconds for them to realise the ball had gone in. Suddenly you hear a roar around the stadium where everywhere else you could hear a pin drop. Nothing else like it.'

Eventually moving on to Middlesbrough in 1992, the same summer he played his last game for Ireland, a cruciate injury ultimately sent Morris down a career path unusual for most ex-footballers. Pasties. Really though, he was just entering the family business. The name of it, after all, is Morris Pasties.

'There were two aspects to it. I was doing some property development at the tail-end of my career at Middlesbrough when my dad became ill. I came and stepped in to help out and I've been doing it ever since. I've done it all. When you're a director of a company, not a huge one exactly, but you have to be prepared to fill the gaps. Do whatever you need to do. I've had days where I've talked about big deals and sold pasties across the counter when a guy's out sick.'

Still though, even after so many years out of the game, football calls.

'I have had a hankering for a lot of years to coach again. That's what I want to do and I'm doing my badges. I remember talking to Bill McNeill up at Celtic and he said, "Football ruins you" – because it gives you so much as a player and nothing can ever match it thereafter.'

Ireland have certainly had very little since to match the moments Morris played through.

'I count my blessings really. These are the highlights of my career. You will take that with you forever. I've got it all on DVD and it's great when your kids are old enough to appreciate it. It has a positive effect and the hair stands up on the back of their neck.'

One more question actually.

The Coca-Cola girls?

'Now that I think about it, they were absolutely outstanding!'

Much like the time with Ireland.

Alan McLoughlin

Heart and graft

Alan McLoughlin is screaming, shouting, jumping up and down. Anything. Anything to alleviate the frustration of not being able to influence events on the pitch.

It's not Windsor Park though. It's not the Stadio Sant'Elia in Cagliari. It's not even the Giants Stadium. It's the press box in Wembley where Portsmouth have dug their studs in to try and keep a fragile 1–0 lead over Tottenham that will, somehow, take them to the 2010 FA Cup final after a season that seemed about no more than survival. And that's survival in the most basic sense with all the club's economic difficulties. But they don't just manage that. They manage another through Kevin Prince-Boateng's penalty. McLoughlin, in his popular role as co-commentator for The Quay radio station, let's go.

'When we scored the second, it is embarrassing when you listen back. I was the only person to do it. All the shit we've had this year though, it was great to have something you can hold your head high about. There's no point doing something like radio commentary for a local city if you're going to do it blandly. You need emotion. And people might say it's a put-on. It's not a put-on. It's nine years. I went through everything with that club. It's two demotions with no money, only 15 players, surviving twice the last day of the season . . .'

It's also the captaincy and the 361 games which put him in the top-10 appearance list for a club whose tapestry he became wound into. Evidently, he was at the epicentre of everything Portsmouth did for almost a decade. The fact that that decade was just before football moved onto a different plane financially means McLoughlin now, among his odd-jobs, spends every Thursday doing removals for a friend's sports company. On the long drives, he admits, Portsmouth's current problems occupy a lot of his thoughts. All of which is why it's such an emotional wringer only watching them now and not being able to do anything about it.

By contrast, it was a role he had long adapted to for Ireland. Over an international career that took in each year of the 1990s, McLoughlin made every single squad he wasn't injured for but spent almost all of that time on the sidelines. He was the epitome of, as he puts it himself, a 'squad member'. Of 42 caps, 18 came as a sub. Yet it took just one of those to ensure he will always be remembered as so much more than a reserve. Just one pristine swing of his left boot to write himself into the mythology of Irish football. A player who hadn't featured in a single moment of the USA 94 campaign produced its defining moment with the equaliser away to Northern Ireland that took the Republic to their second World Cup. Appropriately – and perhaps emblematically – it's all McLoughlin can now actually recall of his time on the pitch.

'I can't remember anything else about the game. I can't remember touching the ball, how many times I touched it. It's all erased. All I can remember is striking the ball, hitting the net, the reaction and then, after the game, people jumping on you and that agonising wait to see if we'd got the right result.'

Infamously, Ireland had to go through an awful lot off the pitch that night to eventually get that point. But so did McLoughlin. Indeed, while his most enduring moment with Ireland may have been marked by adulation, his first moment was characterised by isolation. Far from mobbing him, as at Windsor Park in 1993, most of the Irish squad were seemingly determined to freeze

McLoughlin out when he walked into a Maltese lobby in May 1990.

'I arrive at the hotel with my bag and they're all in the dining room looking at me. If I'm honest, didn't get the warmest welcome.'

He did find out why though – as he approached in a taxi. Jack Charlton had initially brought the more defensive-minded midfielder Gary Waddock to Malta with the plan of including him in Ireland's first-ever squad for a World Cup as the team made the final preparations for Italia 90. Injuries and squad organisation would ultimately deny Waddock that chance though. With Ronnie Whelan and Ray Houghton struggling for fitness in the build-up, Charlton realised he might be left short going forward if Ireland were chasing a game. So McLoughlin, after scoring 17 goals from midfield in the cavalier Swindon side that won the then Second Division play-offs, got the call – if not all the information behind it.

'I hadn't a clue what had gone on. And it wasn't until I was picked up at the airport by a guy called Jack Kelly that he half-briefed me. It was explained Jack had made a decision and changed his mind. I thought Gary had gone home but, unfortunately, as I got out of the taxi, the same taxi was taking Gary to the airport. I did feel for him, it must have been devastating.'

Typical FAI organisation at the time?

'I didn't realise that then. I just thought it was an unfortunate coincidence.'

Naturally, it quelled some of the initial excitement for a 23-year-old unexpectedly plucked from the Second Division to play international football, let alone a World Cup. Particularly when he walked in.

'Most of the lads were upset for Gary. Understandably so. They'd never met me before, I didn't know them. I'd obviously seen them on TV. Heroes of mine really. These were all icons to me and they're all there looking at you. I'm not going to name names but I didn't get the warmest welcome from one or two. But I just thought "fuck it, get on with it, it's not my fault".'

That ice finally thawed in a rather atypical manner. Or, perhaps for footballers, wholly typical.

'"Are you a giver or a taker?"'

'I think that was John Aldridge's first question to me in a broad Scouse accent on the bus after a day or two,' explains McLoughlin. 'I panicked for a minute and said "I'm a giver".'

For the response, McLoughlin adopts an impressive enough Liverpudlian twang.

'"Then you'll fucking do for me, son."

'That was it, Aldo's first words to me. Built a friendship up where we still see each other now. And I'll never forget that from Aldo. Meant a lot to me. The squad didn't know me and the first person to take time out was Aldo, to ruffle your hair up if you like.'

The importance – if not the exact nature – of that kind of gesture to a young player entering such surroundings shouldn't be underestimated. With a mother from Limerick and father from Galway, McLoughlin had spent the summer two years earlier supporting those players at Euro 88. He had also spent the two seasons in between playing in the division beneath them. As such, he was more than surprised at the call. He plainly didn't believe it.

'It was the night before the 1990 play-off final. I got a call into my hotel room about eight. It claimed to be from Maurice Setters but I thought it would be a guy called Ross McLaren winding me up. So I told Maurice to "fuck off" basically, "to stop pissing around" and put the phone down. The phone went again around three minutes later with the irate Mr Setters screaming down the line. So, again, I told him to "fuck off". But it was a genuine call. After the game on Sunday I was to make my way to the airport where my ticket was waiting for me to fly to Malta and I was being included in the squad for the World Cup.

'I hadn't a notion – but what a weekend! Got the call on the Saturday. I scored the winning goal against Sunderland on the Sunday and on the Monday I'm flying off to be involved in the World Cup. It doesn't get any better than that!'

Although McLoughlin would be told half-way through the tournament that Swindon actually weren't to be promoted because of financial irregularities, it did nothing to diminish the experience. Nor did the initial cold shoulders from the squad.

'After Aldo and a few days' training, things got to normal because we were there to do a job really. But, at 23 as I was then, it was the best time of my life. I was training with players who were world-class. I mean Ronnie Whelan was just amazing. Even though he went injured I saw there in just a few weeks the reason why he was a world-class player. It boosted my confidence even playing with these lads. And, obviously then, making my debut against Malta. I did really well in the warm-up game and Frank [Stapleton] equalled the Irish scoring record.'

He didn't have to wait long for his second cap and it arguably vindicated Charlton's decision – however harsh – to bring him in for Waddock. With less than half an hour left for Ireland to equalise Gary Lineker's opener for England in Cagliari, Charlton needed something different. He turned to McLoughlin and started barking.

'"Get forward." That was basically it,' explains McLoughlin of Charlton's instructions as it suddenly dawned on him he wasn't just making up the numbers. '"Get your fucking arse forward, make a difference and keep it fucking simple because if not you'll be off." And that was as simple as it got with Jack!

'I'd only met him a couple of weeks at that stage and I was still trying to get to know his character. Obviously I was in awe of Jack, frightened. If he'd have said go over to that corner flag and stick it up yer arse you'd probably have done it. But I'd heard from the players "you must keep it simple, don't overcomplicate it. He doesn't like that. You have to play to your strengths. If he says do it, do it. Don't do something against the grain."

'Obviously it made a difference in the England game because they'd changed their formation when I came on. We took Aldo off to play one up front with me joining in. So that prompted England to bring [Steve] McMahon on and he subsequently made the mistake that cost them the goal.'

Indeed, McLoughlin himself might have also cost Ireland the goal.

'I was offside. As Kevin [Sheedy] nicked it off McMahon, having trained with Sheeds and seen him play for Everton, I knew his left foot was as sweet as a nut. My job was to get into the box and I just sensed maybe Shilton might parry it and let me tap it in. But I got ahead of the game slightly and was a couple of metres offside. I've seen it again but luckily I didn't get across the line of Shilton and the rules change year on year. I wheeled away and thought "shit" but I looked at the linesman and he was travelling up the line with his flag down. I was more than happy to make my way towards the players and join in the celebration . . . but I panicked for a moment!'

McLoughlin couldn't, unfortunately, have the same impact on his third match. And he admits to a far greater level of anxiety.

'Although I was named as one of the five on the bench against England, I thought "well I ain't gonna get on". So I was relaxed. Then the Egypt game I thought "maybe I will get on". And then you start to think about it a bit more. I came on for 25 minutes and it was dour. Fairly stale on a baking hot day. We didn't get the break. I touched the ball a limited amount of times.'

By that stage, as Whelan got fitter, McLoughlin moved back down from the bench to the fringes of the squad.

'You're getting further into the competition and a bit more quality was expected and I wasn't named in any of the substitutes from then on in. Quite rightly so. But I'd come from playing for Torquay on loan a couple of seasons before to the World Cup. So I just sat back and enjoyed the moment really.'

Or moments as the case was, both on and off the pitch. The World Cup involves an awful lot of waiting.

'Of the six weeks you probably spent four stuck in your hotel room and that's not exaggerating. So, you know, we devised games, throwing oranges around the room, diving across beds. You suddenly become pretty good mates with someone you'd never seen before.

'And I found I was rooming with the mad hatter that is Bernie Slaven. That certainly made the six-week stay eventful. He's amazing. The guy doesn't drink but he's high on life really. He spent most of the six weeks talking to his dogs on the phone, which is hilarious if you're sat in the room. The conversation went as you'd imagine.' – McLoughlin makes a sound that's something like Chewbacca from Star Wars – 'then he'd shout the dogs' names out, getting them to bark at him.

'We stayed in some pretty abject places though. One in Palermo had no air-conditioning. I slept on a camp bed for a week. There was no moaning because everyone knew it was a once-in-a-lifetime experience. But if you train at 10 and finish at 1 and that's it for the day, it's a long stretch. There wasn't Sky TV, it was the normal Italian TV and I think the only excitement we got was in the evening. The old fruity channels came on and some bird took her top off or summat, take her tits out and that made the evening. The whole place erupted. By that stage we hadn't seen our wives and girlfriends for four weeks!

'We were allowed to sunbathe for half an hour per day. Jack would come out and tell you to lie there. He'd come back exactly 30 minutes later, look at you and assess whether you were fair-skinned, tell you to "fucking get up, that's enough". Military-style sunbathing. The games were obviously the big thing though, and that built as the tournament went on.'

Against Romania, Ireland didn't fall. But McLoughlin almost did.

'I wasn't named as a substitute so I decided not to put my boots on. I had a nice new pair of trainers so I kept it nice and casual and didn't tie the laces. They were a bit too big for me but had been given to me by one of the companies so I was delighted with them. I'd never had anything given to me. Then, obviously, when Dave scored we all went bananas and I remember trying to run onto the pitch and was conscious "I'm going to go arse over tit here because these trainers are too big for me", and I remember just shuffling along. But Dave came out of the scrum and came to me. I didn't really know Dave at that stage too well but we were all in it together. And I got a nice picture of that.'

The fact a sought-after player in England's second tier didn't receive his first pair of sponsored footwear until the age of 23 illustrates just how much football has transformed in 20 years. Indeed McLoughlin admits that underlying the collective euphoria were also some purely selfish concerns.

'I was thinking about the bonus going through to the quarter-finals because I'd never experienced that type of money. I wanted to stay on, I was enjoying the trip. I didn't mind the boredom. Training every day with world-class players, I was loving every minute.'

So was the country. Not that McLoughlin was in any way aware of it.

'We were polarised from it. We got a few tapes back, people jumping up in the pub when we scored against England. That was as good as it got. And until we got off the plane . . . it suddenly hits you: Christ almighty, it's meant something what we've done here. And it whets the appetite to be involved. To be part of that. My aim was to get in as many squads as I could with all these great players.'

McLoughlin managed that even if, for the next three years, Italia 90 was to prove an unlikely high starting point in terms of minutes on the pitch. Ireland's newly assured starting XI stormed into the Euro 92 qualifiers by taking Turkey apart 5–0 as the wave just seemed to keep on rolling. McLoughlin did come on in another 1–1 draw against England, just before Tony Cascarino's equaliser at Lansdowne Road. But, with the side so hard to beat and therefore break into, that would prove his only piece of competitive action between June 1990 and November 1993.

'Well the team picked itself in the main. I went thinking if I get on the bench I'll be happy, if I make an appearance – fantastic. Because I knew the squad in and around me – didn't matter what I did at Portsmouth – was world-class. To be part of that higher level was great and the banter of the lads was just phenomenal. It was great to go out with these guys and be treated as equals. That was what it was all about. Didn't matter if you played for Portsmouth or Carlisle, you all went out together, got pissed together. Enjoyed one Guinness, then 10, then 12 and really had a good time.

'There were never cliques. OK, no matter what happens, you can't get a group of 20-odd players sticking together. Cas and the older boys played cards. Myself, Alan Kelly, Roy, Denis [Irwin] and Dave Kelly would hang around together. But, in the main, we had a great time off the pitch and a great time on it. And we knew when to get down to it.

'The pressure for me was probably during training. Because you don't want to look a prat, you wanted to hold your own. "Look, I've got a good touch, yeah

I can score goals but just ain't quite good enough for you guys." But they all respected me, realised I wasn't crap and a decent player.'

That was emphatically proved on 17 November 1993 in Belfast. From a position where qualification had looked a procession, Ireland went into the final game of the USA 94 group needing to beat Northern Ireland or draw and hope one of either Spain or Denmark came out on top in their showdown in Seville.

If that wasn't enough tension, events off the field actually amplified it to unbearable levels rather than render it irrelevant. Three weeks before the game, the Shankill Road bombing killed 10 civilians as well as the IRA member who prematurely set off the bomb. Two weeks before, UFF paramilitaries burst into the Rising Sun bar in Derry and shouted 'trick or treat' before shooting eight people dead.

In Roy Keane's autobiography, he claims some of the English-born players – including McLoughlin – needed some of the background explained. McLoughlin refutes this.

'I was very conscious of it. Both my parents are Irish. I lived in Manchester until I was 19. I completely knew the situation and was no more detached from it than someone living in the South of Ireland. Nothing needed to be explained to me. But, in saying that, it hits you like a ton of bricks when you're in the middle of it. The day before we played, we trained on the pitch and some local lads ran up to the fence as we arrived. They put their hands up pretending to shoot us, like with their fingers, and that hit home.

'Jack insisted on the same routine though. I don't think security were particularly enamoured with us but he insisted on going for a walk on the golf course. There was the threat of a bomb in the hotel so there were tense times. We had armoured personnel, people carrying weapons on the buses dressed up as players. It was difficult and there was the little niggle in the back of your head, "Is someone going to do something stupid?"'

Charlton, as ever, had his own choice of words.

'"Let's get fucking in, fucking out, get the result and get fucking home."

'No team-talk needed really. A quick resume on Northern Ireland, quick thing on set-pieces but impose yourselves onto them. That was it.'

Until they got out there. Then came the catcalls and a whole lot worse. Much of it was saved for the unusually placed Belfast native Alan Kernaghan but, as Townsend recalls in *Andy's Game*, one individual screamed 'Hey Townsend, you fucking English bastard, I hope your mother dies of cancer'. A mere 9,900 Northern Irish supporters – dotted by a 100 undeterred Republic fans – created a spiked wall of noise. And one that seemed to close in on those on the sidelines.

'The safest place was on the pitch. The bench was literally a bench. I could hear it and feel it right behind me. You didn't dare look around and make eye contact. The venom in their eyes shocked me. I remember thinking "this isn't natural". You just get on with it and pray at some stage you get onto the pitch. That was the safest place to be, you could drown out all the noise.'

Undoubtedly subdued by both the sound and Northern Ireland's driven display, Ireland struggled to do as ordered and impose themselves. On the sideline, however, Charlton was stuck on the specifics. Houghton most of all. Any time the star of Stuttgart squandered another ball or chance, Charlton screamed to no-one in particular, 'Look at him! Look at fucking Raymond! Off, get him off. Get him fucking off!'

McLoughlin was to get on the pitch. Just as he came on though so many jeers turned to spiteful cheers as Jimmy Quinn leapt to score a flying volley. America looked a lot further away than across the Atlantic.

Again though, it's odd what goes through professionals' minds even in such extreme surroundings.

'I hadn't scored for Ireland at this stage and I was getting mighty pissed with this. I'd hit the bar once or twice and come close to scoring but badly wanted to.'

So did Ireland, but nothing was happening.

'Jack said, "Get on, influence the game, get forward, see if you can mix it up and keep getting in the box and create something."'

Eventually he did.

With 14 minutes to go, Eddie McGoldrick was hauled down on the right.

Irwin clipped the free-kick in only for Gerry Taggart to clear . . . but not far enough.

'All I remember is the free-kick coming into the box. Big Quinny did me a right favour. He blocked Iain Dowie. And I was a good finisher – 106 goals in my career saw I was – and I practised and practised. I knew what I did to get the ball down quickly from chest to volley was done perfectly. Then it was a matter of relaxing and hitting it as best I could. I had to hit it with my left because I was being closed down on my right. To be fair, that switch takes confidence itself. And as soon as it left my foot I knew Tommy Wright had absolutely no chance. It was always going away from him. And it was gone in a flash.'

Westward ho once more. Not that such a thought even entered McLoughlin's mind at that moment.

'The reaction from me wasn't really, "Oh I'm going to get us to the World Cup". It was, "Thank fuck, I've scored at last". And that was it. That was the emotion. Because it had been playing on my mind. I was a goalscorer, had one in every five games in my career. And I'd gone over three years without scoring and was getting mightily pissed off. The implications of the goal only sank in as the game dragged on.'

Dragged on is possibly the wrong phrase because McLoughlin admits it was a blur.

'As I said, there are only a few things about it all I remember. And the next was the final whistle, people jumping on you, but then that agonising wait to see if we'd got the right result.'

At the same time as Ireland were prematurely punching the air, Denmark were laying siege to the Spanish goal as they looked for the draw that actually would have put both sides in Seville through . . . but, unaware of events in the North, neither could take the chance. After 10 minutes, early Danish pressure saw Andoni Zubizaretta inexplicably roll the ball to Barcelona teammate Michael Laudrup just yards in front of him. Having forced himself into a foul, Zubizaretta was off and 23-year-old Santiago Canizares was on for his international debut. For Sofia '87 read Seville '93 as Ireland's hopes again rested on an international novice. Canizares hadn't even time to warm up but didn't have to wait long to feel the heat. He produced save after unlikely save. And, on the hour, something even more improbable happened. Peter Schmeichel flapped at a corner to allow Fernando Hierro an open goal. It would be enough for Ireland . . . so long as Canizares stayed strong.

He did but was still fortunate a number of Danish players didn't – Claus Christensen missed from six yards and Kim Vilfort from three.

'People were saying we were through. Then someone else said Denmark had equalised but, when it happened, it was amazing.'

Afterwards, McLoughlin told Ger Canning, 'That one was for my wife and my little girl Abby.'

Some of the Northern players would be similarly grounded.

'A few shook your hand, said "well done, hope you have a great tournament". Some just didn't want to know which is understandable. The first thing Jack said was, "Right, let's get the fuck out of here, let's get back to Dublin and celebrate."

'We landed in Dublin and there were thousands at the airport. It was one o'clock [in the morning] and we went straight out on the piss. I hadn't slept but I still had to get back to Portsmouth for training the next morning. I ended up getting a taxi to the airport and then straight to the training ground. Jim Smith took one look at me and told me if I didn't perform on Saturday I wouldn't be going to Ireland again so I had to get to bed fairly sharpish. The wife wasn't very happy either but I needed to put in the performance on Saturday because they paid the wages. I think I did okay!'

Initially, it looked like the goal was going to transform McLoughlin's life and career. Charlton spoke afterwards how he had 'justified his existence'. Every media outlet in the country wanted him. So did the American embassy. McLoughlin and his wife were invited to Ballsbridge for the World Cup draw. But, having driven Ireland to America, McLoughlin frustratingly returned to a role as passenger once there.

'It was a slight disappointment. Obviously Italia 90 was a shock so anything was a bonus. But then I was four years down the line. Certain games I thought I might have been able to affect. Having come on at Windsor Park, making a difference and being in the spotlight, I was then basically put back out of it. I didn't even get an appearance at USA 94. The excitement is great but, unless you're actually on the pitch, it's not as fulfilling. That was the disappointing thing about it. The way it goes – but you just want to play.'

Indeed, the period from the summer of 1994 to the winter of 1995 was probably the nadir of McLoughlin's international career. First, there was the very sudden derailment of the Charlton era. Second, there was the fact McLoughlin again hadn't played a minute of the manager's last campaign. Given the quality in the squad he usually accepted this. But not for the Euro 96 play-off against Holland at Anfield, when Ireland were struggling to keep up with an effervescent Dutch side and Charlton at one stage had seven defenders on the pitch.

'I was probably going to chuck the towel in then. I do love Jack to pieces, think he's a one-off. But I really thought I'd come to the end of the road. We needed a goal desperately and at any point if you're going to bring me on that was it. But when he shouted for Alan Kernaghan that was the final straw. I took my boots off, threw them on the floor and thought "fuck this". I'm not saying I would have got on and scored but, no disrespect to Alan, I was going to affect the game much more in the last third than he was as a defender. So I was gutted. I thought there was no way back for me, that I was only going to be a bit-part player – which I was happy with, don't get me wrong – but at that particular point I was flogging a dead horse. That was as low as I felt playing for Ireland. But whether I'd have taken that step, I don't think I would have . . . but at that moment, no malice towards Jack who gave me my debut, I did feel like that.'

Lucky he didn't keep feeling like that because, within 12 months, McLoughlin was named Irish player of the year having been one of the few to really flourish in the first months of McCarthy's adventurous new era. He was ideally suited to the new manager's surprisingly expansive play.

'Everyone assumed Mick would be a clog-the-ball-forward merchant but I'd seen his Millwall play fantastic football. He made some big decisions and I found myself pushed further into the fold. One thing that happened which was fortunate for me but unfortunate for Ireland was Roy's absence.'

Keane notoriously missed McCarthy's first chance to properly mould his squad, the 1996 US Cup. By that stage, the midfielder had long begun the process of distilling his feral drive into the dynamism that would make him one of the world's best players. Having become Britain's most expensive footballer on signing for Manchester United for £3.75m at the age of 21, he was named Ireland's player of USA 94, had attracted the attention of Diego Maradona for his "balls" and had just been awarded the man-of-the-match award for the 1996 FA Cup final that sealed an unprecedented second double for Alex Ferguson. With so many of the influential figures from the Charlton era no longer around, Keane was surely going to be integral to the next one. Except for the fact he had little respect for Charlton's era and not much more for one of the men most associated with it – Mick McCarthy.

The new manager, however, had an awful lot of respect for Keane the player. That was evidenced by the fact that, despite having watched the new captain walk off in shame after kicking Russia's Omar Tetradze in his opening 2–0 defeat to Russia, McCarthy reached out by again awarding the armband for that tour. At his most erratic as a young man then though, Keane wasn't going to return anything like a compliment. Quite the opposite. He simply didn't turn up with the squad and gave McCarthy no notification. On the day the manager should have been celebrating a fine career with his testimonial, he was instead fielding questions about his errant star. Eventually, Keane released a statement through his solicitor . . . half-way through Ireland's close-season friendly with Portugal.

'Contrary to statements, there is no absence of commitment on Roy's part to playing for his country . . . Furthermore, he has an excellent relationship with his manager Mick McCarthy . . . he endeavoured to make contact by telephone . . . it is Roy's earnest wish he now be left to enjoy, with his family, a few weeks' break from football and to resume playing for his country in a few months' time in the World Cup qualifying competition.'

It was read out to McCarthy by journalists during the regular post-match press conference. There was no disguising his anger. 'I said all along I want to speak to Roy.' The complete breakdown in communication was an ominous omen. McLoughlin, having started the 1–0 defeat to the Portuguese, was a first-hand witness to the moments that got Keane and McCarthy's player-manager relationship off to such a bad footing.

But then he was also a first-hand witness to the moment that got Keane and McCarthy's personal relationship off to such a bad footing. Again it involved a US tournament. Again it involved the senior prefect's inability to influence a junior genius. As a group of Irish players eventually got onto the team bus after closing the trip with a session, McCarthy infamously reproached Keane: 'Call yourself a footballer?'

Response: 'Call that a first touch?'

McLoughlin feels the incident has been afforded undue importance given everything that's happened since.

'It's banter. Mick was a very proud man, Yorkshire man and he isn't going to let no whippersnapper who's just arrived have a bit of a pop at him.'

Often overlooked in McCarthy's mixed early days as Irish manager though, as McLoughlin emphasises, is the amount of games Keane also missed through genuine injury. His cruciate removed him from the close of the France 98 qualifiers and the play-off with Belgium, numerous other niggles from the Euro 2000 campaign.

'Had he been around for the 1997 campaign where we just missed out . . . There was no way I was anywhere near Roy. He was world-class and I filled that space. I played well but we got done in Belgium then done in the last second in Macedonia. Bitterly disappointing.'

McLoughlin never had anything like McCarthy's problems with Keane though.

'We got on fine. I first met him on the trip to America in 1992. I would have called him shy at first. Young lad and I knew the talent because I'd played against him in the FA Cup and I'd played against Chile at Lansdowne Road for his debut.

I just knew it was something great waiting to happen. Pulling people out of situations, wanting the ball, demanding the ball.

'As a player he demanded certain things. Lots of people could be frightened of being involved in an argument, especially younger players. It could be a bit daunting with Roy. Yeah, sometimes he was a pain in the arse but, more often than not, I found him fine. Again, he doesn't suffer fools.

'The one thing I found with Roy was – later on anyway – if you just act normal and don't try and be something you're not then he was fine. I just got on with him and took him for who he was which was, number one, a great footballer and, number two, Roy Keane the lad I used to turn up and treat like everyone else.

'And he looked after me. I went to Wigan towards the end of my career, up there by myself while my family stayed in Swindon, and I'd speak to Roy a lot. He'd say "Come around and have tea with us". I was very grateful for that. I don't speak to Roy now on a week-to-week basis, it's ad hoc. But we'd be fine. I wouldn't claim to be his best mate in the world but we always had a mutual respect for each other and that was it.'

By the time Keane demanded the Irish squad have greater respect for themselves at the start of the 2002 campaign, McLoughlin decided to bow out. At 32, he felt it was no longer worth his while to go back to being the bit-part player. He had served his dues. In more ways than one. It was around then he also ended a long association with Portsmouth. What's remarkable is that, having left the club with a place in their pantheon, he actually started as a pariah with the sound of 'scummer, scummer' reverberating around Fratton Park.

A very amiable and relaxed individual – when not commentating on Portsmouth – McLoughlin has naturally allowed a south-coast twang to invade his Mancunian accent at this stage. He began his career at Manchester United but admits now he didn't quite cut it at the time. From there it was to Swindon Town where his technical ability at the tip of a diamond midfield was ideal for Ossie Ardiles's approach. An astonishing goal haul appeared to take the Robins up to the top flight – until astonishing accounts saw them brought right back down. In demand, and having appeared at a World Cup, McLoughlin was sold to

Southampton for £1m to help settle Swindon's fines. Jibes about his fee were to be the least of his concerns at the Dell though.

'There were people who'd turn around and say "how much?" But there were soon shenanigans about the amount of games I'd played. I was on 26 and they'd refuse to play me. I was told I wasn't good enough and wasn't playing well enough and that's why. It wasn't until I bumped into a Swindon director and asked why I wasn't playing. He asked how many games I'd played and that's when he told me. "Christ, they owe us after 30." At that point you lose respect for people.'

After a loan spell at Aston Villa he went back to Southampton 'in limbo' until Jim Smith asked him to come down the road.

'Desperate to get out, I said yes. Foolishly, I didn't realise the intensity or what Portsmouth were about. It was a big deal, locally, for a million-pound player to move to the local rivals. A big, big story. Obviously Southampton fans will argue differently but there's a more intense feeling in Portsmouth about their football club.

'That was evident the moment I turned up for my first home game against Tranmere. As we came out, Darryl Powell turned to me and told me he couldn't believe I was subjecting myself to it. I thought "it can't be that bad" but I went out for the warm-up and the whole crowd were singing "scummer, scummer!" Any time I touched the ball I thought "what the fuck is going on here?"

'But I managed to set the first goal up and then scored another with my left foot, top corner. Then the next time was an FA Cup quarter-final against Nottingham Forest – Roy was in their team – and we managed to win 1–0 with yours truly scoring the winner. That took the pressure off . . . not fully. The next season, I got 10 in a side that just missed out on promotion to the Premiership by one goal. It did take about a year though.

'But it was the sort of club you could only dream of playing for because Fratton Park is like stepping into a different world, the intensity of the crowd. I'm a working-class lad from Manchester and love the fact they're down-to-earth, honest people. Even now, you'll still get the odd guy calling you "scummer" but

I think I managed to win them over.'

That's an understatement. When Portsmouth's financial situation looked particularly precarious during the 2009-10 season and there were genuine fears for the club's future, McLoughlin was approached to manage a provisional 'Plan B' side akin to other fan-founded teams like FC United and AFC Wimbledon. Quite an endorsement.

Although unlikely to happen as Portsmouth's future now looks some way secured, McLoughlin admits a return to the game would fill 'something missing' from his life. Which is not to say he doesn't keep busy. First, there's his work for The Quay and Talksport for all matters Portsmouth.

'Well you miss being a player, miss the Saturdays. That's why it's great to be part of the Portsmouth situation on the radio because I'm living that moment in the game, "what should he have done?" You talk and think the situation through so that's been a real help. Radio keeps me involved – although I get more nervous doing the commentary than I did actually playing.

'On a Thursday then I deliver equipment for Luis Michael Training. It was set up by two former players, Paul Sugrue and Mark Aizlewood, and it's a government-run scheme encouraging activity for 16- to 18-year-olds. I just deliver the course.'

For a player who made two World Cup squads and appeared alongside genuine superstars like Keane just as Sky Sports began to transform football, that varied level of employment comes as a surprise.

'Well to give you an example, I was in my early thirties or so when I heard whispers about some of our squad [Ireland] earning eight, 10,000, 15,000 a week and thought "that can't be right". Now the car park at Portsmouth around then, if you pulled in in a Mercedes you were very lucky. I was driving a Mondeo.

'And I had a conversation with Tony Cascarino just before the Turkey play-off in 1999 when we both retired and he said to me, 'Macca, someone will be earning, in a few years' time, 150 grand a week." I said, "Not a fucking chance, no chance." He said, "I guarantee it." He was right, I was wrong. And there are players at Portsmouth I know for a fact wouldn't have made the bench in our

The Irish team lines up to take on Spain a few months after Euro 88, when they were arguably at their peak. From left to right: Kevin Moran, Packie Bonner, Ray Houghton, John Aldridge, Steve Staunton, John Sheridan, Tony Galvin, Mick McCarthy, Tony Cascarino, Dave O'Leary, Chris Morris. (*Sportsfile*)

Members of the Irish Euro 88 squad as they were in 2007. Back row, left to right: Gerry Peyton, Liam O'Brien, Kevin Moran, David Kelly, Tony Galvin, Packie Bonner, John Anderson. Front row, left to right: Chris Morris, Ronnie Whelan, Chris Hughton, kit-man Charlie O'Leary, Ray Houghton. (*Sportsfile*)

Tony Galvin on the ball during Ireland's 1–1 draw against USSR in Euro 88. He surprised some of the Soviet players before the match with his knowledge of the Russian language. (*Sportsfile*)

Mark Lawrenson in his early days as a pundit. He eventually entered the media after clashing with the likes of Robert Maxwell as manager of Oxford United. (*Sportsfile*)

Mark Lawrenson attempts to block Maarten Schoenaker during Holland's September 1980 visit to Lansdowne Road for the 1982 World Cup qualifiers. In midfield rather than defence that day, Lawrenson would venture forward to score the winner seven minutes from the end of a 2–1 victory. (*Sportsfile*)

Mark Lawrenson turns out for Liverpool. 'I think playing for Ireland so early in my career was one of the main reasons Liverpool signed me.' (*Sportsfile*)

Liam Brady, Packie Bonner and Kevin Moran are among the vast majority of ex-players to have stayed in the game in some way once they retired, either through punditry, coaching or as an agent. Indeed, only three of the 70 former Irish internationals from 1986 to 2002 have made a complete break from football. (*Sportsfile*)

Liam Brady became Ireland assistant manager along with Marco Tardelli (centre) when Giovanni Trapattoni (left) took over the international team in 2008. 'A great experience.' (*Sportsfile*)

Liam Brady directs from the line during Ireland's 1–1 draw away to Italy in April 2009. 'What pleased me was that I got on very well with the players and enjoyed working with them.' (*Sportsfile*)

Liam Brady at a press conference as Ireland assistant manager. 'I don't even see Trapattoni reading newspapers. Doesn't give a monkey's. That kind of confidence transmits to the players.' (*Sportsfile*)

History is saved. Packie Bonner stopped Daniel Timofte's penalty in Ireland's World Cup penalty shoot-out victory but immediately worried it would have to be retaken because celebrating players ran into the box. (*Getty Images*)

Packie Bonner with Ossie Ardiles, left, and Pat Jennings, right. Many of the Irish players were supporting Jennings as his Northern Ireland team showed the way by reaching the second stage of the 1982 World Cup. (*Sportsfile*)

Members of Ireland's Italia 90 squad celebrate that World Cup's 11th anniversary. Left to right: John Aldridge, Andy Townsend, Frank Stapleton, Tony Cascarino, Kevin Moran, Kevin Sheedy, Paul McGrath, Packie Bonner. (*Sportsfile*)

Steve Staunton and Niall Quinn attempt to stop Roberto Baggio in Ireland's 1–0 quarter-final defeat to Italy in the 1990 World Cup. Many Irish players remain convinced today that they wouldn't have been 'let' win that match. (*Sportsfile*)

Chris Morris holds off Ruud Gullit during the 1–0 Euro 88 defeat to Holland. Ireland were only minutes from a semi-final place. (*Sportsfile*)

The team that started Ireland's first ever World Cup finals match. They would draw 1–1 against England. Back row, left to right: Chris Morris, Steve Staunton, Tony Cascarino, Packie Bonner, Mick McCarthy, Paul McGrath. Front row, left to right: John Aldridge, Kevin Sheedy, Ray Houghton, Andy Townsend, Kevin Moran. (*Sportsfile*)

Chris Morris goes to clear the ball for Ireland at Lansdowne Road. Jack Charlton would specifically instruct his full-backs to hit the ball behind the opposition and *never* pass it straight to the midfield. (*Sportsfile*)

Alan McLoughlin scores the goal away to Northern Ireland that sealed Ireland's qualification for USA 94. Charlton later told him he 'justified his existence'. (*Sportsfile*)

Alan McLoughlin turns out for Ireland in 1999, the final year of his international career. Throughout the '90s he was picked for every single squad he wasn't injured for. (*Sportsfile*)

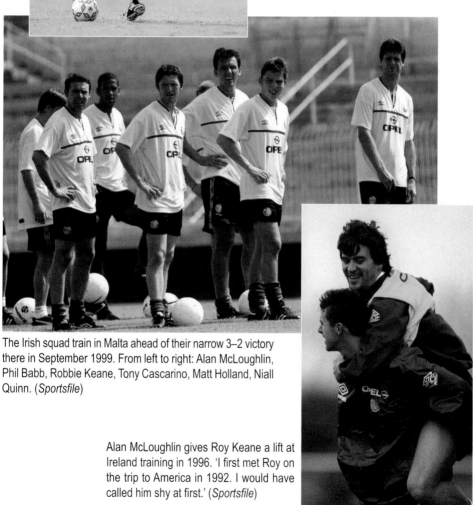

The Irish squad train in Malta ahead of their narrow 3–2 victory there in September 1999. From left to right: Alan McLoughlin, Phil Babb, Robbie Keane, Tony Cascarino, Matt Holland, Niall Quinn. (*Sportsfile*)

Alan McLoughlin gives Roy Keane a lift at Ireland training in 1996. 'I first met Roy on the trip to America in 1992. I would have called him shy at first.' (*Sportsfile*)

Liam Brady plays a pass away to Scotland in February 1987. Ireland's 1–0 victory that night would see many of the players fully come around to Jack Charlton's unconventional style. (*Getty Images*)

Alan Kernaghan in action for Ireland in October 1994. The English-born Kernaghan only qualified for the Republic instead of the Northern Irish team he supported because his grandparents were born in Belfast before partition. (*Sportsfile*)

Alan Kernaghan wins the ball in the crucial World Cup qualifier away to Northern Ireland in November 1993. He would be called 'Judas' and an awful lot worse that night. 'It was probably the worst I heard. You could feel the venom in it.' (*Sportsfile*)

The Irish team that beat Italy 1–0 and claimed the country's first World Cup win during USA 94. Back row, left to right: Roy Keane, Paul McGrath, Packie Bonner, Tommy Coyne, Steve Staunton. Front row, left to right: John Sheridan, Ray Houghton, Andy Townsend, Denis Irwin, Phil Babb. Terry Phelan was missing from the photograph due to a last minute change of kit. (*Sportsfile*)

Alan Kernaghan forces a flying save from Peter Schmeichel during Ireland's 1–1 draw with Denmark at Lansdowne Road in the USA 94 qualifiers. Ireland narrowly qualified ahead of the Danes on 'goals scored'. (*Sportsfile*)

Jack Charlton speaks to Terry Phelan during a 1994 World Cup training session in the Giants Stadium, New Jersey. Phelan, however, feels Ireland's training might have cost them. 'We could have acclimatised better. We could have been in the final.' (*Sportsfile*)

Terry Phelan makes up an Irish defensive wall with Ray Houghton and Andy Townsend to the left, Steve Staunton to the right. (*Sportsfile*)

Terry Phelan blocks Dennis Bergkamp in Ireland's USA 94 match against the Netherlands. Phelan's error, however, would gift Bergkamp the first goal in a 2–0 defeat. 'I just made a judgement error. Bit disappointing.' (*Sportsfile*)

Matt Holland is consoled by Niall Quinn (17) and Damien Duff (9) after missing in the penalty shoot-out against Spain during the 2002 World Cup. 'You have your family there, the fans. You just feel like you've let people down.' (*Sportsfile*)

Matt Holland tackles Patrick Kluivert during Ireland's landmark 1–0 win over the Netherlands in September 2001. 'Probably the best night I've had in Dublin.' (*Sportsfile*)

Matt Holland hits the equaliser in Ireland's 1–1 draw away to Portugal in October 2000. 'The first thing Mick says is "Oi! What were you doing down that end? I told you don't go forward!" Tongue in cheek!' (*Sportsfile*)

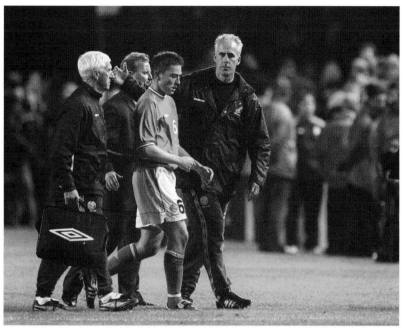

Matt Holland walks by a despondent Mick McCarthy after the 2–1 defeat to Switzerland in October 2002. It was McCarthy's last game as Ireland manager. 'Perhaps we came back with a hangover.' (*Sportsfile*)

Richie Sadlier in his role as CEO for St Patrick's Athletic in 2008. 'I loved elements of the role.' (*Sportsfile*)

Richie Sadlier ousts Russia's Dmitri Khlestov during his solitary appearance for Ireland, the 2–0 win in February 2002. He experienced enough around that time, however, to fill a career. (*Sportsfile*)

Richie Sadlier outjumps Nigeria's Okpala Obinna in the 1999 under-20 World Cup. 'The whole thing was remarkable, something you'd never experience again.' (*Sportsfile*)

championship side, and they're earning 40, 50 grand a week. And I say good luck to them. If I was in their situation I'd be saying "thank you very much". But I'm not. I'm like any other common man now. I've got an income from the pension I invested in, from radio, from Luis Michael.

'People think why you work for your mate doing removals. Why not? I'm a grafter. My old man, when I signed for United at 16, wouldn't let me have six weeks off in the summer. I had to go for two or three weeks to graft in his company. He wanted me to get the blisters on my hand and feel like shit at the end of the day. That's why you should concentrate on your football and get on with it. You get nowt for owt, as he said. You've got to graft and I've tried to convey that to my two daughters. Yeah, I have a lovely pension to fall back on and it pays me a nice dividend. It means we don't starve but I have to work.

'But you get one good contract now you should be set for life. I retired on my 35th birthday, playing for Rochdale against Bristol Rovers. Managed to score a penalty in the last five minutes. That's over 600 games though and it was difficult. I've had various operations. I had a hip replacement when I just turned 40. The one thing that depresses me now is I'm not fit. Where you had a nice toned body now it's starting to droop. So there's a physical toll on your body.'

Not to mention a mental toll.

'After Forest Green – where I did every job except the one I wanted which was the manager's – there was a 10-month spell when I had nothing to do with football. And that was difficult, difficult at home. Which is why I think, even if I earned the money, I would have found some project for my own sanity.

'Christ, if I could walk back into football I would. Don't get me wrong, I've been offered jobs, even with Portsmouth, but that would have meant upping sticks from Swindon and I didn't want to do that with my two girls then in school. I remember talking to Alan Ball, and his big regret was that his kids moved to five or six different schools.'

With the yearning to play, the post-career pressures and the grafting – as he puts it – does McLoughlin have any regrets himself?

'Well, watching that goal in Windsor Park always helps clear my head.

Funnily enough, I don't even have it on tape. I just watched it recently on YouTube. And I'm very lucky to be in a select band of players – Ray twice, Dave O'Leary, Packie, Jason McAteer for the goal against Holland – that will be remembered for something iconic. I never reached the dizzy heights as a player and would never claim to be better than the likes of, say, John Sheridan. But I'm always remembered for scoring that goal. And it was a great goal. I couldn't have hit it any better. You're remembered for iconic moments and I'm thankful I've managed to pull one out of the bag.

'It was worth the ride.'

7

Alan Kernaghan

Northern plights

The walls are shaking with noise. The soldiers lining them are almost growling. Until, all of a sudden, Alan Kernaghan notices a familiar voice and friendly face.

'I came out of the dressing room into the tunnel and there's a boy in the RUC who I knew. He was a friend. Started to talk to me and I said, "Look, you have to get out of the way here in case we're photographed together. Whether it's bad for you or bad for me, I don't want that to happen." That might be paranoid or whatever but I didn't want to get caught in any of those situations.'

The situation Kernaghan already found himself in that November 1993 night in Windsor Park was bad enough. He may have been returning home to Belfast for Ireland's final World Cup qualifier but the welcome back was only warm in the sense that it was hellish. While the rest of the Irish squad were thrown into an event that encapsulated an awful lot of the island's historical and social problems, Kernaghan persevered through a very personal one. Having grown up a Protestant, if only in a mildly cultural sense, he was viewed by Northern Ireland's supporters as a traitor but called an awful lot worse.

And not just on that night. The month before, both during and after Ireland's 3–1 home defeat to Spain, Eamon Dunphy and John Giles gave an analysis of his performance that almost amounted to a character assassination. It drifted down to the Lansdowne Road terraces. Kernaghan was told to his face by more than one supporter that he was 'fucking shite'. Their brazenness was no doubt bolstered by knowledge of his background. And all this while the national team was meant to be a respite from his club troubles where Manchester City supporters chanted 'What are you still doing here?'

The black humour taken out, it's almost a worthwhile question. Surely a player who had been considered good enough to skip ahead several age groups as a youth, who had been one of Britain's most expensive defenders and who, at various stages of his career, acquitted himself adequately against some of Europe's best attackers, must have got fed up? While many other Anglo-Irish players might have been considered effective outsiders, Kernaghan could have been forgiven for feeling like an outcast. No other Irish international ever played with so many issues, and at such an inopportune time. As if to add just an element of farce to all that, he is now an underage coach at Rangers. Is he a glutton for punishment?

Not a bit of it. Kernaghan reacts to the 'embarrassing' sectarian element of the Old Firm divide as he did to all those other difficulties in his career with an admirable determination to just work through it and resolve to 'only remember the better times'. Such a genuine detachment from the negatives is exemplary. He has no time for any of the damaging tribalism that accompanies football. But then that sense of perspective seems to go with Kernaghan's make-up.

First of all, he comes across as quite introspective and thoughtful for a former footballer. And that's just what teammates said. Although very much one of the lads in the Irish camp, an occasional intensity and tendency to berate himself did stand out. Sitting in his Rangers training gear in Glasgow's Radisson hotel the day after the 2009–10 Premier League season ends, the only person he's berating is Didier Drogba for his posturing against Wigan. That dual nature does come out though. He can often be engaged and yet detached in the same sentence, speaking animatedly before suddenly taking 30 seconds to peer into the distance and think about what he's saying.

Then there's his rearing. 'I can't thank my parents enough for bringing me up the way they did. The religious thing meant diddly to me.' Which also explains how he can work for a club whose worst supporters sing gory songs about the Irish without the issue even registering. That's for others to care about.

What many of the bigots who berated him that night in Windsor Park clearly didn't know however, was that Kernaghan cared very much about playing for the North.

'I went to watch all the qualifying games for the 1982 World Cup. They were great times.'

Kernaghan contributed to them in some way having worked as a ball-boy at Windsor Park after turning out for the Northern Ireland schoolboys team. Only an arcane agreement among the four British football associations and the IFA's ludicrous attitude to attempting change prevented him from stepping up to the seniors.

'I was born in England, so were my mum and dad. My dad's family were from Belfast and his father worked at Harland and Wolff. Dad even worked in the docks and my brother was born there but then they moved to England. I was born in Leeds but dad got the chance to be sales manager for the John West Food company and it was back to Belfast.

'So I lived there since about seven and played for Northern Ireland schoolboys. But when it came to playing at any other level the rules only went as far your mother's side or something because it was still the Home Internationals.'

Since neither Kernaghan nor his parents had been born in the North, he couldn't declare. It was a gentleman's agreement among England, Scotland, Wales and Northern Ireland as opposed to anything FIFA enforced. 'So that was me scuppered. My dad contacted the secretary of the IFA and argued with him "Why is this, why can't be this be changed?" From what I am led to believe, the IFA were keen to keep the status quo.'

If it was unfortunate to come across such intransigence, Kernaghan insists he had already got lucky elsewhere. A chance match he turned up for with a friend had a Middlesbrough scout on the sidelines. 'That was the start of it, 13 or 14. Right place at the right time.'

A different kind of opportunism would prove useful for his first role at Middlesbrough. Kernaghan made his debut against Huddersfield at 17 not as a centre-half but a striker.

'It went really well. I had always been one of these people who didn't have a proper position. I didn't score though. The goalkeeper had a blinder. As well as a centre-forward I was a bit of this, bit of that until about 21.'

That versatility, however, proved invaluable to Middlesbrough. They didn't exactly have the money to cover gaps elsewhere in the squad. From the beginning of Kernaghan's time there in 1984–85, the club began to face serious financial problems. As much as £30,000 had to be borrowed from the PFA to pay wages in April 1986 and in May those same out-of-pocket players arrived at Ayresome Park to find the gates padlocked. The liquidator had been called in. With £350,000 capital required just to get a league registration for the following season, the death of the club was even announced on Tyne Tees Television.

'Because I was so young I just got on with it. Unlike other players, I didn't have a mortgage so I just went back to my mum and dad's. And that was that. Steve Gibson came in then though, he was part of the consortium with ICI and it just went from strength to strength. That was the making of the club.'

And it was immediate. Under the strict but strident management of Bruce Rioch, a young squad gave the likes of Gary Pallister, Tony Mowbray, Colin Cooper and Kernaghan himself, their first steps in the professional game and the club achieved successive promotions. By 1988, they were back in the old First Division. From death to high life in two years.

'Yeah, we were on a real roll. We got promoted two years on the trot then relegated and promoted again. It took for you to leave [the club] to realise how good Bruce Rioch was. He'd be in a bad mood and you could tell, so you'd try and keep out of his way. He used to be on my case all the time for different bits.

And that's probably why I didn't like him as much as I should have done but I think it was the making of me.

'Colin Todd was a very good right-hand man too. Real disciplinarian. It was when Bruce left that Colin said I was a centre-half and that was that. I thought of myself as a centre-forward but I never scored enough goals so I think that made the decision pretty easy!'

Kernaghan also took to defending quite easily. So much so that, by the time of the club's second promotion and the first ever Premier League season in 1992–93, he was the Middlesbrough player selected to appear alongside the likes of Ryan Giggs on Sky Sports' advertising campaign. Little wonder he was about to get even wider exposure.

With Mick McCarthy and David O'Leary having retired after the Euro 92 campaign and Kevin Moran expected to soon follow, Ireland were going to have a dearth of centre-halves for the first time in decades. Jack Charlton, however, had been keeping an eye on his old club Middlesbrough and thought the young defender with the Irish-sounding surname would be a fine new choice in the McCarthy mould.

'Out of the blue, Curtis Fleming said he had been speaking to some journalists and told me "Jack's trying to bring you in, are you eligible?" So I sent all the documentation away and that was looked into. It worked out that, because my grandparents were born in Belfast before the division [Partition], I qualified. So it was a wee bit strange.'

To say the least. Even if he didn't give a damn about the social dimensions that led to partition, many on either side did. And, although he couldn't play for Northern Ireland, he was still effectively a self-professed supporter signing for their closest rivals. Like almost everything though, Kernaghan looked at it with simple logic.

'I had no problems declaring because the chance to play international football is rare. I was simply furthering my career. I was fortunate enough to be in that position. So that was what I did. There was no sort of real hard thinking. Fortunately I was brought up not in the political side of it. I don't think it proved a problem really. Maybe a minority of the supporters thought it wasn't right but that was about it really. I dealt with it as I deal with it now – it didn't matter to me.'

Kernaghan's eventual first meeting with Charlton wasn't actually his first encounter with him.

'He'd been manager at Middlesbrough when I'd been an apprentice so I'd cleaned his boots. He'd only come in on a part-time basis but the first time I'd spoken to him was in the hotel for the first game. A squad was put together for a pre-season game against Man United. It was the likes of me and Liam Daish, people on the edges, couple of boys who played in the League of Ireland. I courtesy-called him Mr Charlton and he just went "No, Jack, Jack". My dad was there and he asked my dad for a couple of cigarettes and everything went alright.'

By that stage, Ireland's USA 94 campaign had already kicked off. A World Cup in the New World was a fitting end destination since the qualifying group would contain a few re-adjustments.

First of all, the general dismissal of Denmark's chances turned to trepidation when, having only been allowed into Euro 92 because the Balkan War saw Yugoslavia removed, the Danes went on and won it. Spain and Northern Ireland would then provide fearsome away trips for very different reasons. Latvia and Lithuania, meanwhile, involved journeys into the unknown as they participated in their first international tournaments after the fall of Soviet Communism. Albania was similarly free of the USSR's influence but not its effects. Ireland would find out just how far-reaching they were in the first match in May 1992.

The Albanians turned up in Dublin with no money, no strip, no music-sheet for their new national anthem and, initially, only half their squad. The FAI had to provide them with a loan and Adidas with a donated kit. The rest of their players eventually arrived after a delay in Athens, sparing their FA the ignominy of fielding their under-21s. Albania still held Ireland off until the 60th minute when John Aldridge scored the first goal of the campaign. Paul McGrath sealed the points.

Kernaghan would help keep the momentum going when he made his debut in the second match at home to Latvia. Other than some misgivings in the media about his declaration, Kernaghan thoroughly enjoyed the 4–0 victory.

'It very much established the way things were and how it was run by Jack. The whole country was on a high so it was very easy to fit in. Even in my strange case I was fortunate enough I played pretty well and that made things a lot easier.'

Were there any issues with the squad about his situation?

'Fine, no problems at all. I think like all footballers it doesn't really matter whether they know you or like you. It's if you play well because that's what they're all there for. Footballers are a funny bunch and will accept a lot of things if you're a good player.'

Next up were the European champions Denmark away from home, as Charlton continued his trend of attempting to organise the most difficult qualifiers as early as possible to catch teams cold. Denmark had, after all, caroused through a backline as renowned as Germany's in the Euro 92 final and may have been suffering from a hangover. Ireland duly held them at bay for a 0–0 draw thanks to a superbly disciplined display that saw Kernaghan, his central-defensive partner Moran and Packie Bonner receive particular praise.

'They had some top players. I remember Jack being really concerned about Brian Laudrup but I had a decent game and managed to make a few tackles against him so Jack was quite happy. Kevin was a real hard man. He went up for a header, got smashed in the face with an elbow. Don't know if it was a mistake but I was stood beside him and heard his nose break. There was a slight grunt and then he just got on with it as if nothing had happened. Just frightening. Obviously very intelligent and took that with him onto the pitch. Got himself in the right areas, didn't get caught out and, as I say, was a very tough character.'

That and more was said about a 21-year-old Roy Keane as he rampaged around Spain's Sanchez Pizjuan pitch in another notable 0–0. Kernaghan missed that game through suspension having picked up two yellow cards in his first two caps. Much more significantly though, the Belgian referee missed the defender keeping Aldridge onside for a finish that was then disallowed. Nevertheless, the commanding manner in which Ireland claimed two points in their two trickiest away trips of the group led to a lot of bold claims about booking tickets for the States.

Only McCarthy, as ever, sounded a note of caution on RTÉ. 'What we shouldn't forget, not to take the pleasure out of the result, is that Spain and Denmark are well capable of coming to Lansdowne and getting a point.'

It would prove prescient. As would Charlton's apparently innocuous comments about Northern Ireland. When the group was drawn, he couldn't have been bothered with the usual platitudes. 'I'm not exactly in a flap about Northern Ireland. I won't be losing any sleep about the match against them in Dublin.' In the event, Ireland completely overwhelmed the North in an eight-minute first-half onslaught. Steve Staunton added to Andy Townsend's opener and Niall Quinn's flick by scoring direct from a corner. That 3–0 win was the last match Kernaghan missed in the campaign, denying him the chance to play a first game against the team he considered his first country. But everyone else saw the elements that would add to so much tension to the return game in Belfast.

Northern Ireland's manager Billy Bingham was irate at Charlton's presumptuous – if also precise – remarks, as well as the crowd chanting 'Only one team in Ireland'. So he had a prediction of his own. 'There is a chance that, come the return [fixture], our supporters will be taunting their visitors in a similar fashion with the tune of "You were never born in Ireland". At least our team is of Irish extraction and our players are not mercenaries.'

The die was cast. Denmark would only complicate matters with a 1–1 draw that cancelled out Ireland's result in Copenhagen. Niall Quinn equalised that day with 15 minutes left after a rare Paul McGrath error had allowed Kim Vilfort to lob Bonner.

McGrath, however, would exasperate his manager in a much more concerning way. Charlton had been one of the few senior figures throughout the defender's career to subtly and successfully manage – in the word's broadest meaning – the issues arising from McGrath's troubled childhood and alcoholism. 'He's a special case and we need to look after him,' was the squad line. But they couldn't do so all the time. Having been so celebrated for his performances in

Italia 90, McGrath kept the party going on a week-long binge that saw him miss the opening Euro 92 qualifier against Turkey. 'His knees' was the euphemism always used. But it wasn't needed again for a competitive match until the awkward trip to Albania. That came at the end of the 1992–93 season, one of the most terrific seasons on the pitch for McGrath – he won the PFA Player of the Year – but the most terrible off it as his mental state descended to new depths. His drinking only accelerated as he went on another week-long session which continued over to Tel-Aviv for a holiday rather than Tirana for a match. Charlton could only sigh. 'I hope to meet Paul as soon as possible to talk things over. After all, we're speaking here of the best player in Britain.'

Kernaghan certainly agreed with that, even if McGrath's excellence also came with a more endearing unpredictability on the pitch.

'He was a Rolls Royce of a player. I mean, if you don't train for three or four days then play, you feel it, but he did it all the time. How he managed it was incredible. But he was the most bizarre footballer ever. He would do the most ridiculous things. Like he couldn't kick the ball with his left foot so he would do the most ridiculous pirouettes to avoid it. A fantastic player though.'

He wasn't all that Ireland had to make do without in the heat of Albania though. As an omen of what the players would be up against, each was given toilet rolls, a candle, a towel, a bar of soap and a bottle of mineral water on departing.

'Albania was an absolute toilet. Aw . . . horrible. Horrible place. We were there at the end of the season, it was boiling, no air-conditioning, had to take all our own food. I remember big metal shutters on the windows in the hotel. The condition of the pitch wasn't great and it was roasting. But we came away alright.'

Despite an initially lacklustre performance and the concession of an early goal, the side carved out a 2–1 win. Within a week came the two matches in the Baltic, first Latvia then Lithuania. Ireland won both games narrowly but won them nonetheless. The home game against Lithuania saw Kernaghan score his only goal for Ireland as he added to Aldridge's opener in a 2–0 win.

Characteristically, he doesn't get carried away.

'Yep, one and only goal. Denis [Irwin] free-kick, crossed it in and I was at the far post. Pleased to say the least.'

Most important of all though, Ireland had done what both Denmark and Spain hadn't and won all four games against the Baltic sides. It left them a point in front of the Danes and two ahead of the Spanish. Even better, the last two matches left were on the island of Ireland. Even better still, the side hadn't ever lost a competitive home match under Charlton. Regardless of the fact that Spain were going to be the last team Ireland hosted, defeat simply wasn't considered. So assured did qualification appear for that penultimate match, fireworks were installed at Lansdowne Road.

The only thing that exploded was Spain's attack and Kernaghan's previously cast-iron reputation. The Spanish tore into a tepid Irish team, going 2–0 up within 14 minutes and 3–0 up within 26. For one of the goals, Kernaghan attempted to shepherd the ball out of play only for Julio Salinas to steal it with one touch and strike with the next. It defined a disastrous performance for both Kernaghan and his country.

'We didn't perform. I didn't perform. Maybe we just thought it was going to happen. We never lost at home. You couldn't blame the FAI for the fireworks, you have to do that. I made that mistake and it sort of got worse from then onwards. Whether it was our own doing or they played well . . . maybe it was a bit of both.'

Dunphy and Giles were in no such doubt and singled out Kernaghan. Did it get to him?

'Well I think Eamon Dunphy was a pain in the arse for everybody so I just joined a long list. Probably at the time you maybe think into it too much. But, nowadays, you just think it's somebody's opinion and get on with it.'

That was all Ireland could do. In the process, John Sheridan pulled a goal back that appeared no more than a consolation to leave the final score at 3–1. When it came right down to it on that final November night though, it meant Ireland were on the same points and same goal difference as Denmark but with more scored. That would be enough to qualify.

Both the team and Kernaghan would have to go through an awful lot to get to that stage however. It isn't too much of an exaggeration to argue there's never been so much riding on a single match. On a football level, there was the knife-edge nature to the group and a place in the biggest sporting event of all at stake. On a broader, social level, there was the tension of the Troubles and all that potentially went with that on a poisonous night. None of which was helped by the intimately personal edge to it all.

First, there was the acidic manner in which the two managers' amicable relationship dissolved. When Jimmy Quinn volleyed over Bonner, Bingham turned to Charlton and shouted, 'Does it feel a bit like déjà vu, Jack?' Worse, he then turned another 90 degrees to the crowd and conducted a chorus of 'Only one team in Ireland'.

It was one of the milder chants by a long, long way – as Kernaghan can testify. Because, most of all, there was the gauntlet he had to run through. In any normal scenario, a player returning to his home city to play his first international there in front of family and friends would have been an occasion to celebrate. This was one to be feared.

'It was probably the worst I heard. You could feel the venom in it. "Pope-sucking whore", "your mother's the Pope's whore". That sort of stuff.'

Depressingly, his father and brother heard every word.

'They went to the game but my mother didn't – just for that reason really. They just kept their heads down. Tried to block it out a wee bit.'

As much as a player may attempt to do the same and focus, is that really possible? Surely the abuse is far too intrusive?

'Yeah. You just get on with it. Try and immerse yourself in the game. Sometimes it's as if the whole crowd goes dead bar that one person and you can see them and hear exactly what they're saying. It's difficult not to make a reaction to it. But . . . I mean you'd have some sympathy for Eric Cantona. Very much so. I prefer to remember it [the game] for the outcome and how it came about rather than anything else.'

The outcome, after all, was the high point of Kernaghan's career. He ran to the dressing room when the final whistle was blown and, when it was finally confirmed that Denmark couldn't get the draw they needed in Spain, he burst into tears. Communication problems between Belfast and Seville initially left the final outcome in doubt for some minutes. Kernaghan had some communication problems of his own.

'That was just the start of mobile phones. I had one and tried to ring home and never got through. And to this day my missus still goes on about it, not phoning her.'

What's often forgotten is that after the final whistle Charlton went to present a prize in the Linfield FC Social Club where he received a standing ovation. Another oddity of a night that really did go from extreme to extreme.

Although Kernaghan admits he never experienced emotion on a pitch like qualifying for the World Cup, that feeling would only have been accentuated by the sharp contrast of everything happening around it. And not just at Windsor Park. Because the abuse he received that night and the nature of his performance against Spain were far more in keeping with his career at that point. After seven years of almost uninterrupted highs, a £1.7m transfer to Manchester City at the start of the 1993–94 season represented a peak before a very sharp drop. It was a case of the right move at a very wrong time and the main factor in his drastic collapse in confidence.

City had already sacked the manager who signed Kernaghan, Peter Reid, but the supporters wanted to send chairman Peter Swales the same way. It all contributed to a general sense of chaos at the club.

'I'd gone very much from a team foundation at Middlesbrough to a 'me, myself and I' attitude that I found very hard to get my head around. I enjoyed living there [Manchester] and the lifestyle but in terms of stuff on the pitch I didn't enjoy it at all. Maybe I wasn't mentally tough enough at the time, or selfish enough. I would like to say I'm my harshest critic, I'm very honest. If you ask me if I played well I'd be very honest, yeah I did alright or no I didn't.'

It had to be the latter for most of his matches at Maine Road. Indeed, so bad did it get and so ramshackle were City's attempts to fix the fault lines, they eventually had a squad big enough for two dressing rooms. The one Kernaghan occupied was known as the 'leper colony'. It all only added to the image of a club that was fundamentally dysfunctional.

'Yeah, they shot themselves in the foot a lot. I was there four and a bit years and I had eight managers which is just stupid. There's no way you can build continuity. Alan Ball I didn't particularly get on with. Frank Clark was the best one, my sort of manager and cared for the players. But it was just madness.'

Particularly compared to what was going on down the road.

'There is a big chip on the shoulder about Man United. A lot of the fans didn't like the main Kippax Stand because you could see Old Trafford from it. Me, I just wanted to be happy in my surroundings. On the field didn't feel right. My confidence went and I ended up unable to pass the ball from there to here.'

It couldn't have happened at a worst time, costing Kernaghan an appearance at the World Cup.

'I struggled for form and then Phil [Babb] was in. He played well, no problems with that. Looking back it's a wee bit frustrating that I never got on but that's life. It's not something I sit and moan about. It just happened. A bit was circumstance, a bit was my own fault for not playing well at the time.'

Still a valued member of Charlton's squad, Kernaghan's alternative viewpoint makes for some interesting observations on a World Cup many players considered odd anyway. The tone for that was set in one of the final warm-up matches.

'I remember we went to Germany and there was a do in the hotel. It was a Rose of Tralee type competition. The only one in Germany and we of course walk into it. When we got to Florida then we had trouble with the weather. The Americans being the Americans, they wouldn't let us out when it was raining and there was a chance of thunder and lightning. Jack was going absolutely ballistic because we'd come all this way, training and getting prepared, and they wouldn't let us out on the pitch.'

Staying inside was something they'd have to get used to. Although there was at least one big attraction to that.

'The only thing that helped me get through the boredom was the OJ Simpson case. That broke out just as soon as we got there. I remember being sat there in the room watching the white Bronco with him apparently in the back and that was really the focus everybody had: what's happening with OJ today?'

It is surprising the players had enough energy to be bored given how much the training literally took out of them.

'When we had the two weeks acclimatisation we were weighed before and after training and I think on average we were losing about 12 pounds in a session. And then obviously by the time you got back for the afternoon session you had to be back to normal weight so it was just a case of getting as much drink down as you could.'

The heat, however, raised the temperature in every sense. Anger and irritation became something of a theme of the tournament. Before Ireland started actually playing, there was a series of rows that were abnormal even for high-octane sessions. In the first, Townsend snapped at assistant manager Maurice Setters while Charlton was off on a scouting mission. The media had heard it was Keane though. So, in a moment the infuriated young midfielder would never allow himself to forget, Charlton took the chance to confuse the situation by making Keane tell the relative truth that there had been no row between him and Setters.

Another to-do with Charlton was caused when Kernaghan coincidentally bumped into his own wife at the local shopping mall during a time when the manager insisted the players should be distraction-free and away from their families. A little more culpably then, Kernaghan clashed with McCarthy – who was visiting the camp – at training.

'That was a bit of frustration built up and him saying the wrong thing at the wrong time. I had a go at him – then 10 minutes later I apologised.'

They were all in it together again by the time of the Italy match. Even if the temperatures burned specific memories onto the brain.

'Air-conditioned dug-outs! Then there were the size of the dressing rooms.

Could have a game of five-a-side, they were huge. Little things like that. And Ray's goal and the atmosphere obviously. Tommy Coyne got really bad dehydration so he had blankets over his head on the way back to Florida. He was in bits.'

Coyne's health was hardly helped by FIFA's appalling attitude to water, something which became a particular concern for Charlton. With just 20 minutes gone and his players already gasping in the New Jersey heat, the manager was blocked from throwing bottles on. Incredulity turned to outright anger then when another FIFA official, an Egyptian in a notorious yellow hat, needlessly got involved as Charlton attempted the elementary task of bringing on Aldridge for Tommy Coyne against Mexico. With Ireland 2–0 down and emotions already high, Aldridge exploded. Rather than famous Scouse wit, millions of viewers around the globe caught some infamous Scouse grit. 'I lost it,' Aldridge would later say in a deadpan manner.

'Fuck off you, dickhead! You twat! You dickhead! You fucking cheat!'

On the bench, Kernaghan had a front-row view of one of the most controversial – and comical – moments of the tournament.

'First of all you join in and you're shouting at the officials . . . then you see it and have a giggle. We were laughing our heads off. It was pathetic really. Red tape.'

The incident led to an unexplained fine for Charlton and suspension for the next game against Norway. Ireland needed at least a point to progress from the group. So it was another chance to make history. Not that you could tell from Charlton's demeanour.

'I remember while we were warming up, Jack being sat up in the stand and he had a pint of Guinness, sticking it out the window!

'I was meant to play in that game because Jack thought Paul was struggling but then he changed his mind.'

Ireland got through but Kernaghan still didn't get on. Instead, he and Roy Keane were called for a drug test after the side got a 2–0 beating from Holland.

'I had done my sample but I remember there was a boy called Stan Valckx [the Dutch central defender]. He was sat there with a beer and cigarette. And I just remember him saying, "Have a nice trip home". Felt like turning around and saying, "You cheeky bastard, I hope you get stuffed". He did it quite subtly – but it hit home. I don't think Roy heard!!'

At just 27, Kernaghan remained with the squad thereafter. But so did many others much older, including Charlton himself. There was a small but growing body of opinion that maybe a fresh approach was required. Even Charlton admitted to some apprehension in his *Sunday Press* column. 'I don't know if I want to go through all this again. Maybe I'm getting a little bit weary over the whole business, maybe my thoughts are not as clear as they should be.'

The initial Euro 96 qualification performances however, didn't just wave away those doubts but blew them away. Ireland scored 11 goals in their first three games, making the uncomfortable journey to Riga much easier with a 3–0 win over Latvia and putting four past Liechtenstein. Most tellingly though, the only trouble seen on a return to Windsor Park almost exactly a year after McLoughlin's strike was that in the Northern Ireland defence – Ireland won 4–0. Bingham had gone but, much more importantly, so had an era in the province's history as the peace process gathered pace.

Portugal's visit to Lansdowne Road then didn't quite see such an avalanche of goals but did seem to send out a much stronger message. An apparently irresistible young side featuring Luis Figo and Rui Costa were eventually overpowered 1–0 when goalkeeper Vitor Baia allowed Staunton's cross in off his elbow.

The average age of that first XI though was 29, one of the oldest Ireland had ever put out. Five players were over 30. Only one – Gary Kelly – was under 23. And their bodies were beginning to betray them. Northern Ireland's 1–1 draw at Lansdowne Road the month before could be explained away as an aberration. The same inability to beat Liechtenstein couldn't. 'Ireland drew 0–0 with a mountaintop' as Peter Ball wrote in the *Sunday Tribune*. Thirty-six chances were created in desperation but none were enough to get beyond the groundsman at the local park, goalkeeper Martin Heeb. Aldridge even attempted to outdo Thierry

Henry by 14 years and slap the ball into the net with his hand. For probably the first time in his career with Ireland, Charlton had no answer. At half-time, all he could offer was a shrug of the shoulders. 'There's nothing I can do for you. You'll have to work this one out for yourselves.'

If that game sounded the warning signals for Charlton's method of play in the mid-90s, it probably said even more about his methods of preparation. With the University of Limerick set to award him an honorary degree, Charlton's squad spent the six days in the city before the match, crawling between pubs rather than jogging between cones. The week was perhaps best summed up by Charlton's son John, just a few days before the qualifier, pleading with the squad to 'try not to have more than six pints'.

And it wasn't just what they were drinking. On the eve of the next home game against Austria, Charlton took the squad to Harry Ramsden's chipper for 'one of his famous earners'. It would become infamous. With the players breaking wind and laughing through a training session immediately afterwards, they then ran out of steam the next night. Austria came from behind to win 3–1. They would win by the same score in Vienna before Portugal pulled Ireland apart in Lisbon. After a position of complete control just seven months before, Ireland were now limping apologetically into a play-off against Holland. The Dutch, however, only picked up where Portugal left off and dismantled Charlton's team and tenure terminally.

'It was if someone had let the air out of the balloon. Then we looked back to Liechtenstein, the Austria game. Had we done this, done that. Liechtenstein was one of those games but the Austria game was the big downfall. That knocked everybody.

'But we all had an idea Holland was going to be Jack's last night. I don't think he said anything after but we all knew what was going to happen.'

The FAI didn't when it came to appointing a successor though. As Charlton waved off the maudlin Irish crowd to the sound of 'You'll Never Walk Alone', all sorts were walking in to meet the organisation about the newly available job. Liam Brady didn't think he had a chance but, when the FAI called saying they'd like to consider him, he agreed so long as the interview would be 'discreet and confidential'. He arrived at the Heathrow hotel to be greeted by a media scrum and Joe Kinnear walking out.

'It was laughable, a complete shambles,' Brady later said. 'It emerged Kevin Moran was lined up for the job but a couple of people jumped ship at the last minute and they went with Mick McCarthy. That's the FAI for you.'

Then-president Louis Kilcoyne even publicly admitted that McCarthy hadn't been first choice for the job. He certainly wasn't Kernaghan's.

'The first thing I thought was, "Fuck, well I had that argument with him and he's not gonna pick me". But when he came in he was very good. I think you get these perceptions of how people are and you expect Mick to be a shouter and a bawler but he wasn't like that at all. In a coaching sense and managerial sense he was very different to Jack. Tried to move in terms of professionalism as it were, your diet, what you did before and after training.'

Kernaghan played in four of McCarthy's first five friendlies, where unknowns like Dave Savage and Alan Moore replaced the likes of Sheridan and Moran, before heading off for the US Cup.

'It was good playing in Boston, the atmosphere was good. But we had a much younger team. Some head-the-balls, Mark Kennedy and people like that. Fantastic player. Very much his own man. Did what he wanted to do and not very much thought went into it. So it was different.'

It was the absence of another established figure that gave Kernaghan his second greatest moment in an Irish shirt and a perfect way to close out his international career. With Keane AWOL, Kernaghan was made captain. He led the side to McCarthy's first victory, a 3–0 win over Bolivia.

'It was another good piece of management by Mick. If he's going to get rid of you put him out on a high sort of thing.'

And finally, after four long years, a similar sense of contentment was returning to his club career. Close enough to midnight on a Thursday in September 1997, Kernaghan got a call asking him to come up to St Johnstone. Perhaps illustrating his desperation to get away from Manchester City, he got up at five the following morning to make the long drive north. The money was going to be one-fifth of what he was then on. But there was no accounting for the effect on his mentality.

'I felt very much at home as soon as I went in. I never looked back. My time at Manchester City had been dreadful and I just ended up with a smile on my face again and really enjoyed my football. First game was against Rangers. We lost 2–0. Brian Laudrup scored but all of a sudden I felt very comfortable back in surroundings I enjoyed.

'There was more of a modesty too. The money was nothing and that was just at the time when the big money was coming in. Rangers had people on 30 grand a week and we had people on 300 quid a week. Huge difference. But it grounds you. More honesty to it. A kind of hunger too, a desperation to do well.

'And we had success. Did really well, third in the league. Into Europe. Beat Celtic and Rangers. Got into a cup final and semi-final. Really enjoyed it. It all just clicked. Good friends with some good players, good team bond, it was good fun.'

So much so that Kernaghan stayed in Scotland to become player-manager of Clyde. Although he has since taken a self-enforced step back to gain more experience, there is more credit than debit on his account as a coach. He steered Clyde to second in the Scottish First Division twice in a row, just missing out on the trophy itself.

'I loved it. For two and a half years everything went really well. We missed out on promotion on the last day of the season. Should have won it really, that was down to us. Enjoyed four months at Livingstone then before seven months at Dundee. That was tough. There was a bit of turmoil at the club in terms of financial stuff.'

As an example of how a club that had just come out of administration was forced to operate, the first-team squad were kicked off a local park pitch by a school hockey team more than once.

'It was fire-fighting. Never had a settled team or my own team. It was just what we had. Trying to get rid of the big earners, stuff like that. Dundee is madness. Two clubs 50 yards apart but the fans won't do anything about it. They should just have one stadium between the two of them and get on with it. Our problems were purely financial though and that leads to other problems in lack of unity and stuff.'

It didn't put Kernaghan off though.

'I enjoyed management very much. It's the next best thing to playing. I want to get back into it and have another go. I've got all my badges and stuff.'

It is, however, an unusual – if perhaps typical for Kernaghan – route to take. Starting in it, stepping back, then going again.

'Yeah, I've done it the wrong way around. Jumped off the top board to begin with and now back down at the other end. I'm really enjoying it now. I'll be a much better manager. I do plan to go back.'

After this interview, however, he's going back to Murray Park, to coach Rangers' under-12s. He takes them and the under-17s every evening before running the rule over their matches at the weekend. As such, he's rarely at Ibrox and is content to stay out of the spotlight. You'd think it would have been hard to avoid when it was announced a club that only signed its first Catholic since the Second World War in 1989 had appointed an Irish international. But there was nothing. Yes, he was perhaps lucky that first-team coach Kenny McDowall was arriving from Celtic at exactly the same time but he insists he was the only one to actually bring it up.

'I did mention it, but it was not an issue. Yeah there might still be a silly element there but not at the club itself. The assistant I had at Dundee, he got the job as under-19s coach. There was a revamp at Rangers at the time and he just put my name forward. I've been here three and a bit years. It's a huge operation.'

But an enjoyable one.

'The under-12s are like a sponge. They haven't got an opinion yet. You show them stuff and they'll try it. Whereas the under-17s, they think they know it all. It's funny sitting and listening to them. They give me stick for being ancient.'

The job also still throws up a few unique challenges. One of the under-12s at Rangers is a diabetic, which is something Kernaghan himself had to deal with throughout his career. Although he once had to be revived with a bottle of Coke by a doctor in the St Johnstone team hotel, that was rare.

'I had no problems at all. I inject four times a day. It's obviously changed in the last 10 years, people's perceptions of it. There's over a million every year get it. So it's changing and it's becoming a lot easier to live with. Not that there was any hardship before. Our young boy at Rangers is 11 and it's good for him to be doing what he's doing because so many people can think that's the end of it. It shouldn't stop you doing anything.'

Elementary as Kernaghan makes it appear, it does put some of his previous troubles on the pitch into some perspective. And the game itself. Today, he remains an Ireland fan but is not exactly a fanatic.

'Oh yeah. They would be the first ones I would look out for. Sure that's who I played for. When they've been to Scotland I've gone to watch and that. I've only caught one game in Dublin since I stopped playing. But still, if they're on, that's the game I would watch.

'I don't watch football all the time. There's that much going on. I switch on and off. When I'm at work I'm at work, when I'm not I'm not. I'd be picky about who I'd watch. Hardly going to watch, you know, Portsmouth against Leicester. It's not really going to turn me on.'

One last appearance for Ireland might though. He never did actually formally retire from international football.

'I didn't at all, no . . . still available! Even if I'd have to play on a five-a-side pitch these days!'

8

Terry Phelan

The happy wanderer

A
t the end of it all, only the images stay with us really. The snapshots. Not the anxiety beforehand, nor even the action that created those images. The matches remain half-remembered, but the individual moments are stamped on the memory. Packie Bonner's jump of joy in Genoa. Ray Houghton's innocent roll in New Jersey. And, running alongside the latter, the ultra-focused face of Terry Phelan.

It was a curious way to celebrate. But understandable. As if the emotional intensity had completely taken Phelan over. Psychologists call that phenomenon 'flow', a mental state of operation in which a person – most commonly a sportsman or musician – is fully immersed in an activity. Everything seems to come off, even if they're not completely conscious of it.

Which helps explain that facial expression. Phelan had the same one – if a little more worn – in the immediate aftermath of Ireland's 1–0 win over Italy. The live TV coverage of the match lingered on him in the moments following the final whistle as he appeared to incredulously survey his surroundings. By that stage though, he insists he was fully conscious of it all.

'It was a picture. The fans all around. I'm getting goose pimples just thinking about it now. I couldn't believe I was on the green grass, playing for me country in the Giants Stadium. I could have stood there for 90 minutes more and just looked at it and soaked it in again. Some people say dreams are never true but that was a dream for me and I was going to soak it up.'

Right now, Phelan is soaking up another scene. But he's much more relaxed doing so.

'I'll just open the curtain here. I'm looking right down a harbour. It's sunny, there are mountains around me, it's all green and – again – I'm getting goose pimples. I'm 150 metres from the touch of the water so life can't be that bad.'

Imagine one of the panoramic scenes from *Lord of the Rings* and you're not far off. In fact you're absolutely correct. Phelan currently lives in Dunedin in New Zealand where the films were shot and he works as football development manager for the country's soccer federation.

It may be two months before the 2010 World Cup – the first that the All Whites have qualified for in 28 years – but, as yet in a rugby country, Phelan hasn't noticed any sense of anticipation to match that which he experienced for Ireland in 1994. That will change. What hasn't changed, however, is his resiliently Mancunian accent. Despite literally moving from one end of the world to the other after leaving England, Salford patois peppers his recollections. And Phelan seems to humbly enjoy giving them, in the same way as Alan McLoughlin and Chris Morris.

'We're talking about the happiest moments of my career here and I'm just thankful someone like yourself is asking me about it.'

One thing should be set straight though. Phelan may have been delighted to be involved but he wasn't just happy to be there in a manner Roy Keane would have castigated. Indeed, to hear Phelan talk, Keane would nod approvingly. Ahead of USA 94, RTÉ pundit Paddy Crerand said he hoped 'the Irish people don't think they can win the World Cup. That would be laughable.' Phelan is absolutely serious when he contemplates the complete opposite.

'Why couldn't we have won that World Cup? Beat Italy 1–0, who went to the final and got beat on penalties. So why couldn't we have gone on? We had some household names, world-class players. I just think, the way we played, that 150 mph and closing down, it zapped us in certain games. The preparation could have been better.'

Phelan's attitude perhaps comes from a career of defying the odds. Before Ireland, he was part of a Wimbledon team that overcame perception and size to beat one of Britain's most celebrated teams in the 1988 FA Cup final against Liverpool. And before Wimbledon, he himself overcame perception and size to prove wrong one of Britain's most celebrated players.

'I was only a young boy at Leeds and, God rest his soul, Billy Bremner was a wee bit difficult. He pulled me in to his office one day and said, "Look son, you're too small to play this game." And I turned around and said "Too small?" Billy Bremner was five-foot-five.

'Tommy Hutchison brought me down to Swansea and I said to myself, "I'm not going to let that hamper me." Then the story was that we were playing against Northampton and, who's in the stand, Billy Bremner and Mervyn Day. Billy Bremner turned around and asked, "Who's that little dark chap running up and down the line? Look at that, we'll have to get him." And Mervyn turns around and says, "Gaffer, we let him go three months ago." So sort that one out for yourself.'

That kind of resilience suited the perceived cast of grafters and grunters at Wimbledon when he went there in 1987. Already 21 by the time he experienced international exposure with that 1988 FA Cup win, Phelan didn't win his first cap until three years later. Unlike many other Irish players at the time though, he wasn't someone who got as far as a particular crossroads in his career only to realise international football presented another avenue. He was already immersed by the time he left Leeds and, in any case, certainly didn't consider himself anything other than Irish. Phelan played in the under-18 side – featuring Niall Quinn and Pat Dolan – that beat England's Tony Adams, Des Walker and Michael Thomas in February 1985.

'Oh I was always going to choose Ireland. No disrespect to England because

I grew up there but I always felt Irish. All my family's Irish. On my mother's side from County Sligo. I was brought up between Tubbercurry and Salford, back and forth all the time. A lot of people say, "Oh, you picked Ireland because it was an easier option" but it wasn't. I had to come all the way through the ranks to prove myself.'

Phelan was actually one of only a handful of the 34 players given their first caps by Charlton to have graduated through Ireland's underage system. That was a period when the FAI paid little heed to its youth set-up and it suited Charlton to do the same. The irony of course is that, as one of its few success stories, Phelan probably got his true education in that Irish side's ways at Plough Lane. Wimbledon played much the same style, preached many of the same philosophies and also performed best in the role of underdog.

They weren't an identikit though. When Phelan first joined up with the Irish squad, Mick McCarthy put his arms around him and said, 'Welcome to the family.' It wasn't quite the initiation Wimbledon gave him.

'They used to have little portakabins. And I remember, on my first day, sitting there four hours and no-one ever spoke to me. I was thinking "hang on a minute, what's going on here?" So I sat there for four hours, then this head pops around. "Oh yeah, how'ya Terry. Get changed, we'll have a kick-about." That was the tester.

'Six months I struggled with that. But then there was one game against Newcastle when it just switched on and I just thought "right, let me show 'em what it's all about". After that I never looked back. I was brought into that family.'

That family was, notoriously, the Crazy Gang. And the style of initiation wasn't the only insanity. On one away trip Phelan walked into the lobby of the hotel to find his bed on the other side of the elevator doors.

'If people came in in awful gear you'd have a little bonfire in the middle of the changing room. Or, you know, stripping people and putting them through muddy water. The baptism on their first day. And if you moaned and groaned you wasn't part of the family. Although, to tell you the truth, I used to wear all dodgy gear so mine never got burnt!'

And those who did most of the burning?

'Dennis Wise was the one for it. Vinnie Jones, John Fashanu – he was sneaky about it. Alan Cork. Some wonderful characters about. I'm not saying there wasn't professionalism at Wimbledon but I think we was odd-job boys. They bought me but a lot of the lads were free transfers or on the scrap heap and we got moulded into the Wimbledon way.'

Most notoriously Jones, whose history and style appeared to epitomise the club. Just as Wimbledon had fought their way from the part-time Southern League to the old First Division in eight years, Jones had fought his way there from even further away.

'People just seen him as a loudmouth thug. Don't forget Vinnie was a hod-carrier. He'd done his job and he'd come in. And what a story, from that to the First Division. Very underrated and a great character. Would give you his right arm, Vinnie. Real hard-nut on the pitch but off the pitch a different person, great. He was a born leader. Loved the game. Every game was like his last and a lot of the Wimbledon players played that way.

'Everybody goes on about Robbie Earle and that but the Wimbledon boys were Vinnie Jones, your Brian Gayles, Andy Thornes, Dave Beasants. They was the Crazy Gang. When all them left, the Crazy Gang left. You were never going to get that spirit again.'

Just like the bonding sessions with the Irish team, so many pranks at Wimbledon were clearly the adhesive that set that spirit. And also just like with the Irish team, that spirit fostered a specific – if unpopular – style of football that saw the side reach unforeseen heights. How much of the following sounds familiar?

'You had to have trust, honesty and character. And don't forget we had two of the best coaches about. We had Don Howe who was a mastermind and Bobby Gould. We sort of played the same way as Ireland, hit the channels, hit diagonal balls. I think people couldn't cope because it was a hundred miles an hour and it was in your face. That's the game.'

For a time too, it was a winning one. Specifically in May 1988 when their irreverent attitude was required most. Eleven years before that month's FA Cup final, Wimbledon hadn't even been among the best 92 clubs in England as they hiked through non-league. Four times in that same period, Liverpool had been the best club on the continent as repeat European Cup winners. None of Wimbledon's starting XI had won a single medal in their careers. All of Liverpool's had won several and were that day going for a second league-and-cup double in three years.

Suitably, it was a day of shocks. The night before the final, Wimbledon supporters' mouths dropped as Gould walked his entire squad into the local Fox & Grapes pub to relax them.

Thirty-seven minutes into the final, the football world stopped turning as Lawrie Sanchez headed home a free-kick Phelan won. With half an hour left then, John Aldridge sank to the ground in despair as Dave Beasant produced the first ever FA Cup final penalty save.

'Another dream come true. It was every kid's to play in the cup final and win it.'

Romantic as Wimbledon's rags-to-riches victory was, many football watchers were only prepared to give them grudging respect at best. In arguments that would have echoes during Ireland's assault on Italia 90, some saw it as a travesty that Wimbledon's brute force beat Liverpool's brilliance. Phelan is dismissive.

'People forget, to play that way you had to be a skilful player. It was an art to be able to hit the channels and hit the perfect diagonal ball for people coming on. We worked on things. If you've got people who can adapt to it, are focused doing it and can buy into it, then what was the problem? People think it was just lumped in there. No it wasn't. It was put in there with a purpose.

'We had everything at Wimbledon and I honestly believe after winning the FA Cup if we had gone to Europe [the ban on English teams after the Heysel Stadium tragedy was still in effect] we would have smashed teams. Could you imagine AC Milan coming down to Plough Lane? People didn't know how to cope. Maybe there was a bit of jealousy.'

Other teams certainly coveted Wimbledon's squad.

'We had some fantastic players who went to other clubs for over a million pounds. So we couldn't have been that bad. Nigel Winterburn went to Arsenal, won trophy upon trophy. Dennis Wise went to Chelsea, John Fashanu to Aston Villa. You can go on and on and on.'

Phelan himself certainly did. He eventually signed for Manchester City in 1992 at the same time as Alan Kernaghan. But it could have been further afield.

'I had the chance to go to Man United but they wouldn't pay the money. Could have went to Tottenham, Ajax was knocking on the door and – no-one knows this – Barcelona. I could have ended up at Barcelona. Still have the clipping and everything. That's as true now as it ever was. We spoke to Johan Cruyff and he talked to the club but they didn't want to pay the two and a half million.'

If it seems outlandish that any Irish player other than Liam Brady or Roy Keane could have played for a team who were not just reigning European champions but considered one of the continent's landmark attacking sides, then it's worth considering exactly the type of player Phelan was then. The £2.5m City were eventually prepared to pay made him the most expensive defender in England. A goal against Tottenham in the 1993 FA Cup made him one of the most exciting. Phelan picked the ball up well inside his own half, skipped past five Spurs defenders and then slipped it past Erik Thorstvedt.

'I still get phonecalls about that goal. It's on YouTube. I knew my capabilities. People who played against me knew I was a livewire and it was going to be a hard game. I went to Manchester City and it was a bit disappointing. We never won a trophy and Peter Reid got sacked after a year. If I had known that I probably would never have went. It was awful hard living in the shadows of Manchester United but it was still great.'

Phelan's form was so great he was named Irish Young Player of the Year for 1992. At the age of 25! He had finally made his international debut in a September 1991 friendly win away to Hungary.

'Maybe a wee bit late. That's life. I missed out on the 1990 World Cup when I'd been a regular in the old First Division. So, obviously, there were players in there that Jack thought ahead of me, which is grand. You just have to prove yourself to get in the team. Obviously I sat down there on that first day and thought I would have loved to have gone to Italy and just picked the cones up.'

He might have felt like an apprentice brought along to do just that until McCarthy gave him that embrace.

'It was brilliant. And I'm just thinking "these are just normal blokes". They'd learn you. It was great for me and I only wish I'd played more caps. We used to love going over and playing for your country. What better chance with a team full of top players and buzzing. I mean I was at Wimbledon – I knew what it was all about.

'Ireland was different though because it was your country. We wouldn't have been allowed to do what we did at Wimbledon, which was unique. You couldn't have a bonfire in the middle of the changing room burning the worst gear. We wouldn't go round cutting Jack's grey pants in half or his blue coat. We wouldn't over-step the mark there! Ireland was more controlled. We'd have a laugh and a joke, put golf balls in pints of Guinness so that, when they'd drink it, it would go all over them. The odd bread roll fight. Little pranks like that. You wouldn't see your hotel bed coming down into the lobby on a lift.'

They might do worse to your actual room though. Ahead of Italia 90, one unnamed player made a note of David O'Leary's obsession with cleanliness and decided to test it. He 'deposited a turd', as Niall Quinn has told the story, under O'Leary's bed. One by one, the squad was marched in to see if they could get 'the smell'. Naturally, none of them could. Not even his roommate Quinn who was by then suppressing his gag reflex to keep the joke going.

By Phelan's first World Cup, O'Leary had gone and Jason McAteer replaced him as the squad's main target.

'We used to give a bit of stick out. Jason obviously was a young lad then and raw. He is – well, I hope he is! – a mature man now but I hope his humour hasn't changed. I was a wee bit more reserved and used to watch and listen. A lot of the older lads took you under their wing. I always used to sit next to Packie Bonner on the plane. "Little man, come and sit here." There were a few characters and they were the front-runners. John Aldridge and Tony Cascarino for the jokes. Andy Townsend was the captain and he would always be pulling rank, the do's and the don'ts. The lads would just laugh at him. "Alright then Andy, we're not going out tonight. Yeah right Andy, see you down there." But then you had a few quiet lads who went over there and just got on with the job. Paul McGrath was awful quiet, Mick was the elder statesman and all. But once you got into it you'd have a laugh and a joke.'

The impression given by that Irish squad is of hardened men of the world rather than the cotton-wrapped young millionaires of eight years later. The 1988-94 generation had cards, 2002 computer games. Bridging the gap though were the so-called 'Three Amigos' of Gary Kelly, Jason McAteer and Phil Babb. At 19, 22 and 23 respectively, they – as well as Roy Keane – added an irreverent exuberance to all that experience in 1994. They also brought the average age of the squad down to 28.5. Although it was the oldest panel Ireland had ever sent to a tournament (compared to 25.5 in 1988, 28.3 in 1990 and 26.9 in 2002), at least it wasn't by so much.

The general belief in football is also that a player's peak comes between 27 and 29, the time at which they have just the right balance between stamina and savvy. With 19-year-olds like Kelly providing the energy and 32-year-olds like Houghton the know-how, that was a theory that appeared to be borne out on a collective scale by that Irish side. Containing just the right mix of all those qualities, the team seemed to be at its zenith. It was an impression only hardened by results in the build-up. In April 1994, Ireland went to Holland and beat a side who had recently been ranked second in the world 1–0 with a late Tommy Coyne goal. They then followed it with a 2–0 victory away to defending world champions Germany. Not that you'd expect Charlton to actually be happy with this, as Kernaghan recalls.

'I remember after Germany Jack coming in and going, "What the fuck have you done now?" That was what he said. We were expecting "aw, brilliant boys" but he came in, "Now everyone will expect you to win it [USA 94]." It was a funny angle to come at it from. I would be more thinking "well done" but he looked at it from the total opposite – "expectations are now going to be so high".'

Phelan, however, reckons Charlton's reaction wasn't out of concern for expectations but for Ireland excelling too early.

'We went to Holland and beat them 1–0, went to Germany and beat them 2–0. So what do you think was going through our heads? I remember Jack turning around and saying, "Lads, you're peaking too soon! Leave it to the World Cup!" We're looking at him going, "Does that mean you're saying we could win this World Cup?" I think every lad in that changing room then, well, we went away and treated it as, "Hey, we're here to do a job, we're not here to take part, we're here to win the World Cup." Simple.'

It was the sort of form and feeling that make Phelan's confident assertion completely understandable. And should also perhaps alter the impression of Ireland's eventual 1–0 win over Italy. In virtually any list compiled on the subject, it's always named as one of the great World Cup shocks. With the context which hindsight allows, the result may not have been exactly expected but it was by no means a huge upset.

Yes, Italy were still Italy. And, yes, this was a particular Italy with the reigning European player of the year in Roberto Baggio as well as a defence that had also just announced itself as the continent's best by winning the Champions League with Milan. That formidable back four of Franco Baresi, Paulo Maldini, Alessandro Costacurta and Mauro Tassotti had only conceded two goals in 12 games on their way to the title. But the manager who initially gathered them, Arrigo Sacchi, wasn't quite having the same effect on his country as he had on that club. His approach was in many ways the exact opposite of Charlton's. Although the full month of the World Cup would prove sufficient for Sacchi to get some of his message across, it required the kind of repetition only club football allows compared to the Irish manager's instant impact. When Charlton gathered the team to watch some Italy matches, he noticed the discrepancies. Their off-side trap was a lot looser than Milan's, the link between defence and midfield not as fluid.

'The left-back – Maldini – people call him the best in the world but I'm not so sure. Look what happens here,' Charlton had sniffed before showing the squad footage of Jurgen Klinsmann holding him off then getting around him.

It all clearly had an effect. Italy had only scraped into the World Cup on the last night of qualification by beating Portugal 1–0 at home and, a month before the tournament, were ranked 16th in the world – four places behind Ireland.

So, ahead of the game, the Irish squad were understandably assured and focused. Rebel songs then roused them on the way to the Giants Stadium. The only person who had seemingly weighed it all up – other than Charlton – was Joe Kinnear. In the RTÉ studio he confidently predicted a 1–0 win.

Ireland's first unexpected victory of the night came in the minutes beforehand. With Little Italy so nearby, it was assumed the Giants Stadium would be awash with blue. Instead, thanks to ticketing chaos that eventually led to the FAI's 'night of the long knives' two years later, half the stadium was filled by fervent Irish fans. Charlton had warned the players not to actually go out onto the pitch beforehand because of the heat. They couldn't help themselves. And couldn't but be inspired.

'You come out of the tunnel and all the Italian fans were just behind. Then it's just this wall of green, white and gold,' an audibly emotional Phelan recalls. 'What a picture!'

The second unexpected victory came just before kick-off. When the Irish starting XI lined up in their white away kit, they saw the Italians had done exactly the same. As the nominal home team, Ireland had to rush back into the dressing room and re-do half an hour's worth of preparation in half a minute to get into their vintage green. Phelan was even missing from the team photograph because he was trying to find his socks. Many maintain that tense wait in the tunnel unsettled the Italians. But perhaps not as much as Charlton's tactics.

Ireland had first tried a 4-5-1 formation, with John Sheridan behind the striker, in the crushing defeat to Spain. That didn't inspire confidence. But results wrought in the build-up helped.

'We played it to nullify their midfield,' Phelan explains. 'We had to stop Roberto Baggio getting the ball. Jack kept emphasising that. Teams are playing 4-5-1 now and they talk as if it's a new system. We played one up front, the midfield bombing forward.'

There was a firecracker energy to the Giants Stadium that day and Ireland came out electrified by it. Within seconds, Steve Staunton had dented the advertising board with a snapshot as Italy struggled with Ireland's high balls. The warning wouldn't be heeded.

'It's gone up to Tommy Coyne, Baresi's knocked the ball down, Ray's got onto it and it's just taken a little bounce for him at the right time, half-shin, half-foot.'

In goal, Gianluca Pagliuca – who Charlton had also identified as a weakness – expects it to sail over. He doesn't exactly burst a gut to reach it. The ball bursts the net.

'Bang. There's eruptions. I think you could have heard the stadium from New Zealand. Wonderful. Eleven minutes gone and you're leading the Italians 1–0 in the World Cup group stage, first game. Who would have visualised that?'

The Italians clearly hadn't. As the Irish bench exploded, theirs remained motionless. Then they started bickering. But many Irish supporters probably hadn't expected it either. Before the match, there had been a lot of speculation as to whether an off-colour Houghton would even start. He vindicated the decision with the second most valuable goal of his career and of Ireland's football history. But, on this occasion, even Houghton was overshadowed. And by the other major doubt on the day. In the build-up, McGrath had a lot on his mind as well as a virus eating away at his shoulder. But, with one arm effectively tied behind his back, he proved the antidote to every Italian attack.

Against a backline as iconic as Italy's, McGrath ensured it was Ireland's rearguard who gave the master-class in defending. The 22nd minute encapsulated the extent of his heroics. Three times the ball fell ominously to Baggio on the edge of the box. Three times McGrath battered him back with his body literally on the line. How good was he to play alongside?

'Great. Strong as an ox. I think he was already up there as one of the best centre-backs in the world at the time. He proved it.'

It wasn't all muck and bullets. In fact, so assured was Ireland's defending they were never in too much danger. They even played a bit. Before the qualifiers, Charlton had made a few concessions in the midfield to more attractive football and that came across against Italy. Sheridan hit the bar after Coyne stepped over a magnificent Keane run; substitute McAteer – on his 23rd birthday – nutmegged Baggio. In the end, Ireland cruised to victory. As Keane said in his autobiography, '15 minutes from the final whistle they'd "gone".' The Irish, however, had gone into rapture. They had their first ever win over Italy and first ever win at a World Cup.

At the same time Phelan was soaking up the scenes, George Hamilton was exclaiming, 'This Irish side looks like it's going to go a long, long way in this World Cup.' Amid such euphoria, few would have scoffed. It was probably the performance closest to perfection in Charlton's reign. But that only brought out his old fears in the dressing room. 'Here we go again. You're peaking too soon!' It would prove prescient. Keane argued, 'Ireland's World Cup ended that day in the Giants Stadium.'

The joy had already started to fade during the FAI's disastrously organised post-match reception as thoughts turned to an even more uncomfortable trip back to Florida for the Mexico game. It evaporated altogether when the squad arrived in the Orlando heat. News came through of the Loughinisland massacre; six fans celebrating Ireland's win in The Heights Bar in Northern Ireland were killed by UVF gunfire.

Minds clearly weren't right leading up to the match. In *Andy's Game*, Townsend said, 'There is something about this game, an unease.' At the same time though, Ireland were only increasing their own anxieties. Charlton's justified apprehension about water and heat turned into unhealthy obsession as an effective away match with Mexico loomed. Heads only dropped when the players walked into the Citrus Bowl's 43-degree heat. There was a breeze but weather reports confirmed what they felt: it had blown in from the Sahara. Charlton's gameplan hadn't been constructed for these conditions. Neither had the constitutions or fair-skinned complexions of Staunton or Coyne.

'As soon as you walked out you'd have buckets of water in your boots from the sweat. Had to go back into the dressing room. You're sat there but your adrenaline's pumping and you can't warm up right. It was energy-sapping.'

Predictably, Ireland started decently only to drop off badly.

'The first 10 minutes I put a couple of balls in. We should have been 2–0 up. But I've never felt any heat like it before and you're playing against Mexico who train in that all the time. They keep the ball, they tire you. We're trying to close them down and it zaps us.'

With Ireland lacking the energy to follow lines of play, Luis Garcia scored Mexico's first goal just before half-time. He then added an almost identical second shortly after it. And, other than getting in behind Ireland, the Mexicans were also getting under their skin.

'There was a bit of bad blood. They started to get a bit dirty. I have a picture of two of them around me, one pulling me back, another cutting across. You'd touch them and they'd fall over.'

All of it created the tinder-box for Aldridge to light up on the line. But he was also fired up in the right way. Within minutes of coming on, Aldridge made it 2–1 thanks to a header hammered home with all the anger he could muster. Roles reversed, the Mexicans now felt the heat and Ireland could even have salvaged a draw. They didn't – but Aldridge's goal would prove to be as important as Sheridan's goal in the 3–1 loss against Spain in the qualifying rounds. With Ireland's two goals scored compared to Italy and Norway's one goal apiece, a point against the latter would put Ireland into the second round.

Although suspended for that game along with Charlton, Phelan watched his team claim the necessary point in a 0–0 draw as dreadful as that against Egypt in 1990. Indeed, one of the only memorable aspects of the game for the players was the circus around Charlton's suspension. Handed an ear-piece to communicate with assistant Maurice Setters from the stand, Charlton's road-test was like a scene out of *Phoenix Nights*. Standing two feet away from Setters he hollered 'Maurice. Can. You. Hear. Me?'

Ireland were in the second round for the second successive World Cup but it was a case of many unhappy returns. It involved another match in Orlando and a third against Holland in three tournaments. Although April's win in the friendly away to Holland should have bolstered confidence, it only bred complacency. Many of the squad noticed an edge missing ahead of the game. That feeling only deepened when they started making all manner of mistakes in the opening 10 minutes. In the 11th, Phelan committed a cardinal one. Misjudging his position, Phelan's back header fell badly for Babb but perfectly for Marc Overmars.

'That ball should have gone into row Z. I'd already had a look and there was no-one around and then the next thing Overmars – who I'd had in my pocket anyway – skipped down the line, pulled the ball back to Dennis Bergkamp who smashed it in. Then obviously there was Packie's mistake. But if you don't make mistakes in life you're not human and that was just the wrong occasion.

'And, to be fair, I never think about that. Never enters me mind that I cost Ireland the World Cup or I let me people down. I gave 110% every time I put that shirt on. And I'd played against some of the fastest wingers in the world – Andrei Kanchelskis, Franz Carr – no problem. I'd just played against Donadoni so, hey, Overmars? This is the thing about it. He didn't cause me a problem except for that split-second. So can I say I had a bad game? Not really. I just made a judgement error. Bit disappointing.'

Despite the delight with the win over Italy, those two words ultimately summed up the tournament.

'I was walking around Orlando with the wife and children and I'm like "Shit, I've just played in the World Cup and it doesn't feel like it". We got to the last 16. Not bad for a small country but we could have done better. That's my perception anyway. We maybe needed to adapt our game a little but we didn't. We could have acclimatised better. We could have been in the final. I think that's in the back of everyone's mind still.'

In the end, Ireland were the only team to actually beat Italy in the tournament. But, before Sacchi's side had lost a shoot-out to Brazil in the final, the Irish players had already gone through the motions of a homecoming. Taoiseach Albert Reynolds had insisted on a reception but it was the last thing the players wanted, as Kernaghan explains.

'Because we hadn't done anything – celebrating as a failure as it were – riled everybody.' A tournament in which the finalists were beaten and the second round reached surely can't be considered an outright failure? 'You were associating it with Italia 90 and we fell below that.'

In the meantime, Gary Kelly's excellence and Denis Irwin's class saw Phelan fall out of favour. And the next game he started after USA 94 wasn't an occasion to be celebrated. It was the visit of England – and a hardcore of Combat 18 hooligans – to Lansdowne Road in February 1995.

'I'd played at places like Millwall and you could smell it in the air there was going to be trouble. That's why I couldn't believe where they were.' David Kelly put Ireland into the lead in the 22nd minute but by the 27th the game was off as English hooligans inexplicably seated in the Upper West Stand began to tear it up and throw parts of it down on the fans below.

As one of Ireland's few black players, Phelan was targeted that night as well as at Windsor Park in November 1993. Did it ever affect him?

'To tell you the truth, yes and no. It would really go in one ear and out the other. We grew up on the streets of Salford so we'd heard it all before.'

There is one interesting anecdote among the Irish support that travelled to Stuttgart for Euro 88. Any time John Barnes would touch the ball, one young man bedecked in green would start with monkey chants. After a while, he got a slap on the head and a roar. 'What colour do you think Paul McGrath is?' Everyone around cheered. Phelan concurs that that kind of element was rare to non-existent with Ireland.

'There you go. It's an escape route. And I used to just smile anyway. I'd turn around to them thinking, "Well I'm on the pitch playing and you're paying to watch me play". So it was never an issue for me.'

Ironically, Phelan would then move to a club with a traditional core of Combat 18 support. The far-right would just have to get used to the sort of cosmopolitan side Chelsea were becoming at that stage though. The arrival of Ruud Gullit in 1995 heralded a new era of glamorous continental stars at Stamford Bridge.

'We learnt a lot off the foreigners. But they knew the game too. They was mad as hatters. Vialli, Ruud was always pranking about. Di Matteo, Petrescu. It was funny to hear little Gianfranco Zola give it out to Dennis Wise. Dennis would be on the ground laughing. I remember Dennis taking one of the lads' brand new Mercedes out, took it down to some fields, spun it around, left it full of mud, driven it back and left it outside the changing room. They didn't know what happened.'

It was his form for Chelsea that also saw Phelan recalled by Charlton. As Ireland prepared for the Euro 96 play-off against Holland at Anfield, confidence and personnel were seemingly decreasing by the day. When Staunton broke down in training Charlton went for a walk to ponder what to do next. It was on the streets of Chester he spotted Phelan doing the same. Remembering he had watched him win man-of-the-match against Newcastle the previous Saturday, Charlton decided to throw Phelan back in. On the left of midfield, he was one of six defenders that started that night. Just as Charlton had essentially opened his era against Scotland with a unique approach to his backs, that's how he would close it. But, where once it was a sign of how he could out-think opponents, now it just illustrated how out of touch he was. Against a dynamic young Dutch side that contained the core of the Ajax team that won the 1995 Champions League, Ireland were simply outclassed.

Watching from the bench, Kernaghan sensed an inevitability to it all.

'Holland knew what we were going to do. They knew how to play against us and, the way we play, it was easy for them. Patrick Kluivert got most of the plaudits because he scored the goals and he did look very good on the night but they were fantastic. Too good for us, simple as that.'

Holland's passing produced seven clear-cut chances from which they scored two. Ireland's chasing produced absolutely nothing. Phelan felt the sense of futility from the start.

'They'd gone up a level. They had more than us. I was playing out of position and it didn't work. That was the end of an era – wasn't it? But a new era was starting with Mick.'

Having been given a hammering by a team famous for wearing orange that night, Phelan's next competitive start didn't actually come until an equally dismal defeat in a much more notorious kit of the same colour. As Ireland togged out in Skopje for their 1998 World Cup qualifier against Macedonia, they were handed unfamiliar away jerseys. The Mancunian in Phelan betrays him here as he sounds like Peter Kay doing a 'garlic bread' sketch.

'Orange and black?! Orange and black?! Why?! Was that one of the FAI's gimmicks? It was ridiculous. It was like United with the grey strip against Southampton. Sometimes it can be a psychological thing but we weren't on our game. You can't blame the shirts.'

The players' frustration in a 3–2 defeat peaked when McAteer was sent off for crane-kicking Artim Sakiri. Other than a 1–1 home draw with Romania, that was to be Phelan's last cap for three years as his career entered a prolonged valley period. It began with what transpired to be one of his worst decisions – to leave Chelsea. It wasn't, as many believed at the time, because he fell out with new manager Gullit though.

'I don't know where that has come from. Me family was up in Manchester and I was going up and down all the time. So it was family reasons I moved up to Everton. And I remember the first person that came up to me was Ruud and he said, "I can't believe you've left." Mark Hughes said the same thing, Dennis Wise, Gianfranco Zola. "Stay here Terry. This is going to be a massive club." But, obviously, my family was more important. Yeah, had a few handbags with Ruud but never fell out with him.'

He did, however, fall out with Walter Smith at Everton. Worse, a cartilage problem kept him out for 18 months and there was even talk of retirement.

'I said I'm not retiring, I'm going to battle through it. And, lo and behold, I did. Played a few games at Everton, went on loan at Crystal Palace and it was the best time of my life – those three months. Steve Coppell, fantastic. It was like I was on top of the world again. They were going into administration though so I ended up going to Fulham with Paul Bracewell.'

Although initially 'brilliant' there, the club's subsequent treatment of Phelan – forcing him to train with the youths – even led to a case of mild depression which culminated in visits to his GP.

In 2000, however, came a turning point.

'I'm in America on holiday with my wife and children and get a phonecall.'

Phelan puts on a Yorkshire accent.

'"Is that a Mr Phelan?"

'Yeah, this is Mr Phelan.

'"How do you fancy playing for Ireland again in America?"'

It was McCarthy recalling him to the US Cup.

'We cut short the holiday. I was thinking, "Will I make it to 2002?" but I didn't care. I was putting on that green jersey again.'

Phelan played in all three matches on the tour but, with figures like Keane absent, the true purpose of his recall was to temporarily provide an evolving squad with a touch more experience. He was naturally disappointed when McCarthy then phoned him after America.

'I felt a little bit let down when I got the call that I wasn't going to be involved. I dropped everything to go out there and I don't think the favour got repaid. That's when I felt let down by me country a little bit. I honestly thought I was better than what they had at left-back. More experience, could cope with things better. So yeah, there would be a little bit of regret with Mick over it. But Mick was the manager and you have to make decisions. And I was probably a little bit selfish in that I wanted to play in a World Cup again. I had a wonderful nine years with Ireland.'

Nevertheless, the experience of playing in America again had triggered something in Phelan. In the summer of 2001 he was contacted by North Carolina team Charleston Battery.

'I thought, "You know what, I'll have a look" and I fell in love with the place. It was beautiful – lovely little club. Won a championship there. It was laid-back too. In America a lot of the players had come out of college. The banter was a little bit different but it does fly around.'

Phelan stuck around in Charleston to coach, set up a business called One on One Soccer and, one summer, was even contacted by New York GAA team to improve the panel's fitness ahead of a Connacht championship match against Galway. It was there too that he struck up a friendship with Dunedin native Blair Scoullar. Knowing too well how hard Phelan worked players, when Scoullar returned home to Otago United he mentioned Phelan's name as a potential player-coach.

'I'd always wanted to come down to this part of the world so I jumped at it. It gave me the chance to get into the other side of the game, expand a little bit in a different country with a different culture. So it was ideal.'

Some of the conditions, admittedly, weren't ideal. As manager of Otago he had to adapt to the sudden loss of players to rugby or cricket. So, in 2009, after a four-month stint working with his coaching company in the States, he took his current job with the New Zealand association. It involves training kids up to 20 years of age . . . and attempting to counter the influence of rugby.

'It is a bit hard. It was the same in the States but it [soccer] has got bigger there. It's probably the same a little bit in Ireland with the Gaelic and the rugby. But football is the biggest participation sport in New Zealand at the moment. There are so many kids taking part right up to senior level.'

The only World Cup most people were discussing, however, was still the rugby one taking place in the country in 2011. Speaking then a month after the All Whites had become the only unbeaten team at the 2010 World Cup though, Phelan did notice a change.

'I think a lot of people have started to look at the game a lot more now. I just hope it doesn't stop and we just need to keep the kids active. Football's very structured now. It's very rare to see kids playing in the street, especially down here. Everything's organised for them whereas in my day, you'd be out there all the time. When I was being coached aged eight to 13, I probably had a thousand hours of football in already. But my stuff is getting kids into colleges in America.

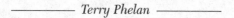

Scouts are starting to come down here now for the under-20 and under-17 lads.'

It's the sort of move, of course, Phelan would only encourage having taken his career to such far-flung destinations himself. Indeed, he's really the only member of Ireland's qualification era to display such wanderlust.

'For me, travelling is an experience. I don't think many players travel as much as myself but I love it. When I'm older, I can say I have travelled around the world. I just try and make sure my kids have a green shirt on and they know their dad played for Ireland and they're Irish. When I do go back over to Europe I try and catch up with a few people for a couple of pints. They're always intrigued by what I'm doing. I've spoken to Packie on one or two occasions and visited Roy when he was at Sunderland.

'I've been down here now five years. And I'll travel anywhere. It's a great learning experience. Maybe one day I can coach in Ireland, a League of Ireland club. Doesn't have to be Barcelona. If the shout ever comes from Ireland, why wouldn't I look at it? The game's given me a wonderful life.'

And off he goes a-wandering.

Matt Holland

Stuck in the middle with you

The madness of World Cups. About a week into the 2002 tournament, FIFA protocol dictated it was Matt Holland's turn to take Ireland's daily press conference. One local reporter put his hand up. What did the team think of the Izumo water supply? Laughs at the back, shrugs at the front. But a sincere face on the Japanese journalist. And, with respect, a response to match from Holland. For a few minutes he elaborated on the importance of hydration in such humidity and how the local infrastructure had been 'tremendous'. Most of his squad-mates would probably have looked on blankly before altering one of the automated responses modern professionals have seemingly been programmed with: 'You can't rule out any water supply to be fair.'

In that sense, Holland was never like most of his squad-mates. He was always media-savvy rather than media-suspicious, capable of offering an honest, considered statement rather than a stock response. It's little wonder he's now presenting programmes rather than just appearing on them as a pundit. It's little wonder either that he gives the impression he's never been overly dependent on an agent. Many of his club and country colleagues often had to be told their obligations on a day-to-day basis. By contrast, Holland seems to live like a normal individual. That could be down to the fact he was preparing for a career in the bank rather than professional football as he entered his twenties. Or it could be down to common courtesy. Either way, he's laughing now about the unfamiliar workload of all of his own paperwork as he is, technically, a freelance journalist. There's a reprieve from it the week he speaks while he attends the Dublin Horse Show to support his wife's equestrian interests. As Holland proved in Izumo – and to butcher a metaphor that does otherwise apply to many modern footballers and the media – sometimes you can lead a horse to water and he'll even tell you how it tastes.

In any case, Holland had already experienced a whole different world of madness in the two weeks leading up to that Japanese reporter's question. It was also probably the most innocuous to answer in all that time. It certainly was compared to questions like whether he was fully behind Mick McCarthy. Or, if it came to a vote, which way would he go on taking Roy Keane back? Most of all, perhaps, there was the question whether he could fill that Keane-shaped hole.

Holland was only two and a half years into his international career by the time of Saipan. Already 28 though, it was just as well he possessed a rare maturity. It was just as well too that his first cap gave him a strong sense of the emotional turbulence to come.

He got it five minutes from the end of the final Euro 2000 group qualifier in Macedonia. Ireland were 1–0 up thanks to Niall Quinn's early header and only needed to close out the game to claim a place at the European Championships.

'I didn't think anything of it at the time. I was coming on late as a time-wasting substitution if you like. Taking off a striker, bringing on a midfielder, just trying to see out time. Sure enough, they got the corner.'

Holland's midfield partner at that moment, Alan McLoughlin, remembers it all too vividly.

'I asked the ref and he said "it's over". The corner was swung in, a bit of confusion. I was at the edge of the box and, as it's come in, a guy takes a run and you just know – you just know – he's going to head it. Then your world seems to drop into slow motion. You're thinking please head it over, please be straight at Alan Kelly, please be someone on the line . . . but it's gone in.'

Goran Stavreski. He was the guy. A *bête noir* to go with Wim Kieft.

'It wasn't the ideal way to get into it,' Holland admits. 'Last touch of the game, it was such a massive disappointment. And then the emotions in the dressing room . . . it was an unforgettable debut but not in the way you'd want it to be.'

As regards the long-term evolution of McCarthy's team though, it was arguably unforgettable in exactly the right way. The lesson from that match would be burned on the squad's collective memory. And, although they would lose the Euro 2000 play-off to Turkey amid a flurry of fists, it would prove the last one before graduation.

In the four years before Stavreski, they had been taught an awful lot. McCarthy, after all, had to turn a new generation of apprentices into internationals while learning on the job himself. To illustrate the extent of the transformation, Jack Charlton had used 58 players in his eight years; McCarthy picked 47 in his first four. As he said himself, 'Unfortunately a number of players were past their best. I now had to do the dirty deed of not picking them.'

Or picking them in the wrong positions. Initial ham-fisted attempts at the wingback system or playing Ian Harte at centre-half saw Ireland scrape into second place of one of the easiest qualifying groups in which they had ever been drawn. The side lost to Macedonia away as well as dropping points to Romania, Lithuania and Iceland at home. A patched-together team ultimately competed admirably in the 1998 World Cup play-off against Belgium but never really convinced as they went out 3–2 on aggregate. There were still too many players past their prime or not enough close to approaching theirs.

McCarthy began to get a sufficient sense of both himself and his team by the Euro 2000 qualifiers. An energetic 4-4-2 formation brought dynamic home wins over World Cup semi-finalists Croatia and a strong Yugoslavia. Against the latter, Mark Kennedy looked like the player he should have become, scoring a brilliant winner. One former English international who played with him at

Liverpool confided that Kennedy could have been an 'Anfield great' had it not been for the hedonistic influence of Neil Ruddock.

Just like Kennedy, Ireland had by then shown real potential but were still not quite the finished article. That was illustrated a little too literally by a complete failure to close out games. Stavreski's injury-time goal was the continuation of a theme as it followed Davor Suker's similarly late strike when Croatia had beaten Ireland 1–0.

Something was still missing. Sometimes, it was the team's sole finished article: the captain. Much had been made of the occasions Keane went AWOL as well as his antipathy towards McCarthy. But genuine injury did keep him out of as many as nine of Ireland's 22 competitive games between 1996 and the Macedonia match. In Keane's absence though, McCarthy had to adapt. But he and the team also required a bit of bolstering. Which is where Holland came in. The new midfielder's career to that point had been as steep a learning curve as McCarthy's.

Holland grew up near Manchester and regularly attended Old Trafford where he idolised Bryan Robson. Coaches recognised in Holland the same determination as the United captain but not the stature as both Southampton and then Arsenal shook their heads at his size. Weekdays in the bank and weekends on non-league pitches seemed inevitable until West Ham gave him another chance. But not on the actual pitch. Holland was pushing 21 and still hadn't made a senior appearance in football. He could have been forgiven for losing hope. Harry Redknapp, however, came up with the sort of deal that fuelled his wheeler-dealer reputation. Knowing his first club Bournemouth had only nine points at the bottom of the old Second Division and even unhealthier figures in their accounts by Christmas of the 1994–95 season, Redknapp offered them the loan of a promising young midfielder, and Holland the opportunity of actual football.

'I remember my debut well. We lost 2–0 at home to Huddersfield. Within two minutes, my shorts had ripped and I was getting wolf-whistles as I pulled them down on the sidelines!'

It wasn't the only time he was caught short. Bournemouth hadn't a bean.

Players were paid as money came in. In such circumstances though, Holland's influence was invaluable. His 16 appearances helped Bournemouth to a 'great escape' – the club shop still sells DVDs about it to this day. And, despite the economics, he was enjoying himself.

'I could have had another year at West Ham but Harry let me go for free because I wanted to play regularly and put myself in the shop window.'

There, he also first displayed his defining qualities: how to lead and speak persuasively. Holland was immediately installed as captain and became Bournemouth players' spokesman in a time of financial turmoil. It wasn't long until bigger names took notice. The £800,000 Ipswich paid for Holland in 1997 solved Bournemouth's problems. Within a year, his old club were in the Auto Windscreens Shield final and Holland – at just 24 – was asked to make his first media appearance as a pundit. His new club were making similar strides though. By 1999–2000, Ipswich were showing the form that would see them reach the Premier League and then the UEFA Cup in successive seasons. Holland's own input, of course, brought higher-level football before then.

'I got a phone call out the blue from Mick. I think George Burley had been in conversation with him about my availability. I obviously wasn't born in Ireland but with my grandmother being from Monaghan it was always talked about. So Mick asked would I be interested in playing. Straight away I said, "Yeah, I'd love to." Then I was picked for a B international at Bray against a League of Ireland team. The showers weren't great, let's be honest! It all went from there really.'

And on to America. In another of the era's ironies, a US Cup had seen Keane and McCarthy first fall out. In 2000 it would allow the manager the opportunity to finish moulding the rest of his squad. On finally getting to spend proper time with the group, Holland noticed a real togetherness.

'I'd been in a number of squads but not involved too much. Obviously, becoming a regular starter on that tour, it just increases the confidence. You feel more part of the set-up. I think the team spirit was phenomenal. Everyone backed each other one hundred per cent. That's one thing I would say about the group of players we had. Mick, terrific manager, got you playing for him and I think all the players felt the same . . . Especially the younger ones, the ones he gave a start to – or maybe showed loyalty to – you could see they would have done anything for him.'

Inspiring that reaction was McCarthy's one undoubted masterstroke for the 2002 qualification campaign. Throughout the previous four years, many players who appeared either not ready or not in the right frame of mind for international football had their confidence chiselled away by the Irish media, supporters or their own club managers. McCarthy, however, only worked to rebuild it. He kept faith with the players having a tough time at the top level like Gary Breen and Ian Harte. And he kept his door open for players having a tough time at club level like Jason McAteer and Kevin Kilbane.

Holland felt the benefit of McCarthy's paternalistic approach first hand. When Ipswich were relegated in 2002, he panicked about whether second-division football would affect him playing for Ireland.

'No,' McCarthy responded. 'I know what Matt Holland is about, so go and make the right decision for you, your football and your family.'

The effect of that kind of reassurance is often unquantifiable. But what it undoubtedly did was create a spirit that is rarely seen in international football. That was in contrast to even the highest-quality nations who, as Roy Keane himself argued, were often 'overrated and fragile'.

Ireland, then, had an effective club team. Throw in a true world-class talent and an awful lot was suddenly possible. Just as important too, that world-class talent had undergone a transformation every bit as deep-rooted as his country's. The cruciate ligament injury Keane suffered in September 1997 clearly enlightened him. In an instant, he realised how short the game was; how he had occasionally been reckless with his rampaging talent; how he now had to make the optimum use of it. The numbers proved it. Keane went from the player with the highest body fat in the Premier League to the lowest. From then, only the very best would do. And often it wasn't enough.

Going into the 2002 campaign then, Ireland were being driven by two very different forces. On one side was good cop McCarthy cautiously helping them along. On the other was bad cop Keane doggedly hauling them along. The chemistry of it all was quite delicate. Too much and the antagonism between Keane and McCarthy could overspill. Too little and the team lacked edge. Just right and they were explosive. And that was the only way to describe the very start of Ireland's campaign, when the tone was set.

Ireland were dropped into one of the most difficult groups. Favourites Portugal and the Netherlands had just proven themselves to be among the best four sides in the fiesta of attacking football that was Euro 2000. Overcoming them was a lot to ask of a team that, only a year before, had struggled to beat Malta. But it also illustrated the extent of Ireland's development. In Amsterdam in July, the Dutch had been unlucky to go out of Euro 2000 having missed five penalties over one long semi-final against the Italians. In the same stadium two months later, they were lucky to even be in the game.

After just six minutes, Robbie Keane plundered a header. After 60, McAteer powered in a second. All the while, the likes of Breen and Dunne were battling hard to keep Patrick Kluivert and company at bay. If they did slip, there was Roy Keane to cover any errors while exhorting the culprits – often ferociously – not to make another. The extent of the Netherland's late onslaught was always going to force a few more though. Jeffrey Talan bundled one back before Gio van Bronckhorst thundered home an equaliser. Two goals apiece and two conflicting emotions at work. A draw might have been a disappointment by the end of the match but would have been a huge boost beforehand.

There, encapsulated, was the knife-edge the Irish squad were on.

After the game, McCarthy accentuated the positives. 'I'm proud of the team because we came here to take Holland on at their own game. I'd have taken a draw before the start.'

Roy Keane, however, wanted to dispel the negatives. Once and for all.

'We have to start giving ourselves a bit more credit. We have good players and you get a bit sick and tired of the whole "well, the Irish will have a good time no matter what the result" stuff. Sure, the fans will be happy tonight and rightly so. But we're professionals and we have to raise our targets a bit. We haven't qualified for a major finals since 1994 and you get into this rut. Sometimes the players even underestimate themselves.'

Throughout the squad, opinion was generally somewhere in between. Certainly for Holland, who watched from the bench. 'Well it was a great result! At the time, it didn't feel that way. The manner felt like a defeat.'

Just like Charlton had in Ireland's last successful campaign, McCarthy arranged for Ireland's two most difficult fixtures to come as early as possible. Next up was Portugal away. Unlike the Dutch though, their velvet movement pulled Ireland all over the pitch. For Matt Holland, at least, it ensured he was introduced.

'I came on as a sub at half-time with the same instructions as Macedonia really: shore up midfield. It is quite ironic when I look back. Mick felt we were getting overrun in midfield. And, sure enough, within 15 minutes of me being on they take the lead. And you're thinking, "Oh no, not again . . . that one wasn't my fault surely."'

In truth though, McCarthy's switch had begun to sway the game. With Holland sitting behind Keane and Mark Kinsella, Ireland countered Portugal's 4-5-1 and clogged the supply lines to Rui Costa, Luis Figo and the scorer Sergio Conceicao. It wasn't from there, however, he made his most meaningful impact. With 18 minutes left and Portugal suddenly not so imperious, Holland ventured forward.

'I remember picking up the ball and I've always enjoyed shooting from distance. So I thought "I'll have a go" and fortunately it found the back of the net.

'Afterwards, coming in, the first thing Mick says is "Oi! What were you doing down that end? I told you don't go forward!" Tongue in cheek obviously. It was a massive result for us. And in a game of that stature to score, it brings you to the forefront I suppose.'

And Ireland to the forefront of the group. Two points from the two most difficult away games were a fine foundation. For a McCarthy team, it was also giddy new ground. Away trips to sides of similar stature such as Romania, Croatia and Yugoslavia hadn't even yielded a goal let alone a point. The table after the opening games was as sure an indication that things were changing just as Mark Lawrenson's goal had been in Hampden Park 14 years earlier.

'Absolutely. I think, also, it gives the squad confidence to get results against the bigger nations. To actually take a two-goal lead against the Dutch and then come back against Portugal, all of it helps the feeling that "actually hang on, we're not getting beat here".'

It stayed that way. Andorra may have had the audacity to take the lead at Lansdowne Road and Cyprus the resolve to irritate Roy Keane to boiling point but his fury ensured Ireland took full points from the four matches after Lisbon. They were four points ahead of the Dutch and one in front of Portugal when the latter visited Lansdowne Road in June 2001. The group stood on a precipice. And, for most of the match, so did the Irish defence. Portugal hit top gear, Rui Costa hit the post but their attack still hit a wall. One that was 178cm tall.

As influential as Keane was over the course of the group, Holland – his midfield partner in the second half – felt this was a particular high.

'Let's not play down Roy's role. Throughout the campaign he was phenomenal. There's no question he dragged us through. And that game, of all games, he was magnificent.'

During the first half, Keane may well have pounded down every blade of grass to block Portugal. Early in the second half then, he produced the goal that summed up his performance. Latching onto a throw, Keane forced the ball off a defender, off the post and in. It wasn't the prettiest finish but, just like the result, he made it count through sheer force of will. In the end, all that could cancel out his excellence was the only other player on the pitch in such fearsomely world-class form. The reigning European footballer of the year, Figo, headed home 10 minutes from time. Keane was clearly emphasising the kind of company in which he belonged.

Whether that, on a personal level, included his Irish teammates was becoming an increasing source of fascination. A growing belief was that Keane barely tolerated the rest of the squad. For their part, any perceived friendships had apparently given way to a fierce respect bordering on fear. Keane's was the door no-one ever dared knock on, the autograph one of the backroom staff forged when a jersey needed to be signed. On the pitch, that perception was intensified by the manner in which he bawled out the likes of Breen and McAteer. Off it, the image was only exaggerated by the caricature of an unreconstructed barbarian the English media were particularly keen to promote.

Only a year before the Portuguese game, after all, he had pursued referee Andy D'Urso with the veins in his temples pulsating. Then there were anecdotes such as when Gary Neville sent around his new number only to get the response: 'So what?' Or when McAteer made the mistake of calling him 'mate'. 'I'm not your mate.'

These, however, are either extreme examples or possibly apocryphal stories with the intended humour taken out. The genial side of Keane was one that was a little too inconvenient for the caricature. And, just like Alan McLoughlin and Terry Phelan, Holland puts forward a more rounded portrayal.

'I've always got on well with Roy. As a player, look, I loved playing with him. His high standards brought out the best in you. I remember in one match he drilled a ball at me from about 10 yards. I miscontrolled and they got possession. From that moment, I thought, "The next time he passes the ball I'd better control it" because he gave me such a bollocking. On a personal level, Roy engaged too. Quite often you'd sit at dinner with him and he'd be very interesting to listen to. On any subject. His experience as a footballer, his funny stories. So yeah, Roy was great in that sense.'

Richie Sadlier, who at that stage was on the fringes of the squad, paints a similar picture.

'We were training on a Sunday and it was fine, jovial – only a friendly on the Wednesday anyway. Keane came that evening and the following morning in training the atmosphere was different. Suddenly the game was important. I was just going, "he's tiny". But I've never seen a bigger man in terms of an effect on lads. It was as if teacher had arrived.

'But, again, he was sound. I remember, for lunch, the only seat free was the one next to me. I look up and there was Keane. I'd never had a conversation with him, shook his hand and he sat next to us. Our conversation went dead because it was me, Steven Reid, Colin Healy and Clinton Morrison talking about the stupid things 22-year-olds talk about. Keane obviously sensed that so he instigated conversation. He was brilliant. It was just four lads chatting. Then when I'd my hip injury I was getting nowhere and I remember one or two people saying, "Why don't you ring Keane? He's brilliant about all that."'

Keane then could be one of the lads as often as he was above them. There was less ambiguity about his relationship with McCarthy though.

'Gary Doherty had been in the squad before me,' explains Sadlier. 'I was in the same hotel with the under-21s and we were there, "What's it like?" And his first response was "Fuck me, Keane and McCarthy hate each other." This was 2000 and no-one had ever really said it. "Really?" "Oh yeah, no time for each other. Keane thinks he's shit, Mick thinks he's a prick." Something like that.'

Despite the tension, that wasn't really too tangible through the 2002 qualifiers. Holland insists, 'I didn't see any evidence of it' and Sadlier concurs.

That's probably down to the truce McCarthy and Keane had drawn in the captain's house ahead of the campaign. Keane privately set out the standards he felt the team needed to meet. Nevertheless, he readily went public when he felt management fell short. There was the call to arms after Amsterdam then the call for improvement after Cyprus when he had seen FAI officials relaxing in business-class as players squeezed into economy on the flight over. Keane's fiercest critics claimed this was all the preening of a prima donna. That was to miss the point though. His ultimate goal, after all, was the collective good. But he often didn't help perceptions. A blatant disregard for McCarthy often led him to fall below standards he himself expected.

Most obviously, there was the manner in which he strolled into the camp a day late ahead of the Portuguese away match, leaving McCarthy to make excuses for him. At training ahead of another international, Breen turned to Mick Byrne and asked, 'What time is Roy coming in?' Everyone laughed. The joke was he did as he wished. Incidents like that embarrassed and undermined McCarthy.

But he indulged them because such relatively minor infractions were more than offset by major influence. Like Quinn later explained, 'The deal with Roy – as it was in a different sense for Paul McGrath – was to get him on to the pitch.'

The story of Ireland's qualification era from 1986 to 2002 is really the story of two monolith-strong personalities. For the first 10 years, Jack Charlton. For the next six, Roy Keane. Amid all the debates about the rights and wrongs of Saipan, there was one undisputable argument. Ireland might have got that far with another manager. They would never have got there without Keane.

He famously imprinted that notion on the popular consciousness as well as on Marc Overmars's leg in the first 30 seconds of the Netherland's return visit to Dublin. This was the acid test for McCarthy's Ireland. With only two group games left and Ireland still four points ahead, a win or draw would all but eliminate the Dutch. One problem though. Ireland didn't just have the failures of the last five years to exorcise but those of the last 50 years. Even in Charlton's time, they had never beaten such high-profile opposition at such a high-stakes stage to actually qualify. And the majority of this match didn't exactly suggest that history was about to change. What is often forgotten about Keane's tackle is that, far from rattling the Dutch, it arguably roused them. Kluivert was almost immediately put through for a one-on-one. He missed. So did Bolo Zenden and Ruud van Nistelrooy. Nevertheless, a Dutch goal seemed inevitable. As did Gary Kelly's red card given the evisceration he was suffering at the feet of Overmars. Keane and Holland had to cover a lot more than even the captain seemed capable of. The question is: how?

'Great question,' exhales Holland. 'A lot of it was down to spirit and total effort throughout. Everyone played their part. When Gary got sent off you are thinking, here we are with 10 men against a team like the Dutch. On the backfoot . . . Roy set the tone.'

Ten minutes after Kelly's red card and 22 from the end of the game, Keane drove out of defence. The ball was fed to substitute Steve Finnan who chipped over for an unmarked McAteer. The first-time finish was immaculate. The emotion indescribable.

For many, the enduring memory of that day was an image. That of Keane reluctantly shaking hands with McCarthy but refusing to look at him, capturing the complexity of their relationship. For anyone who was there, it was the sound. The atmosphere. The electricity.

'The crowd were always good but that day . . . it lifted the players.' And maybe influenced the referee.

'One massively scary moment was when Shay might have given a penalty away. That stands out. My initial reaction was to turn around to the referee . . . and he doesn't give it. We got away with that one.'

Despite the tension, Ireland passed the test. And celebrated accordingly. Mick Byrne cried cheers of joy, Edgar Davids tears of pain. Holland embraced his family.

'We went for dinner, had a few drinks and, yeah, we did let the hair down. It was a great day. Probably the best night I've had in Dublin.' The players met up in Lillie's Bordello and drank until dawn. Keane even joined them, getting up to sing Bob Dylan's 'Positively 4th Street'.

Ireland had to keep on keepin' on though. Cyprus were dispatched 4–0 in the final game but that only brought second place and an awkward play-off against Iran. It was the fourth in four tournaments. For the previous three, Ireland had seen the finish line and 'gulped' as Quinn said. This time, they fancied it. 'That's how much this team had grown up'.

By the build-up, Keane hadn't appeared for Manchester United in almost a month and doctors advised him against air-travel. A deal was struck with Alex Ferguson whereby he would play the first leg at Lansdowne Road and avoid an away match in Tehran if the first leg result was deemed strong enough. In the event, Harte hit a penalty and Robbie Keane volleyed home the clincher.

'The second goal was vital,' says Holland. 'And Shay Given's performance was vital.'

Keane returned to Old Trafford but there was still more to overcome than the Iranian attack. Like the sound – and the fury – of 100,000 Iranian supporters.

'I couldn't believe the crowd. They were in the stadium for four or five hours before the game. Normally you arrive and there's no-one there but that's the only time in my career I can remember walking into the stadium an hour and a half before the game's kicked off and it's full. Hostile. As we were walking to the pitch there were things being thrown at us, bottles, fire-crackers.'

If ever a match required Keane this was it. Earlier in the campaign though, McCarthy had maintained, 'When Roy is missing, we don't miss him that much because of Matt.' An exaggeration it may have been but Holland proved inspirational on the night. As did many other players.

'It was more than professional. People were making runs they didn't need to. Getting bodies back and that's what you need.' Iran got a late goal but it proved irrelevant. Ireland were back in the big time. Eight years of frustration going up in the smoke of all those firecrackers.

'If you look back at the video where we're celebrating you think, "Why am I doing that?" But to be honest, you do just lose yourself. It's all a bit of a blur. I can't remember anything in detail. I was thinking "the World Cup!" It's the pinnacle. Magnificent.'

If also somewhat surreal. While the Irish players danced, many Iranian fans demanded blood. Giant banners of the Ayatolla Khomeini were ripped down and a lot more was hurled on to the pitch.

'It was intimidating. But it couldn't take away from the fact we'd done it.'

Neither could assistant manager Ian Evans's comment, 'We've lost the bollocking unbeaten record.' They had. 16 games hadn't become 17. But had become a World Cup. How, though, could they have a traditional celebration in a country where there was no champagne?

'We were throwing Lucozade over each other!' Holland, a player who only a few years previously had doubted his very future in the game, was going to appear on its greatest stage.

There was the day-to-day matters to deal with in the meantime though: Ipswich's difficult second season. Holland had kept up the run that lead to 223 consecutive games for the club but couldn't halt their slide. Having reached Europe so unexpectedly, relegation was coming around all too quickly. One explanation often put forward for the sudden reversal was that, after a self-contained core group of players quietly scaled such heights, ego and the expanded wages of glamorous new signings tore them apart.

'It'd be unfair to blame the fact we got relegated on players like Finidi George coming in. Yeah, they came in on big money. But we were in Europe. Perhaps the squad wasn't big enough to meet all the demands. Perhaps those coming in had an element but it'd be unfair to blame it totally on that. There were lots of reasons.'

It must be a strange double-think for a professional? In one direction, there's the road uphill to the World Cup. In another, there's a road downhill out of the Premiership.

'No, your club's your job. And once you qualify, it's still seven months away. But then the hype builds and it can't come quick enough. As it got closer I kept reminding myself that I am off to play in the World Cup. When I finally managed to change topics in my head, a friend phones up to remind me. Then it just takes over.'

So did the optimism. Ireland had a superb build-up, beating Russia and the USA as well as destroying Denmark with Duff in particularly sparkling form. Italia 90 nostalgia was high. The squad's official song appeared to capture the mood: 'Here Come the Good Times'. But it also contained the words 'with Keane to lead us there is nothing to fear'. Except maybe Keane himself.

With the panoramic view that distance and hindsight provide, Saipan seemed all so inevitable. On an individual level, Keane had been on edge throughout the 2001–02 season. He had threatened to retire after an altercation with Alan Shearer. His knee was in 'constant trouble', his tolerance for failure very low. Now, he was about to spend four weeks with a manager who he communicated with through a 'middle man', Byrne. So taut were the seams that held their relationship together they were never going to last a month. In the event, they didn't last nine days.

Already, relatively minor issues had assumed major importance in Keane's mind: the travel itinerary, the fact the training equipment arrived a day late, the atrocious pitch. Finally, the absence of goalkeepers in a nine-a-side game. Keane walked. Only talk from Ferguson and his agent Michael Kennedy stopped him from leaving altogether.

For his part, McCarthy appeared to be getting fed up indulging Keane. There was the very quick call-up of Colin Healy, the reference to 'treading on eggshells'. The two were headed in different directions, as rather neatly signified by McCarthy's jaunty cycles around the island, Keane's brooding walks. Saipan was supposed to be about rest and relaxation. It was to experience Irish football's most exhausting emotions.

On Wednesday 22 May, Keane did an interview with Tom Humphries of *The Irish Times*. It wasn't overly sensational and, other than complaints he'd already made, contained jokes at his own expense. In the context of that week though, it was sulphurous. Rage spread through the backroom staff with every reading. McCarthy felt he had to address it. A team meeting was called in the Saipan Hyatt hotel's private dining room on the Thursday evening.

The air was relaxed. Only McAteer and, as a result, Quinn had an inkling something was afoot. As Keane clapped along to a band ironically playing 'Stand By Me', McAteer turned to Quinn and whispered, 'I hope Roy will still be singing when the meeting is over'. Holland, however, insists the rest of the squad were as oblivious to what was about to happen as their captain. They thought it would be an elementary discussion about travel arrangements.

The earth would move alright. The biggest story in the history of Irish sport was about to break.

It started when McCarthy produced a transcript of Keane's interview.

'Roy, I want to speak to you about . . .'

'Who are you to fucking ask questions about me?'

In the eight years since, there's been much commentary about what actually took place next. From sources within the squad, autobiographies and on-the-record evidence, the most agreed-upon account appears to be the following.

For nine pretty much uninterrupted minutes, Keane allows every single incident that has in any way angered him over 11 years to vent with volcanic force. His voice rising to a high-pitched screech, he cuts his relationship with McCarthy apart with clinical precision and in chronological order.

McCarthy's supposed accusation that Keane picked and chose games – like missing the second leg in Iran – has been described as the trigger. Instead, it was McCarthy 'belatedly reaching for any weapon'. As Quinn has said, it probably 'was unfair, probably was a mistake, but the previous nine-minute contribution from Roy was all unfair and all a mistake'. No one other than Keane can remember McCarthy mentioning feigning injury. No one at all, however, can remember the words 'English cunt' either as the 'debacle' reaches its defining moment.

'You were a crap player and you're a crap manager. The only reason I've any dealings with you is that somehow you are the manager of my country.'

'If you don't have any respect for me, then don't play for me.'

'Stick it up your bollocks.'

No response.

'I'll fuck off then. I'll not go to the fucking World Cup. Now you have your excuse. It's all Roy's fault. See ye later, lads.'

And like that, as Kevin Spacey says in *The Usual Suspects*, he's gone. Fittingly, the mood is like a bloodbath at the end of a thriller.

Gary Kelly eventually asks, 'Is that it then, is it really over?' Quinn wonders if the situation is retrievable. McCarthy shakes his head solemnly. Dean Kiely momentarily tries to lighten the tension by declaring 'his service to fill that midfield dynamo role'. Kelly then calls for a round of applause. All but Gary Breen and David Connolly join in. Finally, McCarthy says, 'We go on from here now. We'll go stronger from this. We stick together.' He, Alan Kelly, Staunton and Quinn give an impromptu press conference. Ireland reels.

Quinn is one of the few players from the 2002 squad to have gone so elaborately on the record about the incident. Most declare it off-limits, unwilling to reopen wounds. Many of them initially agreed to speak for this book but then had second thoughts once they realised Saipan was unavoidable. With any raw emotion about the incident long since passed though, almost all will bluntly call the whole episode what it was: a pity. A shame it all had to happen then. This is how Holland feels.

'I don't really want to go into it in too much detail. It happened. It wasn't an ideal situation and everyone would have preferred Roy to have played I'm sure.'

Although most were too stunned to string a sentence together in the immediate aftermath, that didn't last long. Quinn, Staunton, Alan Kelly, Harte and McAteer went to Keane's room to, at the least, wish him well. He shook their hands. Breen and Connolly even offered private support.

Black humour breaks through though. An envelope with 'RIP' is placed on Keane's coach seat. Eventually, the squad start singing their unofficial anthem and that which was played after every positive result at Lansdowne Road in qualifying: 'We're on the One Road'. Holland explains the mentality.

'Well lads will be lads. Exactly that. Once it was happened there was nothing you could do about it. Nothing's forever. You have to move on and that's exactly what we did do really.'

The country, however, simply couldn't. It's almost impossible to overstate the effect the story had on Ireland at the time. Euro 88, Italia 90 and USA 94 had been genuinely nation-unifying events which Ireland had arguably only ever experienced with the visit of the Pope. As such, the majority of the population were gearing themselves up for a long-awaited reprise. Yet Keane's departure traumatically ripped this prospect away. Worse, aside from having to come to terms with this painful new reality, doing so evidently involved choosing one side. Such was the emotion, one column in *The Irish Times* described the whole affair as 'Ireland's Princess Diana'.

If it all seems ludicrously over the top, it's worth considering the news coverage. Pakistan and India were squaring up with nuclear weapons behind their backs, Fianna Fáil were attempting to form a new government, but the only story in town was 'Saipan'. RTÉ had more callers on that Thursday, 23 May 2002, than on 11 September 2001 when the World Trade Center was attacked. In the media, the issue became about much more than a simple personality dispute and the affairs of 24 men in a room in the Pacific. It became about professionalism, the direction of Celtic Tiger Ireland. As with the contrasting euphoria of Italia 90, it seems most of the players never quite grasped this. Even now.

'I think the fact that we were as far away as Japan meant we weren't exposed to the media side of it,' Holland explains. 'We were very sheltered from it and I think that was probably best. We just didn't know what was going on back home.'

Quinn, however, had an inkling. And, once Connolly came to him after speaking to mutual agent Kennedy, he realised how the story had become much bigger than a battle of wills. First, though, he had to go about convincing the squad – most pressingly, Keane's fellow midfielders. In Quinn's book he states, 'Mattie Holland is a gentleman, always quiet and dignified. He's been very upset with Roy and with how he could allow himself not just to miss the World Cup but to cause everyone else the problems that he had. Mattie is a modern professional and he's found Roy's behaviour hard to accept.'

Perhaps that was down to Holland's humble start to the game. Living in Ipswich now, he has many interactions with the club's manager, Keane. Their children even go to the same school. His opinions today aren't necessarily what they were in that emotional week. What he will offer though is an interesting insight into how professionals think even at such moments.

'I was asked a few months ago how I felt when Roy left the squad. And I'm sitting there thinking what do I say? But, the thing is, it means I'm playing. Mick was very loyal. I had been playing alongside Roy and probably felt I deserved to start but, then again, it would have been quite easy for Mick to turn around and say, "Mark Kinsella, you're playing. Sorry Matt." So even though I had been playing you still don't think there's a guarantee with the way it had gone. But then Roy, unfortunately with what had happened, did give me a better chance of playing.'

To his credit, Holland was won around by Quinn. So were most of the squad. All sorts of individuals – from the Taoiseach to JP McManus – began to get involved in a frenzied few days to get Keane back. McCarthy started to yield to the enormity of it all. There was a feeling an agreement was close. On Monday 27 May, Keane was due to be interviewed by Tommy O'Gorman on RTÉ. No-one had organised a feed to the players though. Many of them were on the phone home, the receivers put close to the TV sets.

Keane comes close to tears. He doesn't come close to an apology. And, in the transcript of the interview as opposed to the live images, the sense of contrition is far from obvious. McCarthy sees the words but only feels anger. He all but tells the players 'it's Roy or me'. With that, Quinn convenes the squad again. They're in a hugely difficult position. Hedging their bets, they realise the best they can get out of the situation is to back Mick and play as well they can. A statement is drafted to that effect. The PR man, Brendan McKenna, reads from it before McCarthy's daily media work, making it look as if the players have killed any hope. They apparently haven't though. There's still wriggle room. Thirty-six hours of mixed messages follow. Finally, Keane sends an unambiguous one. It's over.

Ireland's World Cup, however, hasn't even started. They have five days to get their minds in order for the opening game against Cameroon. Arriving at the Niigata Stadium, at the least, jolted them back into World Cup mode. The players' eyes widened at the huge dressing rooms, lit up at simple pleasures like the accreditation badge and moistened when they finally got to see the number of fans who had travelled. This was what the World Cup was all about. Maybe the last two weeks had only been a nightmare. Except for the fact the jerseys were lined up one to five then seven to 23.

Holland himself was doing a lot of talking, Kiely a lot of roaring. Someone had written 'No regrets' on the blackboard. In the huddle beforehand, the new captain, Staunton, repeated it. 'Don't be shy. Express yourselves. Don't anybody hide out there. Remember, no regrets!'

By half-time, however, Ireland had plenty. Patrick Mboma had given Cameroon a deserved lead after they caroused through a beaten-looking Irish backline time and again.

'It was a slow start,' admits Holland. 'Whether it was the occasion, the heat . . . whatever. You can mention as many things as you like. We didn't play well. We came in at half-time and Mick says, "Look at that, no regrets" because we'd probably had a few. And the players thought "let's do something about it".

McAteer does first. He admits he was never fit enough to start but, before McCarthy can explode, Finnan is brought on with Kelly pushed forward. Ireland suddenly have more energy. It creates a great opportunity for Kilbane. He squanders it.. Geremi then does the same. The latter could have killed Ireland. Instead, it completes the turnaround. Given's goal-kick finds Kilbane. He crosses . . . Holland is loitering.

'It was a poor clearance from the defender really and, as it's coming out, I'm just thinking "hit it" really. I've caught it well and it's got a chance.'

Exorcism. Holland's shot slices through the air and into the net, he wheels off arm raised.

'The whole thing takes over, the emotion of it all. For example, I could have planned a celebration. There's no way I would have done it because I wouldn't have remembered. But I knew, when I scored, it was the end where my family were and, for some reason, I went to see them. But for three, four seconds or whatever you lose yourself and all that went through my head was "I've scored at a World Cup". Then my family. Then, once you've calmed down, "we're back in it, now we can win this game".'

Victory for Ireland certainly looked the only likely outcome at that point. Where Cameroon's physical presence initially made them seem awesome, they now only looked awkward. Ireland were snapping into tackles and hungry for the ball. Duff's runs fitted a confident, freewheeling style.

'There's no rhyme or reason to it. I can't sit here and say why but we did step it up a gear in the second half. They were a big team, they were physical. I came up against Marc-Vivien Foe in midfield who is sadly no longer with us. I remember making one big challenge on him in the first half. I did get his shirt as we came off the field. Again, you don't think that a few months later it's going to mean so much.'

The spirit McCarthy had spent six years distilling paid off with an unlikely point. There was no doubt Ireland were a lesser side without Keane but, far from the whole affair exhausting them, all the emotion seemed to energise the team. Holland reversed a refrain heard at the very start of the campaign. 'It felt like a good result. Not a victory.' *The Observer* even carried the headline 'Roy who?' The fans might have wondered about the outcome had Keane been there. The players didn't.

'Didn't even think about it. I think everyone was like that. All I thought was it was a draw against Cameroon. Germany up next.' In perhaps a sign of how much tension had been lifted, the players could only laugh giddily when they heard the Germans had slaughtered Saudi Arabia 8–0.

The 1–1 draw Ireland managed in the second game, by contrast, did feel like a victory. All the more so because it felt like it would never come.

The confidence that had spread through the team like wildfire in the second half against Cameroon stayed burning. What's more, the team bond had only been deepened by the dinner held to celebrate Staunton's 100th cap. Ireland were having the better of the game . . . but still something wasn't quite right. After 19 minutes, Miroslav Klose slipped away from an off-form Ian Harte to head home.

Ireland had belatedly realised Germany didn't deserve the respect given them – but couldn't prove it. As the clock ticked into stoppage time, many players felt that was it. Not just for the game but for the group. A defeat in the second game meant that, the way it was arranged, Cameroon and Germany would surely draw the last match to go through.

'Yeah, we were thinking that. We'd done everything but score. Then you're thinking maybe it's not going to happen. We had chances. But their goalkeeper was superb. We just tried to keep believing.'

It would pay off. In the 93rd minute, substitute Cunningham launched one last ball forward. It could have gone anywhere. It went to Quinn's head. He flicked on. Keane 'did something special'.

'That felt like a win! We were so close to losing, it was against the favourites for the group. That was special. As if we won the tournament.'

When the players got back to their hotel, they were applauded into the lobby. They then did the same for McCarthy. And, afterwards, all drank into the night. It was a welcome reprieve from the routine.

'Yeah, that's the hardest part really. Luckily we were able to see our families then. Otherwise you're just watching DVDs, reading. Some of the boys are playing computer games. We went to the Japanese Disneyland. The one good thing was that we were able to go out shopping without being totally mobbed because we weren't that well known. But it'd only be for half an hour. And that's it. I've been to so many places around the world with football but not really seen any of them because you spend so much time in hotels.'

So much time too, to think about what was next. Saudi Arabia should have been the perfect game to prepare for. Ireland knew a 2–0 win would ensure qualification. But, in six days, an anxiety appeared to afflict the squad. Not even Robbie Keane's early goal to make it 1–0 could ease it.

'There was a strange feeling. I guess over the years we had probably produced our best results as underdogs but this was a game we were expected to win. It took a while to settle down. I remember against Andorra it was the same until Ian Harte scored a penalty. But we had to get a number of goals here and the longer it goes, you're thinking, "Is it ever going to come?"'

The players thought 1–0 wasn't going to be enough and let that be known a little too loudly. Everyone was shouting. McCarthy decided to change things, bringing off Harte, sticking Kilbane left-back and Duff left-wing. It gave the side a little extra ingenuity allowing Breen to poke home the second goal and Duff to finish the job to make it a comfortable 3-0.

Ireland had done the minimum expected. But the maximum dreamed of was suddenly possible. By this stage the mighty France, Argentina and Portugal were out and on their way home. A team as mediocre as Senegal were already through to the quarter-finals. Just a pity, perhaps, Ireland were playing a very competent Spanish team in the last 16.

'They were a good side, no question, and tough to play against. But they weren't the best in the world at that moment. Like a lot of big sides we played against, once you put them under pressure, they're beatable.'

Also like a lot of big sides playing against Ireland at that time, they took the lead. Fernando Morientes ghosted past Breen to nod home. Again though, chasing the game lent an epic nature to Ireland's performance. Robbie Keane and Damien Duff, in particular, began to rampage through the Spanish with stream-of-consciousness runs. Goalkeeper Iker Casillas was keeping Spain in the game. Never more so than when Duff was felled for Harte to hit the resulting penalty straight at Casillas. Ireland weren't affected though.

'Damien Duff was outstanding against Spain. It was another one of those games. You're thinking "It's never going to happen for us." But . . . 94 minutes, whatever it might be, everyone kept going. Everyone had a go. And it happened.'

Fernando Hierro lifted Quinn's shirt almost over his head in the sort of flagrant offence defenders usually get away with. Not this time. Anders Frisk pointed to the spot.

'At the time I thought it was soft. I mean he'd already given one penalty so to give a second was a very brave decision. But, after you see it, it is a penalty.'

Robbie Keane showed further courage and a cool head to slot home. He'd have to do so again. Despite injury reducing Spain to 10 men, neither McCarthy nor the Irish players noticed. By the end of extra-time, the Spanish team carried the expressions of men who knew they'd escaped. And it showed in the shoot-out. Keane's successful first was matched by Hierro. Then Holland put his hand up.

'Mick basically just asked, "Who wants one?" We didn't have an order. A lot can happen in games. Ian Harte taking a penalty, then he's off the pitch. So you can pick five names beforehand but that might change. It's a case of getting the game out of the way to decide. And if you want one, have one. I felt I played well in the tournament, confident. I'd made my mind up. And people say do that. I thought "smash it". Struck it well enough . . . but just a little too much and it's hit the bar.

'It turned out the lowest point of my career. I think, of all the penalties I took, that was the only one I missed. People put a consoling arm around your shoulder but it doesn't help. You have your family there, the fans. You just feel like you've let people down. People say you haven't and that's great . . . but you still feel it.'

He wasn't the only one to miss a penalty though. Both Connolly and Kilbane also did for Ireland while Juanfran and Juan Carlos Valeron failed for Spain. Just five out of 10 penalties were scored. Crucially, the fifth Spanish penalty was rolled in by Gaizka Mendieta. Ireland were out.

Since a miss was as common as a hit in that penalty shoot-out, surely it was some consolation for Holland. His penalty wasn't a Daniel Timofte or a Gareth Southgate. It wasn't the key miss.

'Well unfortunately I didn't get a pizza advert out of it! But I know what you mean. It doesn't make you feel any better. It was still a nightmare moment and unfortunately I have to live with it. And I remember, once we got home, I sat down . . . and the first thing that's on is the penalty shoot-out. It's not something I want to revisit too many times. I've seen the goal a lot more!'

Another argument arose in the aftermath of Ireland's exit that, whatever about Roy Keane's manner of debate, the manner of defeat only proved his point. The tournament had been a success, as author Conor O'Callaghan put it, in a very predictable kind of way. Indeed, once you looked past all the details, all Irish expectations averaged out. The team got to the last 16 and three of their four games were 1–1 draws – in matches they could have won. Losing a shoot-out, however, seemed to validate Keane's mantra – 'fail to prepare, prepare to fail'. As 28 years of Germans unfailingly hitting the net has underlined, penalty shoot-outs are effectively the only thing in football you can thoroughly prepare for. Physically, there's an area of the goal the keeper can't reach unless he stands in the corner. Like golfers, you can train to hit it.

'But how many times do you see golfers missing going down the last at a major?' Holland counters. 'I'm not saying it was pressure or anything like that because I felt confident and made my mind up. There's the crowd. I missed. You can't – as much as you practise, practise, practise – prepare for that moment.'

Although it should have been long over, another element was added to the

Saipan affair by the idiosyncrasies of an odd tournament. What if? The USA were in the quarter-finals, Turkey and Korea in the semi-finals. Had Ireland topped the group, the route to the final would have been Paraguay, USA and Korea. In the end they were the only side to claim either a point or goal against Germany other than the eventual winners, Brazil. What if, indeed.

'No doubt about that. Occasionally I do still think about it. It comes back into my mind. Definitely. But the reception we did get was phenomenal. Something I'll never forget. It helps but, I don't know . . . it's still hard to say how you feel about it all.'

Saipan, seemingly, would have a delayed effect too. The tank of emotion that drove the players through the tournament would empty. They lost the opening two games of the Euro 2004 campaign to Russia and Switzerland with listless displays. The second was to the soundtrack of 'Keano, Keano, Keano!' at Lansdowne Road. As his manager McCarthy stood motionless on the sideline, it was hard for Holland to hear.

'I don't know what went wrong. After beating Finland with a lot of new players it looked like it was going to last. But it didn't. You can only go on performances and that's the nature of football. And, yeah, that night wasn't great. Obviously Mick paid the price with the job. It's difficult. Perhaps we came back with a hangover."

It lasted a few years. Holland eventually retired after another deflating match with Switzerland, Brian Kerr's last as manager as a 0–0 draw eliminated Ireland from the 2006 World Cup qualifiers. By then Holland was at Charlton Athletic, where he was again named captain. His whole-hearted attitude and desire to play every match always earned him a lot of respect. But also a lot of pain.

'When I wake up there's sometimes sore knees, ankle, feet. I played with a lot of injuries when I probably shouldn't have. That just comes from the desire to play football and the way I was built really. I wouldn't have it any other way. I wasn't the most talented payer to walk the earth but I think it's fair to say I made the best of my ability and I don't have any regrets over my career, I don't think.'

He can't say the same about his first spell as a presenter though. By his late twenties he was already experienced as an actual pundit so, when an opening came to front the BBC's regional Late Kick Off show, he was a left-field choice.

'The first couple of weeks I looked very nervous and certainly was. There was a little bit of pressure as it was out of my comfort zone and on the other side of the soda. I was like a rabbit in the headlights. You've got to listen to someone speaking to you in an earpiece and also try to talk to someone else at the same time. I struggle to explain to people how difficult it is. But I think the more I've done it, the more I've got used to it and enjoyed it. It may go further, it may not.'

Holland, at least, has a lot of options. Particularly in the media. Was that down to his late start in the game?

'Not necessarily. I guess football is a very short career. You never know what's around the corner. I've not ruled out coaching for instance. I've started doing my badges. So I guess the key thing was trying to keep as many doors as possible and see which one opened first and see what happens really.'

He certainly doesn't seem the type to be happy sitting around until the next outing on the golf course.

'Oh I would be happy, don't get me wrong! But no, I enjoy going to games, I enjoy working. I couldn't sit down and do nothing.'

What else would you expect of a player who managed to play over 230 matches consecutively?

Must be something in the water.

10

Richie Sadlier

How the other half live

ichie Sadlier is agonising over a decision. Not whether to try to add a
few more precious years to his career with yet another hip operation.
Not whether to finally admit that his career is over. It's much more
mundane. But, at the time, it feels like the world is weighing on his shoulders.
Well, the World Cup is.

It's three months since Ireland have qualified for the 2002 tournament and
three months before they'll set off for Saipan. But, for the squad tonight, it's
party time. February's warm-up against Russia is the first occasion they've
managed to get everyone together since qualifying in the alcohol-free territory
that is Tehran. So they'll be making up for lost time. It's also, however, Sadlier's
first senior call-up and in the morning he'll have his first international training
session.

'I'd never go drinking the night before training. Neither would Colin Healy
and he was the new boy as well. I was in the room with Colin wondering, "What
do we do here?" If it was Millwall I wouldn't even consider going out but
everyone's going and I'd be more comfortable in training having been out on the

piss with some lads rather than meeting them for the first time.'

So in the end he goes. The squad head to Café en Seine. It's a free and easygoing night. Except, Sadlier remembers, for one particularly stern conversation.

'Stan [Steve Staunton] spent a good 20 minutes saying to me. "A lot will happen here with the squad. Just keep it in-house."'

The words would stick. But probably not in the manner Staunton intended. Sadlier got on to play the following Wednesday as Ireland beat Russia 2–0. A career-ending hip injury ensured they were the only 18 minutes of his international football career. And they came in the penultimate year of a mere eight seasons in the professional game. But, from the stories he's willing to tell and honest manner in which he speaks, it may as well be multiples of that.

Sadlier, now 31 and making an appropriate living given his openness as a pundit, isn't just different from many ex-footballers because he's perceptive and self-reflective, he's also different because, going against the advice Staunton gave him, he's willing to break the *omertà* of the dressing room. To give the fans who pay so much a proper insight into what it is they are really supporting.

Some could mistakenly put that down to bitterness. When he did the *Sunday Independent* interview with Clive Clarke in January 2008 that revealed Roy Keane's management consisted of 'going around booting chairs', the then Sunderland boss rang to call Sadlier a 'spiteful cunt'. Quite the opposite. Sadlier excuses that as an angry rant from Keane and, in any case, is generally on the same side as him. The only thing he's bitter about is the hypocrisy of football. He absolutely loves the sport but deplores some of what it's become and what it can do to people.

'I hate the bullshit. Like, some of what you saw on the inside then heard on the outside, it was total bollocks. Fantastic bollocks. Nothing in any way linked to the truth. My impression was that there's so little of the full story ever out there you take it with a pinch of salt.

'Nothing would surprise me. Like, the industry from top to bottom is poison in some ways.'

Sadlier hints at an unhealthy – and sometimes underhanded – obsession with money in a sport already swimming in it. There are accounts of Premier League managers pulling departing players aside to tell them they're due an unofficial cut of the signing-on fee for easing their exit.

Indeed, the explosion of money in football between Ireland's two World Cup qualifications of 1994 and 2002 irrevocably altered the sport. In almost every sense, it made the working-class game the higher classes' pastime. Most of Sadlier's more unsavoury anecdotes come back to cash in some way. Or at least how its influence caused them.

For the majority of the time, Sadlier is good-humoured and relaxed. He even catches himself at one stage and admits, 'Jesus, I'm very ranty today.' And, in the middle of another distasteful tale, he does insist, 'Once you've a ball, cones and teammates, all the bullshit is gone.'

But, while that level of money is there, the stench never really goes away. Sadlier initially noticed it as a mere 20-year-old in his first really big game for Millwall, the 1999 Auto Windscreens Shield final against Wigan.

'It can cause huge friction. The way that bonus structure was agreed at the start of the season, it would be divided between the 14 players for the final. Lucas Neill was one who played in every game but was then injured for the final. So, a month before it took place, the manager said, "Lads, what way do you wanna do it? At the start of the season you signed it this way whereas the likes of Lucas aren't going to get a penny. So you can sign something else." At the start of the season you'll sign anything because you don't think you'll get to finals. In the end we stuck to the original agreement, the 14 on the day, but we had to do a secret ballot because the younger lads didn't want to vote against the senior players. The figure was six or seven grand which to all the younger lads was huge. But I don't think we won a game from the semi-final to the final because the morale had been shot to bits. Bonus discussions split the dressing room.'

They lost that final too, 1–0. The split didn't widen but would be an ominous sign of things to come. In the meantime, it would take the arrival of Mark McGhee as manager in September 2000 to bond the team together again.

And his old-fashioned values allied to a modern approach restored confidence, but also humility. A young team grew up in the right way and won the Second Division, England's current third tier, in 2001.

'We had a load of lads of a similar age, similar outlook. Seven of the team that won the league that year had come through the academy. No-one had agents, no-one had big cars. Just all relatively decent lads out for a bit of craic. And Ray Harford, who's since died, took training. I remember reading about Ray in *Shoot* as a kid. He was assistant to Kenny Dalglish when Blackburn won the league. Just working with him, like – every morning we used to get up to go to training, it'd be a sunny day, you'd turn the bend and the training ground would open up and you'd get a buzz.'

It would last for a few years. With young players like Tim Cahill, Steven Reid, Neill and Sadlier himself honing their undoubted talent over the next few years, Millwall would come tantalisingly close to the top level. In 2002 they were a game from the Premier League as they lost the play-off semi-final to Steve Bruce's Birmingham. In 2004 they were a game from glory as they lost the FA Cup final 3–0 to Manchester United. Even though the club was only on the verge of the big time, however, Sadlier could see they were already behaving as if they'd reached it.

'It's astonishing what football does. When you're going to the local pub you're going to be a big deal because people there support the team and there'd be girls just throwing themselves at you. The social life is different because, every nightclub you go to, you don't queue to get in. You'll know the bouncer or get your agent to ring ahead because the notion of queuing just doesn't compute . . . you get hassled by mere mortals. And then there's usually a roped-off area inside; the club will give you free drinks because they know the more players from the local team are there, the more people will come.

'I remember we went to the local clothes shop and we always got discounts. It always kind of struck me, not that we were millionaires or anything, if you're going to give out discounts give them to students. These are lads who are all on X amount a week but, again, because you're footballers, people do you favours.

Like I bought a BMW one day and then got injured. The dealer kept ringing me asking, "How're you getting on?" not that he gave a shit about me, just because he wanted me to come back when I was upgrading [the car]. Everyone licks your hole.

'There is a huge amount of hassle that footballers have to put up with – like you're surrounded by people all the time – but also a huge amount of responsibility they don't take on. One of the things that maybe sums up what I'm saying: I needed an agent when I thought I was going to get a move from Millwall so I met about three or four. They all said more or less the same thing. "We've got contacts in the media so if there are any stories embarrassing to you, we can always trade off so, instead of the papers writing about you drink-driving or shagging your brother's wife, we'll get one of our players to do an interview. It'll be swapsies and everyone's a winner." Not one of them said, "You sign with us, we'll look after you but we expect you to act a certain way." It's almost "Do what you want. We're here to protect you." And even at the club the notion was that, if you show up on time and play on Saturday – within reason – boys will be boys. There's no accountability at all.'

Eventually, it all has an effect. The most notorious was the number of infidelity stories that came out about the England squad around the time of the 2010 World Cup, from John Terry to Wayne Rooney.

'It's like the Tiger Woods thing recently. If you put to one side that he's married, all that Tiger Woods was was a bloke that had stunning, stunning women throw themselves at him every minute. No-one ever says "no" to you. So there's a real alpha-male thing. Biggest car, rode the most birds, all this kind of stuff.'

What really annoys Sadlier, however, is – just like with Woods – the deceit. All smiles when in reality it's all sleaze.

'It galls me that all it takes for a player to win over the fans is to kiss the badge. Once you give a statement saying "we were shit yesterday, I apologise to the fans", some supporter in a pub will read that and think "this fella cares" regardless of the fact he's spent his entire week in the dressing room going, "Fuck it, 20 grand a week for this shit, this is brilliant. Whether we go up or not – it doesn't matter, it's still 20 grand a week for the next year. And if they want me to go they can pay my contract." That's how players talk and no-one says that publicly. Why would you? There's nothing to be gained while you're in the dressing room. You come out with all these media-trained phrases and it's very easy to come across as someone you're not. That's football. It's bullshit.'

It's one of the reasons why, as a columnist now for the *Sunday Independent*, Sadlier rarely goes to press conferences.

'I find them the biggest waste of time because a manager or player, winning or losing – with the exception of a couple – will come out and you can script it. "Wee bit disappointed, thought we did well."

'Like, we'll sit here in the pub saying, "Jaysus, Bellamy is a mouth or Robbie Savage is a mouth, all these people are outspoken", when all they're doing is telling the truth. That's what I love about [Roy] Keane. He'll come out and call it as he sees it.

'It's probably the clever thing to do – to be boring, to be a politician, swerve every question. But it took balls for Keane to come out and say about Manchester United fans in 2001 that "these people that boo us, they haven't a fucking clue". And that prawn sandwich thing which became famous, but it's true. I've been in loads of dressing rooms where, beforehand, we've said, "If we're not 1–0 up after 20 minutes, these cunts are going to turn on us. They haven't a clue so just stick together regardless." That was the genuine belief within the dressing room regarding the crowd. But if we went out and we won, we'd be "well done crowd, we're all together, one big family". The team just slagged everyone, fans, teammates, managers . . .'

Sadlier was struck by a different disregard for the truth during Staunton's mostly dismal tenure as Irish manager over 2006 and 2007: the manner in which players must toe the line. Criticism scaled new heights with every poor display but the squad had to just keep insisting it was the team's progress that was going up.

'I think the decision to appoint Staunton was beginning to look a big mistake very early in his reign. Despite this, players came out in praise of him, and Staunton himself stuck to the line that things were heading in the right direction. Clearly, that was not the case at all. What else could they say I suppose? Either way, I think the public got very turned off by the whole mess. It's a shame that someone so respected by the public as a player will forever be remembered as a disastrous manager.'

Particularly disastrous were the 4–0 home defeat to the Netherlands, the 5–2 thrashing in Cyprus of all places, and an injury-time winner that spared a draw in San Marino. Boos rang out around Croke Park the night of Staunton's final match, a dire 1–1 draw against Cyprus in October 2007. The team's stock hadn't been so low in a decade, arguably two. But then neither had the players'. Something seemed to happen after Saipan, a souring of the relationship between the supporters and the players.

'I think if you look back over that time, a few things happened alongside it. The rugby lads excelled themselves. Off the pitch too. Footballers were the opposite. The notion that interviews are done begrudgingly came across straight away. Diving, that puts people off. All these factors. And then people were interested in the excesses of their lifestyles. The performances were poor while the earnings were getting bigger all the time.'

Which is essentially the crux of the matter. Although the fan-player relationship seemed to heal to some degree by the shared pain of Paris and Thierry Henry's handball in November 2009, there is that economic detachment. Unlike the Charlton era and even into McCarthy's era when players could genuinely be described as working-class heroes, it's now a lot harder for a supporter who's just paid over €300 to bring his family to a match to relate to multi-millionaires. Especially when those multi-millionaires are underperforming. And especially when those multi-millionaires are complaining about their wages. Ashley Cole is, of course, English not Irish, but the comments in his autobiography about contract negotiations in 2006 appeared to encapsulate the worst excesses of a generation of footballers. Cole was then on £30,000 a week at Arsenal but felt he deserved at least £60,000. One afternoon, his agent phoned to tell him the bad news: the club's chief executive David Dein was only going to £55,000. 'I nearly swerved off the road,' Cole fumed. '"He is taking the piss, Jonathon!" I yelled down the phone. I was trembling with anger.'

For the average person who earns half that in a year let alone a week, it's an impossible mentality to understand. What about for an ex-player who got a taste of it like Sadlier?

'I remember speaking to two older pros and we were talking about club owners as well as a recent transfer, like Ashley Cole. And I remember saying, "Lads, owners are obviously loaded and you've a few quid yourselves. Does it matter, the difference between, say, 55 grand a week and 60? Surely you've gone beyond the point at which you can spend?

'They rubbished my question straight away. "There's a reason owners have the money they have because, every penny, they'll shit on whoever's next to get it." I found that principle hard to get. "But from a dressing room point of view?" I asked. And they go, "Of course it does. If you're better than the bloke next to you, why should he earn more?"

That question would be taken to extremes in Millwall's dressing room during the summer of 2002 though, making the mayhem over the Auto Windscreens Shield final bonus seem mild. That close-season, the football league's broadcaster ITV Digital went bust, leaving a lot of teams – and players – out of pocket.

'We had got promoted the season before so we were all told we were deserving of new deals. Three or four were sorted out, then it was whoever was next in. But then the rest of us didn't get sorted because the chairman Theo Paphitis said, "Lads, the Digital deal's gone bust, we don't have £10m over three years like we thought." So the dressing room was in twitters between lads who had been sorted and lads who hadn't, like the haves and have-nots. That fucking ruined the thing as well. We had all been of a same age, no big car, no egos . . . that was gone. It'd come full circle. There were constant discussions. "Timmy's probably on six grand a week and he's on whatever." If that's not managed properly you can forget it.'

On a much more farcical level, Sadlier cites a Championship match against one continental international who had played in the Premier League and Euro 96.

'He was on 22 grand a week or something. And he was shit. Didn't care. We ran him ragged. And at the end, we'd put four or five past him or something, he's there smiling! He'd just stopped short of telling us what he was doing that Saturday night. Loads of money was floating around and it just got daft.'

It also got deep.

'If you go to watch a 13- or 14-year-old team train you ask, "Why do you want to become a footballer?" "To be fucking loaded." It comes hand in hand. And I remember there was always this thing at Millwall, as soon as you signed your first contract, they kept telling you, "It's a stepping stone; don't think you've made it, keep thinking of the reason you started." And it's because you maybe wanted to play at Wembley or win an FA Cup. "Don't dilute your dreams down to just getting paid." Any old eejit can do that to a certain extent. But, of course, there's a load of lads who aren't playing regularly and it doesn't bother them. They're honouring their contract, they're showing up every day for training. They're not getting a game but, in their eyes, that's not their fault."

As Sadlier intimated earlier, it takes very good management to make players forget all the perks and keep them focused on the most important thing in football: the glory of the game. Adapting to that change in atmosphere and economics is probably Alex Ferguson's greatest achievement. He started winning trophies in 1977 and was still doing so in 2010. In the build-up to the World Cup 2010 in South Africa there was an anecdote doing the rounds concerning the opinions of one former English international when he visited his old national side. The United players there who had come up under Ferguson had a humility and drive about them, the Chelsea players a brashness and arrogance.

'I heard that. And I remember reading a piece by Gary Neville saying a mantra that was drilled into them at United was "you never make it as a footballer, you're always trying to be better". If you're at one of these clubs like Chelsea, they've had five managers since Jose Mourinho left so whose values are in the dressing room? I remember when they got beaten by Inter Milan in the Champions League [in the 2009–10 season], all the papers said, "Ancelotti's gone, the players have lost confidence in him". And I was going, "Is anyone making the players accountable?" I suppose United and Arsenal are the exceptions. They have managers who are unsackable. Otherwise players go, "I'll be here longer than you, mate. My contract's three years, you can be gone in the morning." If it doesn't come naturally to you, it's hard to keep that level of decency.'

Which brings us to the key question: how difficult is it, in that kind of atmosphere, for a top-level player to stay grounded at all?

'Well there are many exceptions – and a lot of them Irish lads. Maybe I'm overly painting a picture that they're all gougers but you have to appreciate that they're living in an industry where if you have an ounce of potential to become one [a gouger] you will.'

Sadlier, for his part, certainly didn't. Indeed his humility makes him insist he was surprised to even get far enough to see the 'gougers'. He thought he was awful on his first trial at Millwall having gone over from Belvedere. But he obviously impressed enough to actually turn down their first offer in order to complete his Leaving Cert. Sadlier eventually joined the club in August 1996 and within seven months had made his debut. It was then he went through enough to fill a full career, let alone four weeks.

'Initially, the team were losing every week and had to do something. Often they did the easiest thing which is look to the youth team for lads who have no fear, haven't been listening to the crowd who have been giving them shit for months. I was one of the ones put in and, the following week, the manager [Jimmy Nicholl] was sacked, 22 members of staff were let go and the club was put into administration. We were all brought in by the administrators and told we were going to have to take a pay-cut. It only ended up 16 quid a week for me so it didn't really matter a shit but there was all sorts in the dressing room. Even the day of my debut there was crowd trouble, a demonstration. We were told to stay in the ground and not to leave because it wouldn't be safe for us to get from the reception door to our car. It's not like some of the bigger clubs where it's all private. It was little more than a public car park surrounded by a gate. And this is all in the first month of my football experience, a month after my 18th birthday. I had nothing to compare it to and thought it was just brilliant. I didn't know what it should have been like. We lost on my debut but that's almost incidental to the story.'

Sadlier would, however, soon feel the wrath of the crowd himself.

'At the start it was hard because they hated me and I was shit. I was 18 and playing with no confidence in a team that was losing every week. Hopeless balls were going to my head and I was just being bullied out of it. I was the boo-boy for a good 18 months to two years. We'd be in a social setting . . . and three out of every four fellas who walk in are Millwall fans. You're there with your girlfriend, or your parents or your mates and they're there, "That's Sadlier isn't it? You're shit. You're fucking shit." And you can't give it back verbally or physically – not that you would because they're all bigger and you're 18 – because you'll get a thumping or you'll lose because you'll get a fine or whatever. That became demoralising because, unlike getting it on a pitch, you can't just run to the centre-circle and drown them out. So when it's bad it's hard. But when it's good it is brilliant.'

'Again, I didn't have six years in the Ajax academy to compare it to. I just thought, "This is league football, this is Millwall." Like, it's the most macho, blokey environment I've ever been in. That kind of changed over the years. Like when Mark McGhee took over. He was the opposite. Fitness coaches, sports scientists, dieticians and very, very good at dealing with people, managing egos. That was probably the best spell of my time at Millwall.

'Even the team that got to the FA Cup final, McGhee had gone by October of that season, but it was his team. They were good lads as well. We had a decent set-up. I can't imagine a team being successful if they all hate each other. I just think you do need a lot of lads who think a lot about each other and, for a couple of years, as a group it was class. We socialised together, we stayed back chatting crap in the canteen for ages. It was all just good craic. No-one had real notions about themselves.'

There were also some right characters. Not least the man who took over from McGhee, Dennis Wise.

'Wise was brilliant. He is what you think he is but there's a very decent, likeable side to him. We'd be out on nights out and he'd get the youngest lad there, only on 100 quid a week, give him 200 quid. "Your bird is there, get her a nice bottle of something, bring her out for something to eat." Not in a room where everyone can see it, just when it's you and him. A decent fella but well able to get himself into trouble as well.

'It was some dressing room. One of the lads, senior pro who'd played in the Premier League, would come in before every game, take his top off, go into the toilet, vomit and then come out shadow-boxing and shouting "feed the bear". When you see that for the first time you're there wondering, "What the fuck is wrong with him?" "Nah, that's what he does." Just his way of dealing with nerves or whatever.

Such personalities, however, helped Millwall pick up momentum and Sadlier to eventually win around the fans. Finally on the other side of the Den's infamous aggression too, he began to relish it.

'That song "no-one likes us we don't care", being at the heart of it was brilliant. No-one wants us to get promoted, police don't want us to get near Wembley for the play-offs . . . there's this real conspiracy thing and, whether you believe it or not, once you buy into it, it becomes great to be a part of.'

Such was Sadlier's form in the Championship that he attracted interest from Sunderland in the Premier League and, of course, his country. In February he was called up to a squad preparing for the 2002 World Cup and there was a genuine feeling he could stay around long enough for a place on the plane. Sadlier just felt like a gate-crasher though.

'Oh yeah, totally. When we went out I had no right to sit down there and be high-fiving. But there were all these discussions then about logistics. Were we going to go with sponsors' cars or someone else, who was going to make the decisions, who does personal appearances? We were all handed sheets asking how many of your family want to go, how many tickets would you want. I found all that interesting, the behind-the-scenes stuff. Never gets spoken about it. But

I remember [Niall] Quinn was handing them out and I go, "There's not really any point in me filling them out." I was embarrassed. He goes, "Shut up you fucking eejit. If my back goes which could happen any day, you're going instead of me." Sure, whatever!

'I don't know how other people deal with their debut. There's the whole thing of "will I be good enough?" but then there's this other element I get which is "will I get on with them? Will I fit in?" Because you just hear about this legendary Irish team spirit. will I fit into that? It's gas. You don't get to levels where you're discussing marital issues or kids or which mortgage to go for. It's just surface stuff, banter about what you do in training, swap anecdotes about nights on the piss. Beyond that you're just talking as lads because you kind of know within a year you mightn't ever work with these lads again.'

Sadlier, unfortunately, didn't. Just three weeks after his Irish debut, he incurred the injury that would eventually end his career. Blocking a shot at Barnsley, he suddenly felt a pain shoot up his hip. Initially, he played through it. But it gradually became more and more difficult to the point he missed Millwall's play-off surge and any chance of making the World Cup. Immediately after Ireland's elimination to Spain a few months later, Niall Quinn name-checked Sadlier as one for the future. Did that deepen the dismay?

'No. I knew the World Cup was possible but I never felt it was mine to lose. Whereas I felt a real part of the team at Millwall and that I'd earned that. It might sound odd but not getting promoted with Millwall that year was much more disappointing than not going to the World Cup because of that.'

Sadlier, however, had already enjoyed a taste of that kind of tournament. In 1999 – just before the Auto Windscreens Shield final – he was called up to Brian Kerr's Irish squad for the under-20 World Cup in Nigeria. The same competition in 1997 had seen the Republic of Ireland side reach the semi-finals. It also provided Irish soccer fans with much-needed solace while launching Damien Duff into the national consciousness too. He was the only member of the 1997 under-20 squad to eventually win a full international cap.

By contrast, the 1999 tournament would feature Duff again, Robbie Keane,

Stephen McPhail, Colin Healy, Gary Doherty and, of course, Sadlier himself. The team may not have excelled to the same extent, only reaching the last 16, but for Sadlier that under-20 World Cup in Nigeria remains an unforgettable experience.

'It was just amazing. I remember when I came home people asking what it was like, all football, football. But football is only a fraction of my memory. The whole thing was remarkable, something you'd never experience again.

'There were security fears, health fears. We'd an armed guard at the end of our corridor. A fella stood there all day with a gun, just outside our room in case someone came up. They came with us to and from the training ground and we couldn't leave the hotel. Then downstairs was full of brazzers.

'We were told not to drink the water and we were asking, "Does that mean we can brush our teeth from the sink?" But then we were playing South Korea in a warm-up and we were scorched. Someone had forgotten the water bottles so all these locals came up with water for us but we couldn't drink them because we didn't get them sealed. At training then one night, about 2,000 kids were watching us, all barefoot, every one of them smiling. So we spent a bit of time messing about with them but then, when it came to training, a couple of kids encroached over the line. They couldn't have been more than 12 years old and the guards put them face down on the ground and leathered them, fucking leathered them.

'It was a real eye-opener. There were open gutters by the shops on the main high street, most of which were shut down when the sun went down because they'd no electricity to light them.'

As for the football itself, Ireland lost the opening match to Mexico and a solitary Rafael Marquez goal before beating Saudi Arabia 2–0 and Australia 4–0 with Sadlier himself scoring in the latter. Then it was to the second round and the hosts Nigeria.

'Eurosport were showing it but both ourselves and the Nigeria team warmed up in the shade of the stand. It was even too hot for the Nigerians so you can imagine how we felt. I didn't last the whole 90 minutes and I don't know how the lads kept going in that heat and extra-time. The football went really well even if it was disappointing to lose the way we did. We did very well in the circumstances but it was an amazing, amazing trip.'

It was on the back of such achievements with the underage teams that Brian Kerr eventually succeeded Mick McCarthy in the senior job. He was appointed in February 2003 on a wave of goodwill. Although the Euro 2004 campaign eventually petered out with a home draw against Russia and a bad-tempered 2–0 defeat in Switzerland, those results could initially be waved away. Kerr, after all, was not yet a year in the role and had impressively picked up the pieces of the group with away wins against the likes of Georgia to put Ireland in with the possibility of qualification before the defeat in Basle. There were also other reasons for optimism. Kerr had coaxed the prodigal son, Roy Keane, to return in April 2004. The 1–0 win that night against Romania was also one of a number of notable friendly results against the likes of Brazil and Portugal borne from Kerr's sense of organisation. The problem, however, was that friendly-match atmosphere remained with the squad in competitive games. There was no vibrancy about the team when required.

Despite a creditable 0–0 in Paris to open the 2006 World Cup qualifiers, a series of damper draws against the likes of Israel and Switzerland saw the group end exactly as the Euro 2004 campaign did – with a slow puncture. Worse, Ireland finished fourth. Sadlier, who was by then working with Kerr in a different capacity as an agent, subscribes to the view that his particular skills were never quite suited to senior international players.

'Given his success with the youths, it made total sense to give him a shot at the top job. Amazingly, nobody – myself included – appeared bothered that he had never worked with senior professionals up to that point. He was a hugely popular appointment in the eyes of the public. Sad for him that it never worked out, but by the end, he had no supporters left, certainly not within the squad anyway.'

Sadlier's work as an agent was one of a number of jobs he tried as he also attempted to come to terms with the end of his career as a professional. As he admits himself, that took an awful long time. So, however, did the eventual admission that his football career was over. Having initially played through pain, Sadlier went for his first hip operation in April 2002. He was taken aback when the surgeon told him there was a 25% chance he wouldn't make a full recovery. He didn't tell anyone, not even his family, as he was effectively in denial for the next year and a half.

'I was living a lie. I couldn't play snooker, walk the dog, bend down . . . a lot of basic stuff. But then I'd cling to the notion that "Jesus, I was on the exercise bike today for 40 minutes and it didn't hurt – so there must be something there" and I'd ignore six days of fuck-all progress. Mad stuff. But it was an addiction. I was hooked on the idea of playing and so fearful of an existence which didn't involve playing.'

In September 2003, at a mere 24 years of age, those fears were confirmed. But still didn't register. Dealing with Millwall getting to that season's FA Cup final was difficult and it would take a degree in sports science and psychology for Sadlier to finally make sense of things.

'I started exploring the whole thing that it wasn't just my job, wasn't just my hobby, wasn't just my earnings. Football was my entire identity. When you're playing, you'll only be asked about a couple of things at any given time but they're all football related. I was thinking, I'm only known as "Richie, your man who plays football", there was no other way of describing me.'

Having studied psychology, Sadlier is now a complete convert. He feels it should be commonly used in football.

'If you ever watch the reasons a manager attributes to a defeat, the percentage that will be psychological will be huge. It'll be "the disallowed goal early on was still in our heads", "we were looking forward to next week's final" . . . they're all psychological and the same manager will just come out and say psychology is for the birds. That's nonsense. They're giving the spiel against what they believe in.'

Once Sadlier finished his degree he was even invited by a lecturer to work in the field of sports psychology with UK athletes. By then he had already tried coaching and agency work and neither quite clicked.

'I was working with Millwall's academy for a few months and enjoyed that, then as an agent. But I never found that rewarding. You're cold-calling players, sitting them down, giving a sales pitch about what the company can bring. There's a little bit of pandering. Again, you're bullshitting. And you're always one tantrum away from six years work wasted. "I'm going to Johnny down the road because he won't give me this shit, he'll get me into nightclubs."

'I found getting the degree very rewarding because it was something I didn't think I could do. I enjoyed all the NLP stuff, which is neuro-linguistic programming. It's also something I can apply to my daily life, dealing with myself and dealing with others. I mean, some of the athletes we worked with – like me – they all kind of present with sporting issues but three sentences later it's non-sporting. Social stuff, family stuff, behavioural. But then the opportunity came up at Pat's [St Patrick's Athletic] to be CEO. I was 29 and told, "Here, run a club, here's your budget." I thought, "I'll never get this opportunity again." A part of me loves taking on things that people or I myself question whether I can do it. I also loved the idea of being back home among my family.

'But I blanked my family, my mates, my two dogs for the entire duration of the job because it took over really. I threw myself into it. It took over from playing really and, because of the nature of the job, I always felt uncomfortable not answering the phone to volunteers because how can you be too busy if they're offering their time for free? But I like that. I like being flat out.

'We got two European runs. One was the strange situation with Steaua Bucharest when they were ordered to play in front of an empty stadium and that actually turned out a punishment for both teams. But there were a load of little things you don't realise happen. Like the morning of the game you agree on the colour of the kits, the director's lunch. Loads of little things, all very dignified.

'I loved elements of the role. It's frustrating that the vast majority of the country doesn't give a toss about the league, but that's the way it is. I suppose I tried to concentrate on the things that we knew we could work on or influence, and not bother with the stuff that's beyond our control. The levels of interest in the Premiership, the Champions League. All those things won't change. I was around during a time of almost unprecedented levels of bad publicity in how clubs were being run, but it was a great experience. I learned shitloads.'

The one constant in Sadlier's professional life since retiring has been his role as a pundit – adding a bit of perspective to all that publicity around football, whatever the level. There's a reason. He's very passionate about it. It started properly in 2006, when an interview with Dion Fanning in the *Sunday Independent* led to a rare opportunity.

'Dion just asked me would I think of doing a column. And I thought it's no harm in saying things in ways that haven't been said before. Like, as an example, I got Ryan Giggs's autobiography because I thought this fella has been through the most interesting dressing room – Cantona kicking the fan, Keane coming back from Saipan, Beckham and Ferguson . . . but when Beckham got hit in the head by the boot all I wanted from that was "he said this and Ferguson said that". All it was was "Ferguson kicked the boot. Had he tried it 100 times he wouldn't be able to hit the target again." I just thought . . . "I've spent 16 quid on this book, give me something!" It doesn't interest me that everyone gets on great because I know they don't.'

Which brings him back to Staunton's words on his first night with Ireland – a little too literally. A few months after Staunton left the Irish job, he met Sadlier at a function. The only words? 'You're on the other side of the fence now.'

'Again, he had this whole football way of thinking – you're either in the dressing room or, to him, you're on the wrong side.

'But I'm actually interested in that job. I'm getting a real buzz out of doing the punditry. Since I left Pat's this is the first time I've managed to strike a balance between having a life outside of what I get paid to do.

'Yeah, I have a load of physical concerns. I've had three operations and there's a load I can't do. But, when I do nothing I'm very sore and when I do too much I'm really sore. It's awkward. My problem is I can't rotate my hip which you do every time you get a ball or turn left or right. But it's all manageable. I don't go running marathons, just have the occasional kick-around when I can. I physically can't play football to any sort of other level anymore. And even back when I was a kid and something was bothering me I'd go out with a ball and come back from that little journey happy again.

'The enjoyment of playing was always the biggest thing for me. It still is. I remember thinking when I finished I would have longed for a day even when I got sent off or booed off or missed a sitter.

'Getting out there, that bit. There's nothing like it.'

11

After the Final Whistle

The Players

Over the course of researching this book and attempting to contact a number of the 70 ex-internationals who played for Ireland between 1986 and 2002, the following conversation took place.

Author: 'Is this . . . (the company name)?'

Woman: 'No, they've gone bankrupt.'

Author: 'Sorry to hear it. It's just I'm wondering is . . . (the player's name) still contactable through this number?'

Woman: 'Well he's a dickhead.'

Author: 'Right . . . em, it's just I'm a journalist looking to get in touch with him for a book about his days playing for Ireland.'

Woman: 'Well I'm his wife and we're going through a divorce. If you want him, he's probably off with his new girlfriend.'

From all those former Irish players, that individual's company wasn't the only business outside football to fail. And it certainly wasn't the only marriage to fail. That particular exchange is an extreme example but it effectively encapsulates the difficulties many footballers face when their playing days end. The career may be a dream but, for many, the aftermath can be a nightmare. Rates of divorce and bankruptcy are far, far higher for ex-players than almost any other profession. So are physical problems. And even before all that – or, really, directly leading to that – there is the adjustment to the simple but searing fact that you're not a footballer anymore. That you are, in the truest sense of the words, yesterday's hero.

To grasp exactly what it means to be thrown from something of a fantasy world to reality, it is worth recalling Niall Quinn's enlightening lament in his autobiography.

'Football does things to people who live it. Football takes them away from their homes at 15 or 16 years of age, tells them that they are special and they are going to be rich and famous, and then football lets their personalities develop – shut off from the real world. When you are a footballer, you grow up competing, listening to dressing-room humour, being flattered and cursed in equal measure. You grow up in largely male company. Your work is a game. Maybe you don't grow up at all.'

And, maybe, you never quite come to terms with finishing. When ex-footballers are asked what they miss most about the game, the banter of the dressing room is mentioned so many times as to have become a cliché. As with many clichés though, it only sounds like one because it's so true it barely needs repeating. Boys, quite literally, become men in dressing rooms. As Quinn all but states, it's the cement they build their lives with. Then, suddenly, it's stripped away. Almost all of the players interviewed for this book, no matter how well-adjusted, spoke in some hushed manner about the camaraderie of a professional side and all that goes with it. Terry Phelan was particularly poetic.

'I always say to the young lads here [New Zealand] when I'm training, enjoy every little bit of it. Enjoy putting your kit on, lacing your boots, warming up, cooling down, the banter . . . because it doesn't last long.'

Chris Morris echoes Phelan. 'The day-to-day banter and that fun you get at training and working, you're never going to get that again and there is nothing to match it.'

Alan McLoughlin, meanwhile, is even blunter. 'I like my job but it doesn't give you the buzz of getting your kit on, getting out, banter with the lads, being fit.'

Now imagine that daily enjoyment being enhanced by isolated moments like Stuttgart '88, Genoa '90 or New Jersey '94. Most people's lives just don't have those kinds of instantaneous highs. To paraphrase Nick Hornby in *Fever Pitch*, real life doesn't have Ray Houghton moments. But then it doesn't have some of the ensuing lows either. McLoughlin mentioned 'being fit' and that physical cost of a football career, of course, is often cited. Again, almost every player mentioned waking up with pains and aches, of having to go for frequent medical check-ups. Most infamously, Dave Langan has been registered disabled. McLoughlin and Sadlier's stories aren't quite that staggering, but they have found their movement in retirement greatly affected by their exertions as players.

'I'll have a load of long-term concerns,' Sadlier explains. 'I've had three operations on my hip and there's a load I can't do. But I knew it at the time. After I had my first operation they said, "Listen, you can retire now or go for broke and have another operation which may extend your career to your late twenties but the downside is in the long term you'll have trouble." And at the time I was 22 or so, I thought I'll deal with my later life then so I said I'd have the operation. I knew this was coming so it's manageable. But when I do nothing I'm very sore, when I do too much I'm really sore. It's awkward.'

McLoughlin hasn't just had operations but a hip replaced.

'And that's at 40. And the one thing that depresses me now is I'm not fit. Where you had the nice toned body, now it's starting to droop a little. You think you're the person you were 20 years ago but time and age have caught up. It's difficult.'

The key word there? 'Think'. Because, as with so much else, the true toll isn't physical but mental.

'When I finished football it was shocking,' McLoughlin stresses. 'There's a real knock-on effect. You're used to getting up every day, testing yourself training, camaraderie with the lads. But you're not there. You're at home. Things get tense there because of the mindset you're in, as you can imagine.'

It's for that very reason above all else, both McLoughlin and Sadlier believe, that so many marriages fail. Of the nine players interviewed for this book who have been married, three have been divorced at least once. They are a rare sample though. For most footballers the number is a lot higher than 33% as Sadlier explains.

'The PFA statistic is that something like 60 to 70% of all marriages which existed the day a footballer retired are over within five years. It's huge. There are a load of glib ways of saying it, like the bird is unhappy because she isn't going out with a footballer any more or whatever. But I think, the behavioural adjustment, you can't but become something different.'

McLoughlin elaborates. 'I wouldn't say it's like a bereavement but it certainly edges on "what is the point?" That's what I did. "What else will match that? What else will stimulate me like that did?" You're just sitting around. You miss being a football player, you miss the Saturdays. You have to learn and understand quickly because, if not, you could find yourself in a difficult position.'

Sadlier's readjustment was perhaps more severe than most given that his career was ended at just 24 but he does feel his own experience should be instructive for all ex-pros. Indeed, having studied sports psychology, one particular epiphany stood out.

'The first thing players should do is counselling . . . I started exploring the whole thing that it wasn't just my job. It was my entire identity and everything. Like I said earlier, when you're a player you'll only ever be asked about a couple of things at any given time but they're all football-related. I'd say 99% of what people talked to me about was football. I was just a bloke who played football so the assumption then is I love talking about football and I'll have the answer to football questions. And then when you stop playing it's like, what else do I do? What else can I do, what else do I want to do?

'And if you ask lads what they'll do when they're retired they just go "don't know" and hope it'll be okay. Okay, a lot of the modern ones, they've enough money that they don't have to work. They have their mortgage paid but there's no structure.'

McLoughlin has seen that in many former teammates.

'I know lots of lads who retired, some not as fortunate as me. I have been sensible with my money. I had a lovely pension to fall back on and work. But I know lads, they've nothing to do with football anymore, didn't pay their way and it's psychologically different. A real bind. They're divorced and half of their money is out the door, pissed it away or gambled it away.

'Now, once you get to 35, 36 and had a reasonable career, you won't have that pressure. One good contract can set you up for life. They won't have that financial pressure. But, even if I had that money, I would have found some project for my own sanity.'

It's not that way for all ex-players of course. You just have to look at the examples of Mark Lawrenson, Liam Brady and Packie Bonner from this book. They didn't just become elder statesmen in their Irish teams but have evidently become similar figures in different areas of the modern game.

All of those reasons above, however, are clearly why so many stay in football in some way. A perhaps unfair description would be that they're clinging on to it by their fingertips. But Sadlier describes it as an 'addiction'. And it's worth considering the post-career statistics of the 70 retirees to have played for Ireland between Jack Charlton's appointment in 1986 and the end of the 2002 World Cup.

Of the 70, 20 have some form of punditry or media work as their primary income (from the players featured in this book – Lawrenson, McLoughlin, Matt Holland and Sadlier); 35 are in coaching or management (Phelan, Alan Kernaghan, Brady); two are in some way involved in football administration (Bonner). That's 81% still directly involved in the framework of the sport. Even three who have branched out in terms of what they actually do have stayed connected in terms of who they do it for. Kevin Moran is an agent, Phil Babb runs a publishing company which prioritises a football magazine while Jon Goodman – the former Wimbledon player who won four caps with the Republic in 1997 – is a sports scientist specialising in his old profession. A tiny minority have made a complete break. And those who did all had atypical late starts in professional football. John Byrne is a chiropodist, Tony Galvin a civil servant and Chris Morris runs a family food business.

Galvin was rare in that he had gone right through third-level education before entering the game and, as such, said he always 'intended on doing something else'. Morris meanwhile explained of his own retirement, 'I don't think anything can match being a footballer. It's just a fantastic career. You have to accept when that's over to fulfil your goals in other ways.' Morris has largely done so. But his next step? Get his coaching badges.

'I have had a hankering for a lot of years now to coach again. It obviously depends on what opportunities come along but I would like to get involved in the pro game if I can.'

That comment and those of many others would appear to some way fit Sadlier's description of an addiction.

McLoughlin: 'To be completely detached from football would be a disaster for me . . . Radio keeps me involved. I still think there's something missing. I'd like to be back in football if I could.'

Alan Kernaghan: 'If you get away from the game totally I imagine it could be a bit depressing . . . we're fortunate that there are more jobs for the likes of us in football. It's a good way of trying to stay in the dressing room.'

Kernaghan, however, is among a few interviewees who feel there are more prosaic explanations. 'The game is all a lot of us know.'

'It's all I do,' Phelan simply repeats. 'Football, football, football and more football. No use going into the clothes business because I know nothing about clothes, no use going into furniture because I know nothing about furniture. All I know is that little round ball.'

Liam Brady expands.

'I think there's a kind of process. When you finish playing you will get the chance to do something in football and then, depending how successfully you do it, that dictates whether you're going to stay in it for longer. I didn't do so in management but Arsenal saw me as the right person to run their youth policy.

That was 14 years ago.'

Brady may have stayed in the same area all that time but the sport he serves didn't. Around the period both he and Arsene Wenger joined Arsenal in the autumn of 1996, all the money flowing into the game began to transform football from a mere sport to an effective arm of the entertainment industry. Wages went into the stratosphere, sportsmen became celebrities. And, as such, their lifestyles went from that of working pros to pampered stars. Indeed, the level to which modern players are indulged will perhaps only increase the extent of readjustment they will require as retirees. As an example, there's an illustrative anecdote about an agent attempting to sign up a Premier League player. The agent gave a pitch about potential sponsorship deals and all the assorted accoutrements. The player's single deal-breaker?

'Will you do me Tesco's?

'Sorry?'

'You know, me shopping? I need someone to do me shopping.'

That more cosseted lifestyle of the modern pro was even noticed in researching this book. When attempting to contact players, the later an individual began his career the harder he was to talk to – almost across the board. There were more buffer levels to go through, more individual numbers to ring. Older players would, on the whole, answer calls immediately or phone back straight away and prove very helpful. Younger, more recent retirees required more reminding. Some would even agree to meet yet, when the time came to organise an interview, calls would just go unanswered. On speaking to many, however, the impression is not of impoliteness or disregard. Merely a lack of responsibility. As other players have emphasised, most modern pros have agents and people at their clubs dictating diaries for them. Even Matt Holland – who, it should be reiterated at this point, was perfectly polite – has admitted to filling in his first pieces of paperwork once he retired.

The majority of ex-Irish internationals who actually played on stages like the World Cup, however, mostly missed out on anything approaching that kind of money or lifestyle. And their opinions on it are interesting.

'I have to bear in mind what I earned in the mid-90s was 10-fold what players a decade before did,' McLoughlin admits. 'But now we've got to a stage where modern players are earning 100-fold of what I was earning. I say good luck to them and don't begrudge them a penny. The only thing that galls me sometimes is when I look at someone who can't even change play earning 30 grand a week.

'I mean, even the cars we had at Fratton Park, you didn't look any different from your average man. But now there are Hummers there, SLs. I went to Blackburn and El-Hadji Diouf got into a chrome-covered Mercedes. That's half a million pounds worth of car. I wouldn't even have even turned up in that, I'd have hid it in the garage. So ostentatious. His car was probably worth more than half the streets in Blackburn.'

McLoughlin and his generation, of course, were always close to the average man in almost every sense. From what they earned to where they celebrated. Interestingly, they feel a similar disconnection from today's players as the fans.

'It's a them-and-us situation now, rather than us-and-we. It's difficult but that's how it's progressed. And what we mustn't forget is not all players earning that money are ostentatious. Plenty of lads at Portsmouth like David James and Marc Wilson were grounded, very approachable. So not everyone should be tarred with the same brush. I just hope it doesn't spiral out any further.'

Galvin, who is detached from the game to a greater degree, is even more effusive.

'The perfect example is the night after we beat England. The room was packed full of people I'd never met before. That was great. Nowadays, supporters don't get to meet players. You don't see them, don't meet them, apart from outside the ground getting their autographs if you're lucky. That's sad. They're like pop stars.'

Kernaghan concurs. 'I think that bond between the player and the supporter has gone. I'd like to get it back but it's very easy to sit here criticising players because they're on good money. I wish I was one of them. So I understand from sort of both sides. But I think some of them could do themselves a favour by coming down a notch or two.'

Brady, of course, has been on both sides of the fence having worked so closely with the current Irish team as assistant manager under Giovanni Trapattoni. Accordingly, he offers an alternative viewpoint.

'Well, you know, that gap is not necessarily their fault. That's the way football has evolved and that's perhaps a consequence of all the things that go with being a top player nowadays. At the same time, I never saw any problems as regards any of the players in the Irish set-up. Players will generally moan about things. Irish players are not too different. I was probably exactly the same. It doesn't matter how much money you get, you're fed up being in the hotel, fed up being away from home. You're only a young man basically, so you have to realise it's your profession and these are the sacrifices you have to make. And, having said that, I think it's an argument people bring up when results go badly. You don't hear it if results are good.'

Which is perhaps the whole point. When the success eventually ends, the fans can turn on the players . . . but then – as some of the cases above have shown – when the career eventually ends, the players can turn on themselves. When it's at its peak, football is the profession none other can replace. At the least, playing for Ireland provided its players with more than one peak . . .

The Team

The Irish dressing room in the summer of 1985: resignation, despair. The team have just drawn 0–0 at home with Norway. The manager Eoin Hand has his head in his hands. He's complaining about the media, the fans, saying he's going to pack it in. Liam Brady has to tell him to pull himself together. The lament 'it's never going to fucking happen for this country' is heard again. Yet another campaign is about to pass without qualification at the end of it. The 20th in succession. Fifty-five years. Worse, this time they wouldn't even get near it. Denmark would come to Lansdowne Road and win 4–1, Ireland would finish fourth of five in the 1986 World Cup qualifying group and the fans would boo.

This is a low.

The Irish dressing room in the summer of 1988: regret but very definite pride. Of course, it could just as well have been the summer of 1990 or 2002 or even 1994. In every squad, the players – to different extents – could revel in their performances at an international tournament. The managers could hold their heads high. The media would fete the team, the fans sing their names. There were three qualifications out of four over eight years, four out of eight over 16. World champions would be beaten, Ireland would reach as high as eighth in the FIFA world rankings. And yet, after every tournament, more than one player would express the belief that the achievements could have been even greater, more ground could have been broken. There's speculative talk of semi-finals, finals, even titles. Just read Packie Bonner, Chris Morris, Terry Phelan and Matt Holland in these pages. How expectations change. These are the highs.

The ultimate high of course, both emotionally and statistically, was reaching the last eight of Italia 90. It's a performance that actually deserves even more credit when placed in its proper context. Consider this. That Irish side were only the fourth team with a population of less than 4m to reach the quarter-finals in the history of the World Cup. The first to do so were the champions of 1930 and 1950, Uruguay, and they were soon followed by both Northern Ireland and Wales in 1958. All those achievements came, however, in a time when the football world was a lot smaller and a lot less competitive. Until Uruguay again reached the World Cup semi-finals in 2010, there is at least an argument that Ireland's passage to the quarter-finals in 1990 was one of the World Cup's most impressive showings when taking into account population against relative performance in time and place.

Along the same lines, Ireland is one of the smallest countries to reach non-consecutive World Cups. That may not sound impressive but involves a very limited pool producing two different squads of sufficient quality to compete. Just five players, after all, crossed the bridge to be picked for both the 1994 and 2002 World Cup tournaments. The only countries smaller than Ireland to manage the same feat were Slovenia (2002 and 2010) and, again, Northern Ireland (1958,

1982 and 1986). But neither had a 100% record of reaching the second stage in their tournaments as Ireland did.

Those are sociological stats that put a different spin on Ireland's achievements. But they don't change the key question: how? How did the team go from such a low to such a series of highs? How did the players go from resigning themselves to never making it at all to regret about not making it even further in competitions? The answer, of course, is a lot more complex than Jack Charlton arriving like a football Saint Patrick to drive the shakes out of Ireland. In essence, the elements were always there. They were just never aligned.

The first was the quality of the panel. Right since the FAI was first formed in 1921, Ireland had produced a stream of players considered among the most legendary at their high-profile British clubs: Johnny Carey, Tommy Eglington, Con Martin, Billy Whelan, Charlie Hurley, John Giles. The country just never had the supporting cast to complement such stars. That was always going to be the case with such a small population, particularly one in which football was also competing with rugby and Gaelic games. But, in other ways, the issue of population – and perhaps using it to praise later achievements as above – is something of a red herring. From the 1950s on, Ireland had one of the biggest diasporas alongside the most liberal citizenship laws in the world. Charlton wasn't the first in the FAI to realise this but was the first to ruthlessly exploit it. It helped to create an effective golden generation of players.

They still required strong leadership though. Giles had given the team a taste of it for the 1978 World Cup qualifiers when only dubious decisions in Paris and Sofia denied Ireland qualification. They were the first of a series of refereeing controversies over the next 10 years. Many players, most ardently Liam Brady, have argued they were all evidence of something deeper. Whether they were or not is something of a moot point though. Throughout football history, there is a reason why similar controversies like Diego Maradona's Hand of God are agonised over when as-blatant incidents – like Nigel De Jong's crane-kick on Xabi Alonso in the 2010 World Cup final – end up forgotten. The ones that are remembered happened to losing sides. They become part of the tapestry of tragedies. Mature, complete teams have the winning mentality to ensure such incidents don't become an issue. Ireland at that stage, as Brady also admitted, lacked that mentality.

What's also often forgotten is that similar misfortune befell the side between 1986 and 1988. They lost three of the highest-quality players in both the side and Europe – Mark Lawrenson, Jim Beglin and Brady himself – to serious injury. At any other time in the team's history that would have ruined Ireland's chances. Instead, it barely registered. Because, alongside a strong squad Charlton had helped deepen, the new manager had created a collective unit for which individual incidents or players never accrued the same importance. He had instilled that mentality.

The notion of Charlton just coming along and bullishly imposing his will is, of course, one that fits his gruffer image. In truth, both his personality and the process were much more nuanced. To go with the mindset, Charlton also had a meticulous tactical mind. He had taken note of a lot of the trends in international football and then devised a system to forcefully exploit them. But, aside from a set-up that worked generally, Charlton was also excellent on specifics. Every player featured in this book who played under him testifies to his aptitude for spotting a weakness or quirk in the opposition that would turn a game. And, despite the expressed purism of some of those players, they were all far more desperate to progress. As such, they were prepared to buy into some of the blunter elements of his style.

That was most evident in, as Giovanni Trapattoni put it 20 years later, the 'little details'. From being a soft touch, Ireland were suddenly very hard to break down. They also excelled at set-pieces, an area many international managers ignore because they have so little time to work with their teams. In such circumstances, corners and free-kicks executed properly could suddenly have a disproportionate impact.

The net result of all this were those unprecedented highs which were so great for Irish people to celebrate. But not necessarily to watch. With that style of putting teams under pressure, matches became battles to endure rather than games to enjoy. After the elimination from Italia 90, Charlton had remarked that his team should get some credit for showing the game a different way to go. Among others, Jeff Powell in the *Daily Mail* was astounded by this.

'Go where, exactly? To proclaim caveman attrition and crass long balls as the panacea for football 2000 betrays how bigoted a convert Charlton has become to a primitive philosophy gaining ground after ground in England for its capacity to destroy rather than delight, stifle not surprise, diminish instead of decorate the greatest game of all. The irony is that Charlton's miserly style of football is a denial of the spirit of the people behind the team . . . While Dublin prepared a hero's welcome, it felt here as if a shadow had been lifted.'

His sentiments were later echoed by Pele, an ex-player accustomed to playing the populist. 'I love your fans but not your football.'

Those same fans had for years got used to watching World Cups as neutrals. Had they done the same in Italia 90 it would have been hard to disagree with either Pele or Powell. The above statistics on population when it came to those performances may be hugely impressive. The actual statistics relating to the performances themselves much less so. In 1990 Ireland reached the quarter-finals without winning a game. Over the course of nine World Cup matches between then and 1994, they only scored four goals. Less than one every two games. Three of those matches – the two 0–0s with Egypt and Norway and the 1–1 against England – are routinely recalled as among the worst the competition has ever seen. Draws, meanwhile, became the default result. As Paul Howard has written, 'You'll never beat the Irish but there's a good chance you won't lose to them either'.

But then the important point is also that Irish fans had got used to watching World Cups as neutrals. It was going to take something different, if not necessarily popular, to initially change that. Many of the arguments which raged about Charlton's Ireland returned when Greece unexpectedly won Euro 2004. Their manager Otto Rehhagel applied many of the same pragmatic principles. But then the country went and joyously celebrated one of sport's great upsets, even if no-one else did. Why, after all, should a smaller team conform to customs if it means winning some friends but not many games? As the crowds at the height of the Charlton era proved, nothing sells like success.

The one caveat to all this in Ireland's case is that, once the mental breakthrough had been made for Euro 88, the side probably had enough players who could achieve success with a purer style. Charlton did make some concessions. For the Euro 92 campaign, for example, he instructed a full-back to fill in in the centre when the team was attacking, allowing another midfielder to break forward. And the matches against USSR in 1988, Northern Ireland at home in 1993 and Italy in 1994 also saw some occasionally swashbuckling football. But the method never changed too deeply.

As Brady argued earlier in this book, 'Giles . . . would have availed in a creative sense of the players that were available to him at the time.' Whether Ireland would have enjoyed the exact same success in such circumstances is, unfortunately, a theory that will never be put to the test. But it is hard to believe that a manager with any sort of competent CV couldn't have got a competitive level of performance out of a first XI that, at its height, featured players as accomplished as Packie Bonner, Denis Irwin, Terry Phelan, Paul McGrath, Kevin Moran, Roy Keane, John Sheridan, Ray Houghton, Kevin Sheedy, Niall Quinn and John Aldridge. There was barely a weakness. In every other era of Irish football, the team was dominated by a few indispensable players. If they were missing, so were Ireland's chances. In Charlton's time, it didn't seem to matter who was out. The squad always covered it. But then the counter-argument is the manager's very approach did too. His teams didn't rely on individuals. By the early 1990s, which was the most important: the squad or the system? In that sense, it's a question that's almost impossible to answer.

Ironically, that system brought an end to Charlton's peak period prematurely. Its intensity couldn't keep up with the parallel advances in international football. The USA 94 campaign encapsulated this. It brought one of Ireland's most joyous celebrations but also most depressing deflations. The 1–0 win over Italy seemed to show how far the side could go, the defeat to Holland how far behind they were. At once, the tournament illustrated how effective

Charlton's approach could be but also how out of touch he was.

In a further irony, one of the very icons of the Charlton era would be inspired to go down a totally opposite route. Mick McCarthy had been the player to boast that Marco van Basten wouldn't be able to 'pirouette with a limp', that he had proudly committed the most fouls at Italia 90. But, as manager, his first mission statement was that the team would pass the ball properly.

That wasn't the only alteration McCarthy had to accommodate. A drop in the quality of players available was a big change. Alongside that, it would take him a while to find his feet. Ultimately though, McCarthy would emulate Charlton in another manner. Just like his predecessor, he would give his Irish team an element otherwise missing from international football: a club spirit. It ensured the team kept together where other, more talented teams would crumble. Ireland's preparation for the 2002 World Cup was, after all, among the most disastrous in memory and probably worse than France's for 2010. They still made it to the second round. France didn't.

It was also to McCarthy's benefit, of course, that some of the players his era brought in – and who correspondingly bought into his era – were of undoubted quality. Robbie Keane was famous among the 2002 squad for annoying Niall Quinn with all the songs from 1990. He was nine years old during the tournament. Along with Damien Duff and Richard Dunne, he represented the Italia 90 generation of young fans. It was another, under-acknowledged legacy of the Charlton era and a bonus for a football association that hadn't exactly shown the greatest interest in youth development during that time.

Another member of the squad was infamously bypassed by the FAI's junior set-up altogether. It was to McCarthy's benefit too that the player's sheer will made sure he wasn't to be held back. The fact that Roy Keane wasn't showbiz and didn't score too many goals ensured his exact value was often underappreciated outside both Ireland and Old Trafford. Despite famously dragging Manchester United to the 1999 Champions League final with his performance in the semi-final against Juventus, for example, it was his teammate David Beckham who came second in that year's world player of the year awards behind Rivaldo. Keane, apparently, wasn't glamorous enough to gather that kind of attention. It said an awful lot about his effect and who noticed it though that, when Louis van Gaal had to vote for FIFA world player of the year in 2001 – just two months after his Dutch team's defeat at Lansdowne Road – he went for Keane.

The captain's passion, the manager's paternalism and their mutual antagonism created a potent but delicate chemistry. But for a very brief time it also put forward the argument that the sum of this Ireland's parts was maybe as good if not even better than Charlton's. Most obviously, they qualified for a tournament. At that tournament, however, they scored more than a goal a game. Along the same lines, they didn't just get results off, but beat very high-profile opposition in genuine high-stakes matches. When a home draw would have all but sealed qualification, Charlton's Ireland lost to Spain; McCarthy's beat Holland. And it was all done by going toe to toe with top teams and playing in a largely freewheeling style. As McCarthy emphasised after the 2–2 draw in Amsterdam, 'We came here to take Holland on at their own game.' His Ireland even went one game short of Charlton's record run of 17 unbeaten matches. There's a salient fact about the match they eventually lost though. It came in Iran – when Roy Keane was missing.

That delicate chemistry made it, in some way, ultimately inevitable that he would be missing for the 2002 World Cup itself. Perversely, its energy temporarily propelled the team to a creditable World Cup performance. Thereafter though, there was a delayed reaction. Two depressing defeats saw McCarthy follow Keane out of the Irish squad a lot quicker than expected. And for the next few years, something seemed to be missing from the Irish set-up beyond Keane's world-class talent. Something elusive. A lot of different approaches were tried to restore it. First of all, in the manner the French federation does, the promotion of a successful youth coach to the senior job in Brian Kerr. Then the opposite by trusting a managerial novice in Steve Staunton. One FAI chief executive, Fran Rooney, even attempted to artificially recreate an Italia 90 atmosphere with flag-days and other marketing wheezes.

It wasn't until the pain of Thierry Henry's handball that the feeling seemed to return though. Giovanni Trapattoni took Ireland to the brink of the big time again. And he did so in part, as Brady explained, by instilling many of the same basic qualities Charlton did: concentrating on the 'little details'.

It's apt. Because, whatever of the debates over philosophy, Ireland's 'qualification era' from 1986 to 2002 did provide a few fundamental blueprints and lessons for the success of mid-tier nations.

For a start, basic organisation can have a surprisingly spectacular effect given the erratic nature of international football. The 2010 World Cup emphasised this. Charlton underlined it. Likewise, much of the talk about the Irish 'spirit' may sound hackneyed but there is clearly something concrete to it. Anyone who can distil it – as Charlton, McCarthy and to some extent Trapattoni managed – will see the side overcome further shortcomings.

On a broader level, the relative golden generation of players Ireland benefited from between 1986 and 1994 is something most mid-tier nations have to wait decades for. Charlton's pool of players seemingly arrived by a few accidents of fortune rather than any focused plan beyond exploiting citizenship laws. There was no real youth development framework to speak of. Installing one can at least help to lessen the wait. Bonner explained in this book how the FAI is belatedly attempting to do so. The relative weakness of the Irish domestic league should actually create an opportunity here in that it requires enhancement anyway. The opening should be there to construct a pyramid structure for young potential players in the same manner as Germany and the world champions Spain have implemented and England haven't.

Ultimately, though, it all illustrates that the successes from 1986 to 2002 need not just be nostalgia to bask in nor enjoyable memories to relive . . . but templates to get it right once more. Maybe then a nation will hold its breath again.